WELCOME

SIMON THURLEY Chief Executive of English Heritage

When I joined this organisation, I set myself the task of visiting all of the properties, sites and monuments in our care. All 409 of them. Almost three years later, I've finally managed it, and feel privileged to have had the opportunity. I don't think the importance of this collection can be over-emphasised. They represent real, tangible connections with thousands of years of England's history and, I believe, help to inspire an enthusiasm for the past in everyone – young, old, expert, enthusiast.

For me that inspiration is found as much in the smaller, lesser known sites such as Rushton Triangular Lodge in Northamptonshire – a fascinating piece of 16th-century architecture that remains one of the most extraordinary buildings in Britain – or Lanercost Priory, in Cumbria – the hauntingly beautiful remains of a 13th-century Augustinian monastic house – as in the more iconic properties such as Stonehenge or Osborne House.

This year English Heritage celebrates its 21st birthday, and travelling the length and breadth of the country has given me time to consider the significance of our role. No other organisation is responsible for the guardianship of such a wealth of material, and if it wasn't for the work of our staff, and the support of our members, over the last two decades much of it wouldn't have survived.

The content of this guidebook is a testament to that work.

We've listened to what you've said and you should see some welcome changes in this edition; clearer opening times, a safety symbol to show properties where extra care needs to be taken, especially when supervising children, sites which you can hire out for a special occasion and, in response to the many requests for better legibility, there's larger print size, more black text and white backgrounds.

When planning a visit, don't forget that children go free with members. There's no better time than childhood to be introduced to the excitement of history or simply to run free in our many gardens and open spaces. And with around 500 history related events this year, from battle re-enactments to falconry days, you're bound to be able to create a day out that everyone can enjoy. This year many of our coastal sites will be joining in the SeaBritain 2005 celebrations, commemorating the Battle of Trafalgar, so do look out for details in *Heritage Today* magazine and on our website.

If you want to keep up with the very latest do visit **www.english-heritage.org.uk** You'll find a host of information from property opening times, education initiatives and archaeology projects to conservation campaigns and advice on period house restoration. You can also subscribe to our monthly email newsletter, packed with seasonal ideas for days out, special offers and event highlights.

Some must-see attractions for this year include our newest addition, Birdoswald Fort in Cumbria, completing another link in the history of Hadrian's Wall, the organic garden at Audley End, the atmospheric Merlin's Cave at Tintagel and the magnificent sub-tropical gardens at Belsay Hall.

I am delighted to welcome you to the 2005 edition of our handbook. I hope it inspires you, as it did me, to go out and enjoy some of the best of what England has to offer. And I hope that in the decades to come, together we can continue to make our past part of our future.

SIMON THURLEY

3

www.english-heritage.org.uk

HOW TO USE THIS HANDBOOK

NAVIGATE YOUR WAY AROUND THE HANDBOOK AS EASILY AS POSSIBLE

This handbook gives details of all English Heritage properties and other properties to which English Heritage members receive special discounts. Property entries are colour-coded by region (see map opposite for breakdown), and are listed alphabetically within these regions.

Website listings are on all site pages should you prefer to look electronically for property details. We recommend that you visit the website before you visit for the latest events information and last minute property updates.

A full listing of the properties is provided in the front section of each region, with a regional map showing the counties and key towns/cities.

More detailed maps can be found on pages 256-268.

Photography
We have included as many photographs as possible to give you a feel for the site.

Essential information such as opening times, admission prices for non-members, contact details and travel directions are included for each property. We have also included postcodes where possible.

Symbols show the facilities which are available, from catering and toilet facilities to whether a property is available for corporate or private hire or licensed for civil wedding ceremonies. The key is on the inside front cover.

Details of OS map references are provided for easy location of each property, with specific map numbers and co-ordinates (OS LandRanger maps).

www.english-heritage.org.uk

YOUR MEMBERSHIP

MAKING A DIFFERENCE

Every penny from your membership makes a difference to our work in conserving England's historic environment. We appreciate your support and urge you to continue helping us to preserve England's heritage for future generations. In return, we hope you'll gain a great deal of enjoyment from your membership.

THE BENEFITS OF MEMBERSHIP

English Heritage has over 400 historic properties in its care, and as a member, you are entitled to visit them all for free as many times as you may wish. But the benefits of membership don't end there; you are also entitled to free or reduced-price entry at more than 100 other historic attractions and a wealth of special events, and you will receive our award-winning quarterly magazine, *Heritage Today*.

CHILDREN GO FREE

English Heritage believes in encouraging an enjoyment of history early, and this is reflected in our children go free policy. This allows free entry for up to six accompanying children (under 19) per member, within the family group. However, children should be carefully supervised, as historic sites can be hazardous.

For non-members, discounted family tickets are available.

ENJOY BRITAIN'S HERITAGE

Whether you're on holiday or local, you can use your membership card to visit more than 100 historic properties in Scotland, Wales and the Isle of Man. As an English Heritage member you are entitled to free or reduced-price entry to Cadw (Welsh Historic Monuments), Historic Scotland and Manx National Heritage properties. During your first year of membership, you pay just half-price – each year after that it's completely free.

For listings of properties in the care of Cadw, Historic Scotland and Manx National Heritage, see pages 250-253.

MORE PLACES IN ENGLAND

• Your membership card will also give you free or discounted entry to many other sites in England. Please see the Other Historic Attractions section in each region. **Please note:** discounts will not apply on days when events are held at these properties.

CONTACT US

If you have comments or views to share, contact Customer Services on **0870 333 1181** or write to:

English Heritage
Customer Services
PO Box 569
Swindon
SN2 2YP

Alternatively email **customers @english-heritage.org.uk**

English Heritage membership makes a lovely gift.

Call 0870 333 1181 or visit **www.english-heritage.org.uk/ gift** for more details.

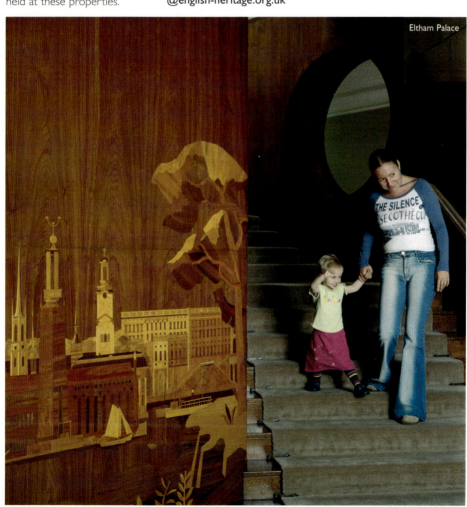

Eltham Palace

For more information on how your membership can make a difference, please visit our website **www.english-heritage.org.uk/membership** or call Customer Services on **0870 333 1181**.

ABOUT US

INTRODUCTION TO ENGLISH HERITAGE

WHO ARE WE?

English Heritage was established in 1983 as the Historic Buildings and Monuments Commission for England. We are the Government's leading adviser on the historic environment and are sponsored by the Department for Culture Media & Sport (DCMS).

As well as working closely with the DCMS, we operate with other Government departments, including the Office of the Deputy Prime Minister (ODPM) and the Departments for the Environment, Food & Rural Affairs (DEFRA) and Trade & Industry (DTI).

WHAT DO WE DO?

The history of England is preserved in the many ancient buildings and sites throughout the country – our job is to protect and promote this historic environment. From the earliest traces of human settlement to the most significant buildings of our own time, we want every important historic site to get the care and attention it deserves. By employing the best architects, archaeologists and historians, we aim to help people understand and appreciate why their historic environment matters.

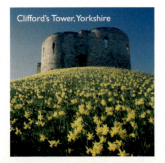
Clifford's Tower, Yorkshire

WHO ARE THE PEOPLE?

Sir Neil Cossons is Chairman and Simon Thurley is Chief Executive. A team of 16 commissioners, who change every four years and come from a wide variety of backgrounds, help them.

If you want to find out more about what happens at our Commission meetings, you can look up the minutes at **www.english-heritage. org.uk/minutes**

HOW ARE WE FUNDED?

English Heritage is funded partly by the Government, and partly by revenue earned from our historic properties. Over a quarter of our income comes from membership, donations, fund-raising and the Lottery. Every penny counts and there are many ways that you can support us. Choose to pay your membership by direct debit as this keeps administration costs low. Sign up to Gift Aid, this enables us to recoup 28 pence from every pound given. Purchase a gift of membership as a wonderful present, or introduce a friend to English Heritage, by taking them along to a site or enjoying one of our many events together.

WHY IS OUR WORK IMPORTANT?

We believe that future generations should have the chance to enjoy England's historic environment. This can only happen if we begin to preserve and protect our historic sites now. As well as undertaking the work ourselves, we are able to provide assistance to others.

We are also an organisation that campaigns to improve and preserve the historic environment. Our recent *Save Our Streets* campaign called for support in helping to clear the clutter from our streets. Visit **www.english-heritage.org.uk/ saveourstreets** for more information.

We hope that the information we provide at our sites, as well as through our Outreach and Education programmes, will encourage people to value the importance of England's historic environment.

Through our role in the planning system, we are able to ensure that any changes made to England's architectural heritage serve to enhance and protect it.

HOW ARE WE DIFFERENT FROM THE NATIONAL TRUST?

The National Trust is a charity, while English Heritage is partly funded by the government and has wider responsibilities with national and local government. Our role is to preserve the extraordinary legacy of buildings, ancient sites and monuments that without attention would otherwise be overlooked and fall into disrepair.

We welcome approaches for filming and commercial photography at our sites, which often appear in films, television programmes and photo shoots. All queries and requests should be made to Sarah Eastel Locations on 01225 858100 or email info@film-locations.co.uk **www.film-locations.co.uk**

Stonehenge, Wiltshire

ENGLISH HERITAGE AT WORK

A GUIDE TO THE DIFFERENT TYPES OF WORK WE DO

ARCHAEOLOGY

As the national archaeology service for England, we set standards, promote innovation and provide detailed archaeological knowledge of the historic environment.

In 2002, we took on responsibility for the historic wrecks and submerged landscapes in, on or under the seabed within 12 miles of the English coast. Our policy paper on the management of maritime archaeology, *Taking to the Water*, is available on our website.

More information on our archaeological work can be found at **www.english-heritage. org.uk/archaeology**

BLUE PLAQUES

What do Sir Christopher Wren and John Lennon have in common? They both have Blue Plaques erected in their honour.

The Society of Arts began the Blue Plaques Scheme in London in the 19th century, and it passed to London County Council in 1901. English Heritage has been running the scheme since 1986, and we are now extending it across the country on a region-by-region basis. To qualify for a Blue Plaque, a person must have been dead for 20 years or have passed the centenary of their birth.

In partnership with Handheld History, we have recently developed commentaries on a selection of Blue Plaques, which are available direct to your mobile phone.

To find out more, please visit **www.handheldhistory.com**

If you would like to know how to nominate someone for a Blue Plaque, go to **www.english-heritage.org.uk/blueplaques**

PHOTO (TOP): Traditional materials and techniques were used alongside the latest methods in our award-winning restoration project for the Albert Memorial.

Hill Hall, Essex

CONSERVATION
In addition to listing buildings, we also designate monuments and landscapes for protection. For example, monuments such as ruins, earthworks or burial sites may be scheduled as a monument and subject to special control.

We also work with Local Authorities on designating Conservation Areas. These are usually areas characterised by architectural and historic features that are worth preserving or enhancing.

England is fortunate to be home to a number of World Heritage Sites, including Stonehenge and Hadrian's Wall. We work with UNESCO to devise management plans for these unique places.

Battlefields are also important sources of archaeological and historic interest, and there are over 40 such landscapes on the *English Heritage Register of Historic Battlefields*. We keep a similar register for parks and gardens, which includes the country's most important green spaces from country house gardens to hospital grounds.

Find out more about our conservation work at **www.english-heritage.org.uk/conservation**

EDUCATION
We are a national leader in education about the historic environment. Each year we welcome over 500,000 pupils, students and teachers to our sites completely free of charge. Our expert advice, inspiring resources, courses and events, support teachers at all levels and link to history, citizenship and other curriculum subjects.

OUTREACH
We are committed to engaging new audiences in learning from, enjoying and valuing the historic environment. Our team of Outreach Officers is leading a range of exciting, creative projects with hard-to-reach audiences across the country, including young people, ethnic communities and people with disabilities. Projects range from oral history projects to community archaeology digs, youth theatre projects to creating community heritage gardens. The team also works with the Civic Trust to broaden participation in Heritage Open Days.

GRANTS
We give grants to individuals, local authorities and voluntary organisations to undertake urgent repairs and to conserve and enhance the historic environment. We also advise the Heritage Lottery Fund on the allocation of Lottery money to worthwhile schemes which do not fit our own grant criteria.

Find out more at **www.english-heritage.org.uk/grants**

LISTED BUILDINGS
We recommend buildings of special architectural or historic interest to the Secretary of State for Culture, Media and Sport for listing. Listing means that any changes made to either the internal or external structure of a building are subject to stricter planning regulations.

Most listed buildings date from before 1840, but we also recommend some buildings from after this date. Modern buildings need to be of significant importance, and normally over 30 years old before they are likely to be listed.

There are three categories of listing: Grade I; Grade II* and Grade II. Grade I and Grade II* buildings are of outstanding architectural or historic interest, and of particularly great importance to the nation's built heritage.

More information on current listed buildings and how to suggest a building for listing can be found at **www.english-heritage.org.uk/heritageprotection**

View details and images of England's listed buildings at **www.imagesofengland.org.uk**

Belsay Hall, Northumberland

POLICIES

One of our key responsibilities is to develop robust policies to enable national and local decision makers to protect and promote the historic environment.

We gather the evidence to support these policies. Published annually as *Heritage Counts*, it can be viewed at **www.historic environment.org.uk**

We play an important role in international conservation, advising the Government on the designation and management of World Heritage Sites in the UK, and campaigning in Brussels and Strasbourg on behalf of the historic environment.

Down House

STATUTORY ADVICE

We advise Local Planning Authorities on listed building planning applications. Buildings need to change to thrive in the modern world, and we work proactively with these Local Authorities to ensure that this change recognises the historic potential of the building.

We publish an annual *Buildings at Risk Register*, with information on listed buildings and scheduled monuments which are 'at risk' from neglect and decay. We also award grants to Local Authorities, to undertake urgent repairs on these buildings where necessary.

PROPERTIES

We currently look after over 400 historic sites, which are open to the public. Our properties include historic country houses, palaces, ruined abbeys, prehistoric settlements, burial sites, castles, statues and Roman remains.

At many of these sites we provide visitor centres, exhibitions and educational resources. England has an extraordinary array of important historic monuments, and our property list includes Stonehenge, Hadrian's Wall, Dover Castle, Apsley House and Rievaulx Abbey.

PUBLISHING

We publish a range of conservation leaflets offering practical advice and guidance on specialist or technical topics. A catalogue is available free of charge online at **www.english-heritage.org.uk /publications** or by calling Customer Services on 0870 333 1181

We also publish guidebooks to most of our sites, as well as a wide variety of titles, from academic works to archaeology and architecture. See page 17 for more details.

RESEARCH

Our research and training programmes increase understanding of the historic environment,

helping us guide its management in an informed and sustainable way. We concentrate our fieldwork and analysis on poorly understood building types as well as on specific sites and areas.

For more information email **buildingshistory@english- heritage.org.uk**

TRAINING: CRAFT & SKILLS

Traditional skills are at risk of dying out in the UK, and there are currently less than 40,000 craftsmen with the necessary specialist skills, to maintain our historic environment. English Heritage provides training for these essential skills, including thatching and stonemasonry.

This means there will always be a continuing reservoir of skilled craftsmen and women to help maintain England's half million listed historic buildings and *Buildings at Risk*.

i For more information on any issues relating to English Heritage, please visit our website **www.english-heritage.org.uk** or call Customer Services on **0870 333 1181**.

Travelling performers in Taplow,
Buckinghamshire – 1885

NATIONAL MONUMENTS RECORD

ENGLISH HERITAGE ARCHIVE

The National Monuments Record, English Heritage's extensive archive based in Swindon, is open to the public. It includes an amazing collection of over eight million photographs of historic buildings, streetscapes, gardens and archaeological sites from the ground and from the air. The pictures cover the whole of England and date from the 1840s to the present day.

The archive also holds a database of more than a quarter of a million archaeological monuments and excavations in England, as well as thousands of plans, drawings and reports.

This is a public resource, and English Heritage is delighted to welcome visitors to consult these records and our reference library, by visiting our search room in Swindon.

Our Outreach Centre holds workshops and tours to help you make the most of our material. Please call 01793 414797 for details.

If you can't make it to Swindon, there are many other ways you can access our resources:

www.english-heritage.org.uk/ viewfinder – view historic images from our collections.

www.imagesofengland.org.uk – view images and descriptions of England's listed buildings.

www.english-heritage.org.uk/ pastscape – view information on England's archaeology and historic buildings.

To find out more please call 01793 414600 or visit our website at **www.english-heritage.org.uk/nmr**

Farrier at Soham, Cambridgeshire – 1948

OPENING TIMES

Public search room:
Tue-Fri   9.30am-5pm
(tel 01793 414600 for details)

HOW TO FIND US

Direction: Kemble Drive, Swindon, SN2 2GZ

Train: Swindon ¼ mile

MAP   Page 257 (2J)
                OS Map 173 (ref SU 145850)

SUPPORTING ENGLISH HERITAGE

HOW YOU CAN HELP

We depend increasingly on donations from individuals and voluntary support from the private sector and the Lottery. We are very grateful to all our members and supporters; last year you raised £38.4m to help us conserve and restore some of this country's most culturally important and iconic sites. Thank you.

Donations from members and visitors have helped us to make significant improvements to many of our properties over recent years. One such project is Tintagel Castle in Cornwall (pictured). Funding raised through donations helped us to do much-needed development work at this site, including improved access routes and new steps to the beach and Merlin's Cave, enabling more people to enjoy all aspects of this magical site.

If you would like to make a donation, you can do so when you renew your membership, or at any of our sites, or you can now donate online at **www.english-heritage.org.uk/donate**

There are many ways to support us: from making a donation to pledging a legacy in the future. Visit the Membership and Support Us pages on our website at **www.english-heritage.org.uk/supportus**, telephone our Development Department on 020 7973 3798 or email us at **development@english-heritage.org.uk** to discuss how your gift can support our priority projects.

PROJECTS SUPPORTED BY DEVELOPMENT FUND IN THE PAST TWELVE MONTHS

The following is a list of projects supported by the English Heritage Development Fund in the past twelve months:

Clifford's Tower
New interpretative scheme.

Tintagel Castle
Improvements to access routes and new steps.

Bolsover Castle
Installation of The Twelve Caesars series of historic paintings in the second floor rooms.

The Home of Charles Darwin, Down House
Temporary exhibition on Emma Darwin.

Lindisfarne Priory
New display and improved visitor access.

Muchelney Abbey
Display of pottery, stonework and metalwork and new introductory interpretative panels.

Tilbury Fort
New interpretative display.

Helmsley Castle
New visitor centre.

Prudhoe Castle
New exhibition.

Tintagel Castle

Queen Mother's Garden – Walmer Castle

HIRING A PROPERTY

CREATE A MEMORABLE OCCASION FOR YOUR HISTORIC DAY

What could be a more stunning setting for a wedding reception, birthday celebration, anniversary dinner or corporate event than an historic English Heritage property? Celebrations can now be arranged at 14 English Heritage sites, some of which are also licensed for civil wedding ceremonies.

Experienced Hospitality Managers are on hand to help plan and fine-tune all arrangements. You can also be assured that carefully selected suppliers are dedicated to providing the finest service. So if you want a special theme for a party, contemporary styling to impress business colleagues, unusual menus or an entertainer to enliven proceedings, our Hospitality Managers can help make it happen. Whatever the choice, every event will provide special memories for years to come.

Properties available for hire are marked with a 🇹 symbol throughout the handbook. Those also licensed for civil wedding ceremonies are marked with a 🔔 symbol.

VENUES AVAILABLE FOR HIRE

Venues also licensed for civil wedding ceremonies 🔔

LONDON

Chiswick House 🔔
Tel: 020 7973 3292

Eltham Palace 🔔
Tel: 020 8294 2577

English Heritage
Lecture Theatre
Tel: 020 7973 3421

Wellington Arch
Tel: 020 7973 3292

EAST OF ENGLAND

Audley End House
and Gardens, Essex
Tel: 01799 529403

EAST MIDLANDS

Bolsover Castle 🔔
Derbyshire
Tel: 01246 856456

SOUTH EAST

Deal Castle, Kent 🔔
Tel: 01304 209889

Dover Castle, Kent
Tel: 01304 209889

Osborne House,
Isle of Wight
Tel: 01983 203055

Walmer Castle 🔔
and Gardens, Kent
Tel: 01304 209889

SOUTH WEST

Old Wardour Castle,
Wiltshire
Tel: 01305 820539

Pendennis Castle 🔔
Cornwall
Tel: 01326 310106

Portland Castle 🔔
Dorset
Tel: 01305 820539

St Mawes Castle 🔔
Cornwall
Tel: 01326 310106

For more information on exclusive hire, please contact the Hospitality Manager on the telephone numbers shown, or visit the website: **www.english-heritage.org.uk/hospitality**

BOOKS AND GIFTS

AN ECLECTIC MIX OF GIFTS

BOOKS

Our Publishing Department produce a wide range of popular history books, including titles on historic cookery, garden history, architecture and military history. For more information please call 0870 429 6658 or visit our online bookshop at **www.english-heritage.org.uk/books**

A Journey Through Haunted England – Simon Marsden

Hardback	£17.99
ISBN	185074 9302

Julian Richards

Hardback	£9.99
ISBN	185074 9264

Please also see p269

GIFTS

We have shops at most of our properties, selling an eclectic mix of gifts including gardening implements, picnic and travel accessories, children's toys and historic fancy-dress costumes, games and puzzles and organic sweets and biscuits.

Some sites also have unique ranges of jewellery and ceramics that reflect their history and setting.

MEMBERS' OFFERS

English Heritage also works with a number of partners to bring new and exciting offers to our members and customers.

For every booking or purchase made, each partner gives a donation to English Heritage to help us in our work of protecting the historic environment.

These offers include:

English Heritage Mastercard
Tel: 0800 015 2204

UK Discovery Weekends with Hilton Hotels
Tel: 0870 520 1201

English Heritage Overseas Traveller Breaks
Tel: 020 7752 0000

Virgin Balloon Flights
Tel: 0870 787 4978

Endsleigh Insurance
Tel: 0800 085 8836

English Heritage Hotel Breaks in the UK
Tel: 0870 901 7818

To order any of our books please call 0870 429 6658 or order online. To buy other gifts, visit our onsite shops or visit our website at **www.english-heritage.org.uk/shopping**

www.english-heritage.org.uk

Audley End House and Gardens, Essex

ADMISSION CHARGES

ESSENTIAL TIPS BEFORE YOU VISIT

MEMBERS

Entry to English Heritage sites is free to all members on presentation of a valid membership card. You will also be entitled to free or reduced entry to a range of events and other non-English Heritage attractions (listed at the back of each regional section).

CHILDREN

All children under five gain free entry to our properties. English Heritage members can also take up to six children (under 19), within the family group, into our properties at no extra charge. Unaccompanied children aged 16 or over can gain free entry on production of their parents' membership card. There may be a charge for children at the non-English Heritage properties listed in this guide.

NON-MEMBERS

There are three levels of charges for non-members shown in the handbook.

For example:

Adult	£2.50
Concession	£1.90
Children (under 16)	£1.30

The concessions apply to senior citizens, jobseekers and students with relevant ID. Prices may vary from the example shown above.

FAMILIES

Family tickets are available at some of our larger properties, and in most cases family tickets are valid for two adults and three children. This may vary at sites not managed by English Heritage; please call in advance to confirm their policy.

GROUPS

Discounts of 15% (10% at Stonehenge) are available for groups of eleven or more visitors.

Call Customer Services on 0870 333 1181 for a copy of our Group Visits Guide. We recommend that groups of visitors book in advance when planning to visit a property.

EVENTS

Please note members may be charged when events are being held at a property (check Events Listings in Heritage Today for details). Opening times may also vary when a public or private event is held, so please check with the property before you travel.

PLANNING YOUR VISIT

ESSENTIAL TIPS BEFORE YOU VISIT

The Handbook is designed to help you get the most out of your visit to any English Heritage site. In this section we cover a range of information which should help you plan your trip.

ACCESS

We are committed to ensuring our properties are enjoyed by and are accessible to all. In this handbook we have used the ♿ symbol to indicate that at least some areas of a property are accessible by wheelchair. However, for a more thorough guide to accessibility and the special facilities on hand at many of our properties, you may like to refer to our *Access Guide*, which is available free of charge. In the *Access Guide* we offer an honest assessment of those landscapes and buildings that have the most to offer visitors with disabilities. For example, sites with alternative routes for wheelchair users or with features such as scented gardens, tactile objects/displays and specially created audio tours.

Some of these features and facilities will also be of interest to families and carers with young children, or to those who like to include both children and grandparents in their days out.

Information on parking and drop-off points is also included in the guide, as well as an indication of some of the obstacles you may encounter around each site, such as steep steps to a castle keep or grounds that may become waterlogged in wet weather.

If you have any more questions about a particular site, we encourage you to call in advance. Our staff will be happy to help. Companions of visitors with disabilities are admitted free to all English Heritage properties.

Information on our sites can also be obtained by fax. For individual site fax numbers, please telephone or email Customer Services.

The *Access Guide* is available in large type, braille, on tape and on disc by region, or on our website.

Please visit **www.english-heritage.org.uk/accessguide** to download your free copy. Alternatively, please call 0870 333 1181 or minicom 01793 414878.

You can also email **customers@english-heritage.org.uk**

CATERING

Refreshments are available at restaurants and tearooms at some sites, and these are often attractively located within the historic buildings themselves. Visitors are also welcome to picnic in the grounds of many sites. Please check individual listings for details of properties with catering facilities.

CYCLING

Call Sustrans on 0117 929 0888 or visit **www.sustrans.org.uk** for route information.

DISPLAYS, EXHIBITIONS AND VISITOR CENTRES

At many sites, there are display panels explaining how the property appeared in the past, often with the help of reconstruction drawings or interactive displays. Other sites play host to temporary exhibitions of paintings and sculptures. Some sites also have visitor centres which feature exhibitions, interactive audio-visual displays and shops.

DOGS

Dogs are welcome wherever possible. Please see listings for individual restrictions. Guide and hearing dogs are welcome everywhere.

EDUCATIONAL GROUP VISITS

Visiting historic sites is an important way of inspiring school children and adult learners about history. We actively encourage these visits by providing free entry to our sites for pre-booked educational groups. We also provide a range of resources to enable teachers and students to get the most out of their visit.

English Heritage follows the Department for Education and Skills' Guidelines on Health and Safety on Educational Visits. We require you to have at least one adult to every six children in a group containing pupils of school years one to three. The ratio could go up to one to fifteen for years seven and above. For further information and an education pack call 020 7973 3385 or visit **www.english-heritage.org.uk/education**

FAMILIES AND CHILDREN

We welcome families with children of all ages. Many of our sites include special features, exhibitions or educational facilities suitable for children.

Some properties offer baby-changing facilities. For safety reasons, babies cannot be carried in back carriers at certain properties. Health and safety guidelines recommend that up to six children can be accompanied by one adult, with a lower ratio for pre-school children. However, you are responsible for the children's supervision and safety at all times, and we would advise that judgement is used with regard to a sensible adult to child ratio, especially at more hazardous sites marked with a ⚠ symbol in this guide.

FAMILY LEARNING – NEW FOR 2005

This year, look out for an exciting range of resources we are developing at many of our sites. Already featuring at over 50 sites, we hope they will enhance enjoyment and understanding for all the family. The resources range from free children's activity sheets and back packs to book boxes, 'very big books' for younger children – as well as interactive Discovery Centres. See individual property listings in the handbook for indication of where family learning resources are currently available.

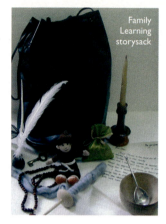

Family Learning storysack

GUIDES AND TOURS

Audio guides are available at more than 50 of our sites. They enable you to learn more about the sites, and can be controlled to provide more or less information to your preference. In exceptional circumstances, for instance when an event is taking place in key areas of the property, audio guides may not be available. To check for special events see *Events* section of *Heritage Today* magazine or visit **www.english-heritage.org.uk** or call Customer Services. Guidebooks are also on sale at manned properties or through our postal service – call 0870 429 6658.

PHOTOGRAPHY

Non-commercial photography is welcome in all our grounds. For conservation reasons, it is not permitted inside some properties.

PUBLIC TRANSPORT

All public transport information is correct at time of going to press. We are grateful to Barry Doe for providing this information. If you have any comments or suggestions, please call 01202 528707.

SMOKING

Smoking is not permitted inside any English Heritage properties.

TOILETS

Toilets are available on or near many English Heritage sites. Please check individual listings.

YOUR SAFETY

Due to their historic nature, some of our sites have features which could be hazardous – such as steep slopes, sheer drops, slippery or uneven surfaces, steep/uneven steps and deep/fast-flowing water. Please pay attention to all safety notices on site.

We have inserted a ⚠ symbol against these sites in this handbook, but if you are in any doubt about the layout or features, please call the property before you visit. We want you to enjoy our properties, so please take care when you visit and remember to wear suitable footwear.

We encourage children to have fun, but please ensure they are supervised at all times.

Our staff are always willing to advise on safety issues. Please prevent fires and do not climb on monuments at any of our sites.

Find out the latest information by visiting our website **www.english-heritage.org.uk/visits** or call Customer Services on **0870 333 1181**.

CELEBRATING HISTORY

THIS YEAR'S EVENTS

Every year English Heritage holds hundreds of events at sites all around the country.

We stage the biggest event programme of its kind in Europe, and the amazing settings make each event a memorable experience. As an English Heritage member, you will have either free or reduced-price admission to most events.

We always make sure there is plenty for children to do and many of the events relate to key stages of the curriculum so they might even help with homework!

We have included just a few highlights for 2005 on this page:

FESTIVAL OF HISTORY
13 & 14 August
Kelmarsh Hall,
Northamptonshire

Following a hugely successful event in 2004, with record visitor numbers and a fantastic programme of activities, we have responded to your feedback and found a stunning new historic setting for the Festival. Check our website for details.

THE KNIGHTS' TOURNAMENT
This year you'll be able to follow the adventures of your very own knight! We will be running a nationwide tournament to test the jousting, archery, falconry and sword fighting skills of brave combatants. Festivals will also feature music, children's activities and historic talks.

EXPERIENCE DAYS
Treat yourself or a friend to a truly memorable experience. We offer the unique opportunity to spend time at one of our beautiful properties, participating in a variety of specialist activities. This year's programme includes falconry, sculpture, bodice making and photography.

TOURS THROUGH TIME
From ornate interiors to romantic ruins, architectural delights to hidden battlefields, take an in-depth look at some of England's most fascinating historic sites on these fully guided historical tours. Places are strictly limited. Book early to avoid disappointment by calling Brookland Travel.
Tel: 0845 121 2863.

SEABRITAIN 2005 CELEBRATIONS
Join us to celebrate England's rich maritime heritage, and the 200th anniversary of the Battle of Trafalgar. Our extensive programme includes: Tribute to Trafalgar, Thunder of Guns, Sea Spectaculars, Viking Battles and Tall Ships Parties across the country.

EXCLUSIVE MEMBERS' EVENTS
EH members also get exclusive access to our range of popular members' events – including behind-the-scenes visits, champagne receptions and guided tours and lectures.

NEW FOR 2005
English Heritage events are about bringing history to life for everyone. In 2005 we will be introducing a number of events with a contemporary twist, including light shows, dance festivals and outdoor cinema.

For details of our events, tours and members' activities, check the latest issue of Heritage Today, visit our website **www.english-heritage.org.uk/events** or call Customer Services on **0870 333 1181**.

Detail of a giltwood marble
top table – Chiswick House

LONDON

Everywhere you look on London's streets you will see the history of this great capital city imprinted on the landscape and architecture. From Roman ruins to elaborate churches, elegant town houses to ornate palaces, London offers them all. And away from the hustle and bustle, you can find peace in the quiet squares, narrow alleyways and beautiful parks.

www.english-heritage.org.uk/london

PROPERTIES

SEE INDIVIDUAL LISTINGS FOR DETAILS

CAMDEN
Kenwood House

GREENWICH
Eltham Palace,
Wernher Collection at
Ranger's House

HAMMERSMITH
Chiswick House

KINGSTON-UPON-THAMES
Coombe Conduit

RICHMOND
Marble Hill House

SOUTHWARK
Winchester Palace

TOWER HAMLETS
London Wall

WESTMINSTER
Apsley House, Chapter House
and Pyx Chamber, Jewel Tower,
Wellington Arch

Comprehensive
map of our sites
PAGE 258-259

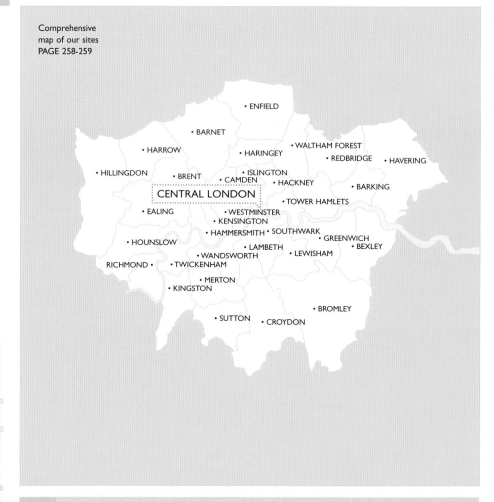

• ENFIELD

• BARNET

• HARROW

• WALTHAM FOREST

• HARINGEY

• REDBRIDGE

• HAVERING

• HILLINGDON

• BRENT

• ISLINGTON

• CAMDEN

• HACKNEY

• BARKING

CENTRAL LONDON

• EALING

• WESTMINSTER

• KENSINGTON

• TOWER HAMLETS

• HAMMERSMITH

• SOUTHWARK

• HOUNSLOW

• LAMBETH

• GREENWICH

• BEXLEY

• WANDSWORTH

• LEWISHAM

RICHMOND •

• TWICKENHAM

• MERTON

• KINGSTON

• BROMLEY

• SUTTON

• CROYDON

i For bus and public transport information, call Transport for London on **020 7222 1234**.

Battersea Park

CELEBRATING LONDON

London possesses a unique treasure chest of garden squares, waterways and great buildings. English Heritage properties convey this diversity with Apsley House at Hyde Park Corner, Kenwood in Hampstead and the Art Deco extravaganza of Eltham Palace in south London.

One of the most important tasks of English Heritage is to help preserve the best of the capital's historic fabric while embracing the demands of modern life.

A good example is the conversion of a disused 1930s cinema in Harrow into a health club. The building retains an important role in the community as well as its stunning exterior and magnificently decorated interior.

This year, also with the help of English Heritage, the famous Roundhouse in Chalk Farm will be repaired and adapted for use as a creative centre for young people.

Sometimes historic buildings can provide the impetus for the best new design. An excellent example is to be found in Duke of York Square, Chelsea. Here a beautiful adaptation of a former 1803 military complex has opened up an area 'hidden' from the public for over 200 years. It now boasts a new public square and retail buildings – all carefully designed to complement its historic character.

In 2005 the Kings Cross 'Regent Quarter' redevelopment will see similar improvements, with the refurbishment of existing old buildings and opening up of new public spaces and thoroughfares.

However, it's not only buildings which are preserved. Last year the restoration of Battersea Park's 19th-century sub-tropical gardens was completed – the first gardens of their kind in Britain. In addition, the riverside promenade and the 1951 Festival of Britain Pleasure Gardens have been given a new lease of life.

In a constantly changing city, London's historic fabric is a real stimulus to new design and ideas.

www.english-heritage.org.uk/london

APSLEY HOUSE HYDE PARK – W1J 7NT

Right in the heart of London at Hyde Park Corner is Apsley House, home of Arthur Wellesley, the first Duke of Wellington, and his descendants. For over 200 years, this important property has been known colloquially as 'No. 1 London', as it was the first house to be encountered after passing the tollgates at the top of Knightsbridge.

The Waterloo Gallery

Apsley House was originally designed and built by Robert Adam between 1771 and 1778 for Baron Apsley – from whom it takes its name. It passed to the Wellesley family in 1807 and was first owned by Richard and then his younger brother Arthur Wellesley – the Duke of Wellington.

The Duke of Wellington is most famous for defeating Napoleon at the Battle of Waterloo in 1815, but this was only the culmination of a brilliant military career. He was also a major politician, rising from representing a small Irish constituency in 1790 to Prime Minister in 1828.

The current look of Apsley House is the result of alterations made by the Wellesley family. The Corinthian portico and two bays of the west wing were added in 1828. Perhaps more importantly, many rooms were redesigned to reflect the Duke of Wellington's rising status. These provided the perfect backdrop for entertaining, particularly the annual Waterloo Banquets which took place every year to commemorate the great battle.

Inside Apsley House you will see many aspects of the first Duke of Wellington's life and work, but it is his amazing art collection that is most famous.

The Duke of Wellington
by Sir Thomas Lawrence

Hung throughout the first floor are works by Velazquez, Goya, Rubens and Van Dyck. Many of the paintings originally formed part of the Spanish Royal Collection and came into the possession of the duke after the battle of Vitoria in 1813. A colossal nude statue of Napoleon by Canova dominates the stairwell at the centre of the house.

Throughout his military career, the duke was presented with a vast collection of silver gilt and unique porcelain as trophies from grateful nations. Many of these collections can be seen in the Museum Room. Wellington's victories are celebrated in fine British craftsmanship in the magnificent Wellington Shield, designed by Thomas Stothard, and the impressive candelabra presented to the duke by the Merchants and Bankers of the City of London.

When the seventh Duke of Wellington gave the house to the nation in 1947, the family retained the private rooms, which they still use today. This makes Apsley House the only property managed by English Heritage in which the original owner's family still live.

Duke of Wellington enthusiasts may also be interested in visiting the spectacular Wellington Arch which is situated opposite Apsley House (page 35) and the elegant Walmer Castle (page 74) which was the duke's country residence.

www.english-heritage.org.uk/apsleyhouse

New for 2005

We have created a special Wellington Boot activity pack designed for families to do together. The activities will help visitors find out more about the vast array of objects owned by the Duke of Wellington.

NON-MEMBERS

APSLEY HOUSE

Adult	£4.95
Concession	£3.70
Child	£2.50

JOINT TICKET WITH WELLINGTON ARCH

Adult	£6.30
Concession	£4.70
Child	£3.20
Family ticket	£15.80

OPENING TIMES

24 Mar-31 Oct, Tue-Sun & Bank Hols	10am-5pm
1 Nov-31 Mar, Tue-Sun	10am-4pm
Closed	24-26 Dec and 1 Jan

HOW TO FIND US

Direction: 149 Piccadilly, Hyde Park Corner

Train: Victoria ½ mile

Bus: From surrounding areas.

Tube: Hyde Park Corner, adjacent

Tel: 020 7499 5676

Family learning resources available.

MAP	Page 258 (4E)
	OS Map 176 (ref TQ 284799)

CHAPTER HOUSE AND PYX CHAMBER

WESTMINSTER ABBEY

Built by the royal masons in 1250, the Chapter House of Westminster Abbey was originally used in the 13th century by Benedictine monks for their daily meetings. It later became a meeting place of the King's Great Council and the Commons, predecessors of today's Parliament.

A beautiful octagonal building with a vaulted ceiling and delicate central column, it offers rarely seen examples of medieval sculpture, an original floor of glazed tiles and spectacular wall paintings. The 11th-century Pyx Chamber was used as a monastic and royal treasury.

Chapter House free to EH members. Under the care and management of the Dean and Chapter of Westminster.

OPENING TIMES

Throughout the year;
Mon-Sun   10am-4pm
Closed   Good Fri,
              24-26 Dec and 1 Jan
May be closed at short notice on state and religious occasions

HOW TO FIND US

Direction: Through cloister from Dean's Yard

Train: Victoria and Charing Cross both ¾ mile, Waterloo 1 mile

CHAPTER HOUSE AND PYX CHAMBER

Bus: From surrounding areas

Tube: Westminster and St James's Park stations both ¼ mile

Tel: 020 7654 4834

MAP   Page 259 (4F)
           OS Map 177 (ref TQ 299795)

CHISWICK HOUSE

CHISWICK   SEE OPPOSITE PAGE

COOMBE CONDUIT

KINGSTON-UPON-THAMES

Coombe Conduit is made up of two small Tudor buildings connected by a passage underground. Water was once supplied to Hampton Court Palace via this tunnel.

Managed by the Kingston Society.

OPENING TIMES

Apr-Sep, every 2nd Sun   2pm-4pm

HOW TO FIND US

Direction: Coombe Lane on the corner of Lord Chancellor's Walk

Train: Norbiton ¾ mile

Bus: 57 Kingston – Streatham

Tel: 020 8942 1296

MAP   Page 258 (4E)
           OS Map 176 (ref TQ 204698)

ELTHAM PALACE

LONDON   GO TO PAGE 30

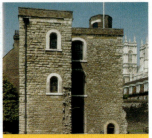

JEWEL TOWER

WESTMINSTER – SW1P 3JX

The Jewel Tower, or 'King's Privy Wardrobe', was built c.1365 to house the treasures of Edward III. One of only two buildings of the original Palace of Westminster to survive the fire of 1834, the tower features an original 14th-century ribbed vault. Today, it is home to *Parliament Past and Present*, a fascinating exhibition about the history of Parliament, which now includes new exhibition panels. The remains of a moat and medieval quay are still visible outside.

NON-MEMBERS

Adult	£2.60
Concession	£2.00
Child	£1.30

OPENING TIMES

24 Mar-31 Oct, daily	10am-5pm
1 Nov-31 Mar, daily	10am-4pm
Closed	24-26 Dec and 1 Jan

HOW TO FIND US

Direction: Located on Abingdon Street, opposite the southern end of the Houses of Parliament (Victoria Tower)

Train: Charing Cross ¾ mile, Victoria and Waterloo, both 1 mile

Bus: From surrounding areas

Tube: Westminster ¼ mile

Tel: 020 7222 2219

MAP   Page 259 (4F)
           OS Map 177 (ref TQ 301793)

CHISWICK HOUSE

CHISWICK – W4 2RP

Chiswick House is recognised as one of the most glorious examples of 18th-century British architecture. The third Earl of Burlington (1694-1753), who designed the house, drew inspiration from his 'grand tours' of Italy.

Burlington was a promoter of the Palladian style originally pioneered in Britain by Inigo Jones, and sought to create the kind of house and garden found in the suburbs of ancient Rome. To do this, he employed William Kent to create sumptuous interiors to contrast with the pure exterior.

An exhibition and video tell the story of the house, grounds and Lord Burlington, including his 'grand tours'. As you walk through the house, you can take in the splendour of the beautiful painted and gilded ceilings, and discover the lavish Red, Blue and Green Velvet rooms.

The historic rooms display paintings and furniture that combine Burlington's original collection with stunning loans to recreate the look and feel of the house as Lord Burlington and his guests would have experienced it.

The classical gardens are fascinating and a perfect complement to the house. There is level access to most of the grounds (except for Terrace Walk owing to a gradient.) Look out for the unique statues in the Italianate gardens.

www.english-heritage.org.uk/chiswickhouse

🍸 Available for corporate and private hire.

🔔 Licensed for civil wedding ceremonies.

NON-MEMBERS

Adult	£4.00
Concession	£3.00
Child	£2.00

OPENING TIMES

24 Mar-31 Oct, Wed-Sun & Bank Hols.   10am-5pm

Closes at 2pm on Sat

1 Nov-31 Mar Pre-booked appointments only.

HOW TO FIND US

Direction: Burlington Lane, W4

Train: Chiswick ½ mile

Bus: TfL 190 Hammersmith – Richmond; E3 Greenford – Chiswick

Tube: Turnham Green ¾ mile

Tel: 020 8995 0508

Disabled access (ground floor; wheelchair stair-climber to first floor, please call to confirm use prior to visit).

Dogs on leads (restricted areas only).

Parking (off westbound A4).

MAP	Page 258 (4E)
	OS Map 176 (ref TQ 210775)

ELTHAM PALACE GREENWICH – SE9 5QE

When textile magnates Stephen and Virginia Courtauld built their 1930s Art Deco mansion by the Great Hall of medieval Eltham Palace, they created a masterpiece of 20th-century design.

The entrance hall

The stone bridge and moat

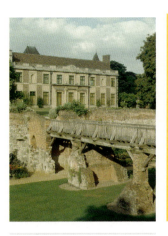

Built as a house with all the latest modern conveniences, the Courtauld's home came with under floor heating, a centralised vacuum cleaner and a built-in audio system.

The new Spotlight display brings together discoveries from the Courtauld era, including original furniture and family photographs.

As you leave the opulent 1930s house and enter the medieval palace, the interior presents a striking contrast. The Great Hall was built for Edward IV in the 1470s, and Henry VIII spent much of his childhood here.

Completed in 1936, the exterior of the house was built in sympathy with the original building, using a red brick design inspired by Hampton Court Palace. However the interior of the house was, and still is, a showpiece for glamorous 1930s design. Today visitors can revel in the eclectic mix of French-influenced Art Deco, ultra-smart ocean-liner style and cutting-edge Swedish design.

The dining room is a tour-de-force, with pink leather-upholstered chairs, bird's-eye maple veneered walls and a silver ceiling. It is entered through black-and-silver doors portraying animals and birds drawn from life at London Zoo.

Even more exotic is Virginia Courtauld's vaulted bathroom, lined with onyx and gold mosaic, complete with gold-plated bath taps and a statue of the goddess Psyche. Luxury also emanates from the centrally heated sleeping quarters of the Courtaulds' pet ring-tailed lemur, Mah-Jongg.

In the 19 acres of beautiful gardens which surround the palace, you can find elements from both the 20th century and the medieval period. Features include a rock garden sloping down to the moat, a medieval bridge, herbaceous borders inspired by modern designer Isabelle Van Groeningen, a formal sunken rose garden and plenty of picnic areas. The garden is special at any of time of year, but visitors will delight in the Spring bulb display and the wisteria cascading over the classical pergola in Summer.

🎬 *The Gathering Storm* and Stephen Fry's *Bright Young Things*.

www.english-heritage.org.uk/elthampalace

🍴 Available for corporate and private hire.

🔔 Licensed for civil wedding ceremonies.

NON-MEMBERS HOUSE AND GARDEN	
Adult	£7.30
Concession	£5.50
Child	£3.70
Family ticket	£18.30

NON-MEMBERS GARDEN ONLY	
Adult	£4.60
Concession	£3.50
Child	£2.30

OPENING TIMES

1 Apr-31 Oct, Sun-Wed 10am-5pm	
1 Nov-21 Dec, Sun-Wed 10am-4pm	
1 Feb-31 Mar, Sun-Wed 10am-4pm	
Closed	22 Dec-31 Jan and 18 Jul

HOW TO FIND US

Direction: **Off Court Rd SE9, Junction 3 on the M25, then A20 to Eltham**

Train: **Eltham and Mottingham, both ½ mile**

Bus: **From surrounding areas**

Tel: 020 8294 2548

Disabled access (and parking via Court Yard entrance).

Family learning resources available.

Parking (signed off Court Rd).

MAP	Page 259 (4F)
	OS Map 177 (ref TQ 424740)

KENWOOD HAMPSTEAD – NW3 7JR

Set in splendid grounds beside Hampstead Heath, this outstanding house was remodelled by Robert Adam between 1764 and 1779. He transformed the original brick building into a majestic villa for the great judge, Lord Mansfield. The richly decorated library is one of Adam's great masterpieces and a feast for the eyes.

The library

Kenwood House holds a fascinating collection of important paintings by many great names including Rembrandt, Vermeer, Turner, Reynolds and Gainsborough. The paintings are beautifully displayed against the backdrop of Kenwood's sumptuous interiors, and an audio tour is available providing detailed information on both the pictures and how they were brought together.

The first floor displays a very different collection of paintings. The Suffolk Collection includes magnificent portraits of Elizabethan and Stuart men and women by William Larkin,

Van Dyck and Lely, given by the Hon. Mrs Greville Howard in 1974. Brewing magnate Edward Cecil Guinness, first Earl of Iveagh, bought Kenwood House and gardens in 1925. When he died in 1927, he bequeathed the estate and part of his collection of pictures to the nation.

The parkland surrounding Kenwood has been redesigned by successive owners of the estate, and was particularly influenced by the master English landscape gardener, Humphry Repton. Set high on a hill, the views of London from these tranquil grounds are stunning. Visitors can also enjoy the lakeside walks and meandering woodland paths, which provide a superb backdrop for the famous summer concerts.

The music room

Most of the grounds are accessible by gravel path and grass, but wheelchairs users will need strong pushers to manage the slopes. The Brew House Café makes a great place to stop for lunch or a cup of tea.

www.english-heritage.org.uk/kenwoodhouse

 *Notting Hill, Mansfield Park* and *101 Dalmatians.*

OPENING TIMES

24 Mar-31 Oct, daily	11am-5pm
1 Nov-31 Mar, daily	11am-4pm
Closed	24-26 Dec and 1 Jan

The Park stays open later, please see site notices. House and grounds free; donations welcome. Pre-booked group tours available.

HOW TO FIND US

Direction: Hampstead Lane, NW3

Train: Hampstead Heath 1½ miles

Bus: Tfl 210 ⇌ Finsbury Park – Golders Green

Tube: Archway then 210 bus

Tel: 020 8348 1286

Disabled access (ground floor only; toilets).

Dogs on leads (restricted areas only).

Garden shop and house shop.

Parking (charge). Disabled bays. Mobility service available on request.

Restaurant (The Brew House Café open all year; serves home-made food throughout the day).

Please note: Kenwood hosts regular events, garden tours and acclaimed summer concerts.

MAP   Page 258 (3E)
       OS Map 176 (ref TQ 271874)

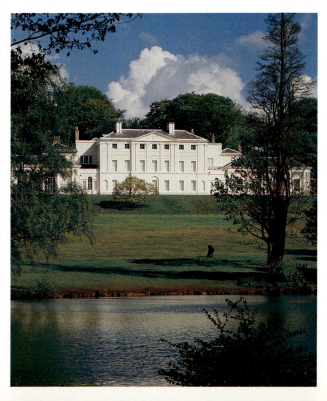

RANGER'S HOUSE – THE WERNHER COLLECTION

GREENWICH PARK – SE10 8QX

Built around 1700, Ranger's House is an elegant Georgian villa, which was the official residence of the 'Ranger of Greenwich Park'.

The house is situated on the borders of Greenwich Park, and the Meridian Line passes through its grounds. Today, it is home to the Wernher Collection – a stunning display of medieval and Renaissance works of art, all purchased by the diamond magnate Sir Julius Wernher (1850 – 1912).

Arranged within the panelled interiors of this graceful mansion, the Wernher Collection presents a glittering spectacle – a sumptuous arrangement of silver and jewels, paintings and porcelain.

Nearly 700 works of art are on display, including early religious paintings and Dutch Old Masters, minute carved Gothic ivories, fine Renaissance bronzes and

silver treasures. Together, these pieces reveal the genius of medieval craftsmen and the unparalleled quality of Renaissance decorative arts.

With the Cutty Sark, Greenwich and Blackheath all nearby, Ranger's House makes a great day out.

www.english-heritage.org.uk/ rangershouse

16th-century infant Christ pendant

NON-MEMBERS

Adult	£5.30
Concession	£4.00
Child	£2.70

OPENING TIMES

24 Mar-30 Sep, Wed-Sun & Bank Hols	10am-5pm
1 Oct-21 Dec & 1- 31 Mar Pre-booked appointments only.	
Closed	22 Dec-28 Feb

Please phone the house for additional opening times

HOW TO FIND US

Direction: Chesterfield Walk, Blackheath SE10

DLR: Cutty Sark

Train: Blackheath, Greenwich, Lewisham and Maze Hill, all ¾ mile

Bus: 53 Trafalgar Sq – Plumstead

River: Greenwich Pier

Tel: 020 8853 0035

Toilets (including disabled)

MAP	Page 259 (4F) OS Map 177 (ref TQ 388769)

WELLINGTON ARCH

HYDE PARK – W1J 7JZ

Situated in the heart of Royal London at Hyde Park Corner, the Wellington Arch is a landmark for Londoners and visitors alike. George IV originally commissioned this massive monument as a grand outer entrance to Buckingham Palace. It was completed in 1825 by architect Decimus Burton, and moved to its present site in 1882.

It is possible to climb to the balconies just below the spectacular bronze sculpture, which sits on top of the imposing monument. The statue is the largest bronze sculpture in Europe and depicts the angel of peace descending on the chariot of war. The glorious views over London's Royal Parks and the Houses of Parliament make the climb to the top well worth the effort, and there is a lift available for less able visitors.

Inside the Arch, three floors of exhibits tell its fascinating history – including its time as London's smallest Police Station – as well as providing information on many of London's other well-known statues and memorials.

Apsley House, opposite the Wellington Arch, was the London home of the Duke of Wellington and is also managed by English Heritage.

www.english-heritage.org.uk/ wellingtonarch

Ⓣ Available for corporate and private hire.

Display inside the Arch

NON-MEMBERS

Adult	£3.00
Concession	£2.30
Child	£1.50

OPENING TIMES

24 Mar-31 Oct, Wed-Sun & Bank Hols	10am-5pm
1 Nov-31 Mar, Wed-Sun	10am-4pm
Closed	24-26 Dec and 1 Jan

HOW TO FIND US

Direction: Hyde Park Corner, W1J

Train: Victoria ¾ mile

Bus: From surrounding areas

Tube: Hyde Park Corner, adjacent

Tel: 020 7930 2726

♿ Ⓔ Ⓣ 🔲 🔲 🔲 ⚠

Please note: Exclusive group tours are available every Mon, with talk, slide presentation and refreshments on request (small charge).

MAP	Page 258 (4E)
	OS Map 176 (ref TQ 284798)

KENWOOD

HAMPSTEAD   GO TO PAGE 32

LONDON WALL

TOWER HILL

This is the best-preserved piece of the Roman Wall which once formed part of the eastern defences of London (Londinium). Built c. AD200, the wall defined the shape and size of London for over a millennium.

OPENING TIMES

Free access

HOW TO FIND US

Direction: Located outside Tower Hill Underground station, EC3

Train: Fenchurch Street ¼ mile

Bus: From surrounding areas

Tube: Tower Hill, adjacent

MAP   Page 259 (3F)
         OS Map 177 (ref TQ 336807)

Visit **www.english-heritage. org.uk** for up-to-date events information and the latest news.

MARBLE HILL HOUSE

RICHMOND – TW1 2NL

A lovely Palladian villa set in 66 acres of riverside parkland. Marble Hill is the last complete surviving example of the elegant villas and gardens which bordered the Thames between Richmond and Hampton Court in the 18th century.

NON-MEMBERS

Adult	£4.00
Concession	£3.00
Child	£2.00

OPENING TIMES

24 Mar-31 Oct, Sat   10am-2pm
Sun & Bank Hols   10am-5pm
1 Nov-31 Mar
Pre-booked appointments only

HOW TO FIND US

Direction: Richmond Rd, Twickenham

Train: St Margarets ½ mile

Bus: From surrounding areas

Tube: Richmond 1 mile

Tel: 020 8892 5115

Café (Coach House Café, March-Oct).

Disabled access (exterior & ground floor only; toilets).

Dogs (restricted areas only).

MAP   Page 258 (4E)
         OS Map 176 (ref TQ 173736)

RANGER'S HOUSE – THE WERNHER COLLECTION

GREENWICH   GO TO PAGE 34

WINCHESTER PALACE

SOUTHWARK

Part of the Great Hall of Winchester Palace, which was built in the early 13th century, is still visible, including the striking rose window which decorates the west gable. Unfortunately most of the 13th-century palace, house of the Bishops of Winchester, was destroyed by fire in 1814.

OPENING TIMES

Free access

HOW TO FIND US

Direction: Next to Southwark Cathedral and the Golden Hinde replica ship; corner of Clink St and Storey St, SE1

Train/Tube: London Bridge ¼ mile

Bus: From surrounding areas

MAP   Page 259 (4F)
         OS Map 177 (ref TQ 325803)

Sign-up on-line for our email Members' Newsletter at **www.english-heritage.org.uk**

If you would like more information on properties, events and membership please call 0870 333 1181 or email **customers@ english-heritage.org.uk**

OTHER HISTORIC ATTRACTIONS

DISCOUNTED ENTRY TO OUR MEMBERS (DISCOUNTS MAY NOT APPLY ON EVENT DAYS)

THE ALBERT MEMORIAL
KENSINGTON – SW1

Her Majesty the Queen reopened the Albert Memorial in 1998, after one of the most ambitious conservation projects ever undertaken by English Heritage. It took four years to repair structural damage to the memorial, which meant stripping the monument to its cast-iron core and rebuilding it with all the original elements conserved. A fully-guided tour provides exclusive access behind the railings of the site.

Managed by the Royal Parks

ENTRY

Tour (EH members)	£3.50

Discount does not extend to EH Corporate Partners

OPENING TIMES

Daily. Guided tours only from 7 Mar-18 Dec, Sun   2pm & 3pm

Call to book tours. Group bookings at other times by prior arrangement.

HOW TO FIND US

Train: Paddington 1¼ miles, Victoria 1½ miles

Bus: From surrounding areas

Tube: Knightsbridge ½ mile, South Kensington ½ mile

Tel: 020 7495 0916 (10am-4pm)

MAP   Page 258 (4E)
       OS Map 176 (ref TQ 265797)

DANSON HOUSE
KENT – DA6 8HL

The most significant building at risk in London in 1995, now restored for the nation by English Heritage, and opened to the public for the first time in 30 years by Bexley Heritage Trust. Built for Sir John Boyd, this is one of Sir Robert Taylor's finest villas, with additions by Sir William Chambers. The restored 1760s interiors include a magnificent dining room scheme of 19 paintings by Charles Pavilion, and a rare George England organ.

ENTRY

A 25% discount on entry to English Heritage Members, accompanied children free (one with each paying adult)

OPENING TIMES

Good Friday – Oct 30th Wed, Thur, Sun and Bank Hols

Guided Tours	11am – 5pm
Last entry	4.15pm

HOW TO FIND US

Train: Welling Station ½ mile

Bus: 89, B16, 486 Or B13 from New Eltham (Eltham Palace)

Tel: 020 8303 6699

MAP   Page 259 (4F)
       OS Map 177 (ref TQ 473752)

KENSAL GREEN CEMETERY
KENSAL GREEN – NW10

Kensal Green Cemetery is one of seven cemeteries which were established to cope with the huge population explosion which London experienced at the height of the Industrial Revolution. It houses some spectacular pieces of Victorian Gothic mausoleum architecture and some illustrious residents, including Prince Augustus Frederick, Duke of Sussex (the sixth son of King George III) and his sister Princess Sophia. English Heritage manages the cemetery buildings, and has recently restored the Dissenters' Chapel.

There are plans to restore the Anglican Chapel and some of the monuments. Tours, arranged by the Friends of Kensal Green Cemetery, are given every Sunday at 2pm. These include a visit to the catacombs on the first and third Sunday of every month (under 12s not admitted to the catacombs).

ENTRY

Tour (EH members)	£4.00

Discount does not extend to EH Corporate Partners

OPENING TIMES

Daily

HOW TO FIND US

Train/Tube: Kensal Green, adjacent

Tel: 07951 631001

MAP   Page 258 (3E)
       OS Map 176 (ref TQ 231825)

37

LONDON STATUES

In 1999, English Heritage assumed responsibility for the maintenance of 47 statues and monuments within central London, including the Wellington Arch, which you are invited to explore (see page 35).

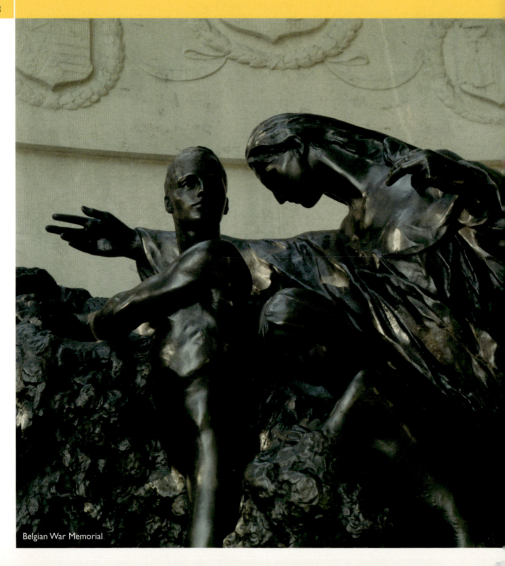

Belgian War Memorial

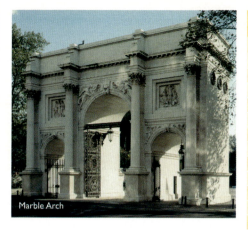

Marble Arch

Statues provide a fascinating insight into the preoccupations of the period. Many of them are associated with wars and military campaigns, such as the Napoleonic Wars, the Boer War and the two World Wars. Royalty is also well represented, with examples throughout the city from Charles I, 1633, to Edward VII, 1921

A leaflet giving more information about the intriguing history of London's statues and memorials is available free of charge from English Heritage. To obtain a copy of Kings and Queens: Royal Statues & Memorials in London, call English Heritage on **0870 333 1181**.

Statue of King George III

THE CAPITAL'S MONUMENTS

Viscount Alanbrooke	Whitehall, SW1
Queen Anne	Queen Anne's Gate, SW1
Belgian War Memorial	Victoria Embankment
Simon Bolivar	Belgrave Square, SW1
Duke of Cambridge	Whitehall, SW1
Colin Campbell	Waterloo Place, SW1
Carabiniers Memorial	Chelsea Embankment, SW3
Edith Cavell	St Martin's Place, WC2
Cenotaph	Whitehall, SW1
King Charles I	Trafalgar Square, SW1
Queen Charlotte	Queen Square, WC1
Clive of India	King Charles St, SW1
Christopher Columbus	Belgrave Square, SW1
Crimea Memorial	Waterloo Place, SW1
Thomas Cubitt	St George's Drive, Pimlico, SW1
Lord Curzon	Carlton House Terrace, SW1
Duke of Devonshire	Whitehall, SW1
Edward VII	Waterloo Place, SW1
General Eisenhower	Grosvenor Square, W1
Sir John Franklin	Waterloo Place, SW1
General de Gaulle	Carlton Gardens, SW1
King George II	Golden Square, W1
King George III	Cockspur St, SW1
General Gordon	Victoria Embankment
Earl Haig	Whitehall, SW1
Sir Arthur Harris	St Clement Danes, WC2
Lord Herbert	Waterloo Place, SW1
King James II	National Gallery, Trafalgar Square, WC2
Duke of Kent	Crescent Gardens (locked), Portland Place, W1
Baron Lawrence	Waterloo Place, SW1
Machine Gun Corps	Apsley Way, W1
Montgomery	Whitehall, SW1
Lord Napier of Magdala	Queen's Gate, SW7
Marble Arch	W1
Florence Nightingale	Waterloo Place, SW1
Samuel Plimsoll	Victoria Embankment
Lord Portal	Victoria Embankment
Sir Walter Raleigh	Old Royal Naval College, Greenwich, SE10
Royal Artillery Memorial	Apsley Way, SW1
General de San Martin	Belgrave Square, SW1
Captain Scott	Waterloo Place, SW1
Viscount Slim	Whitehall, SW1
Lord Trenchard	Victoria Embankment
George Washington	Trafalgar Square, WC2
Duke of Wellington	Apsley Way, W1
Wellington Arch and Quadriga	Apsley Way, W1
King William III	St James's Square, SW1

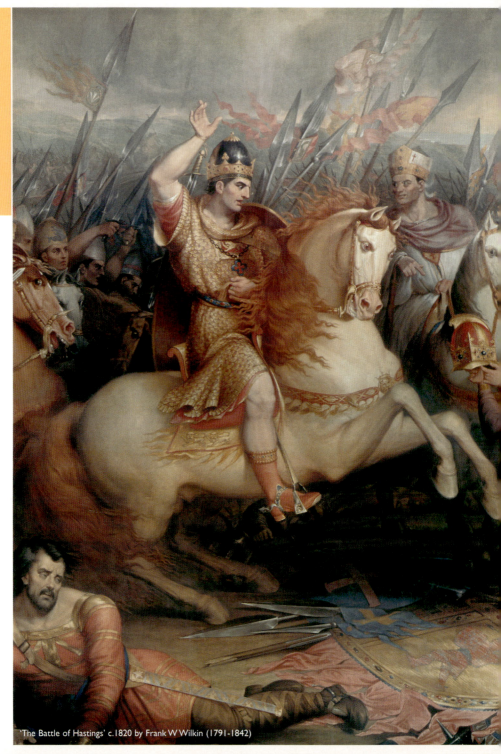

'The Battle of Hastings' c.1820 by Frank W Wilkin (1791-1842)

SOUTH EAST

The history of the South East is as diverse as the famous people associated with it. This region has been influenced by its close proximity to mainland Europe and its vulnerable shoreline.

PROPERTIES

SEE INDIVIDUAL LISTINGS FOR DETAILS

BERKSHIRE
Donnington Castle

HAMPSHIRE
Bishop's Waltham Palace, Calshot Castle, Flowerdown Barrows, Fort Brockhurst, Fort Cumberland, Hurst Castle, King James's and Landport Gates, Medieval Merchant's House, Netley Abbey, Northington Grange, Portchester Castle, Royal Garrison Church, Silchester Roman City Walls and Amphitheatre, Titchfield Abbey, Wolvesey Castle (Old Bishop's Palace)

KENT
Bayham Old Abbey, Conduit House, Deal Castle, Dover Castle and the Secret Wartime Tunnels, Dymchurch Martello Tower, Eynsford Castle, Faversham Stone Chapel, The Home of Charles Darwin (Down House), Horne's Place Chapel, Kit's Coty House and Little Kit's Coty House, Knights Templar Church, Lullingstone Roman Villa, Maison Dieu, Milton Chantry, Old Soar Manor, Richborough Roman Amphitheatre, Richborough Roman Fort, Reculver Towers and Roman Fort, Rochester Castle, St Augustine's Abbey, St Augustine's Cross, St John's Commandery, St Leonard's Tower, Sutton Valence Castle, Temple Manor, Upnor Castle, Walmer Castle and Gardens, Western Heights

OXFORDSHIRE
Abingdon County Hall, Deddington Castle, Minster Lovell Hall and Dovecote, North Hinksey Conduit House, North Leigh Roman Villa, Rollright Stones, Wayland's Smithy, Uffington Castle, White Horse and Dragon Hill

SURREY
Farnham Castle Keep, Waverley Abbey

EAST SUSSEX
1066 Battle of Hastings, Abbey & Battlefield, Camber Castle, Pevensey Castle

WEST SUSSEX
Boxgrove Priory, Bramber Castle

ISLE OF WIGHT
Appuldurcombe House, Carisbrooke Castle, Osborne House, St Catherine's Oratory, Yarmouth Castle

Comprehensive map of our sites
PAGE 258-259

BUCKINGHAMSHIRE

OXFORDSHIRE
• OXFORD
• HIGH WYCOMBE

BERKSHIRE

READING •

SURREY
• GUILDFORD

GILLINGHAM •

KENT
• MAIDSTONE

• BASINGSTOKE

DOVER
FOLKESTONE •

HAMPSHIRE

WEST SUSSEX
CRAWLEY •

EAST SUSSEX

• SOUTHAMPTON

• RINGWOOD

WORTHING •
• PORTSMOUTH

HASTINGS •

EASTBOURNE •

• NEWPORT

ISLE OF WIGHT

Dover Castle

GREAT DEFENCES OF THE SOUTH EAST

The coast of South East England has always offered a point of weakness for invasion, and the great wealth of Roman remains here is a reminder that Richborough was Britain's front door to the Roman Empire. The area retains evidence of Roman settlement, but it is the invasion by Duke William of Normandy in 1066 for which this area is most famous. The Battle of Hastings, commemorated by Battle Abbey, changed England forever.

Castles also abound, both along the shoreline and inland. Some, like Portchester Castle, have served as palaces: others, like Carisbrooke Castle where Charles I was held captive, as royal prisons. Spectacular Dover Castle, with its hidden network of secret wartime tunnels, has always played a leading role in defending England. Like many other south-eastern coastal fortifications, it has helped shape the destiny of the nation down to the present day.

Other cultural influences have come from further afield. Among the most decorative examples is Italianate Osborne House, where Queen Victoria also created the Durbar wing to reflect her love of India.

As well as caring for this price-less legacy, English Heritage also works with a number of partners in the area to enable the past and present to work together.

Over the past year, we have worked to ensure that people from any background can learn from, and enjoy, the historic environment. Among the sites that were open for Heritage Open Days this year were two unique war memorials in Brighton and Woking, which reflect the tremendous contribution of the Indian Army during the First and Second World Wars. English Heritage Outreach Department is currently developing an exhibition with ex-servicemen of pre-Partition India living in Slough. Exploring the importance of such war memorials, the exhibition will open at Slough Museum in April 2005, and will then tour the South East.

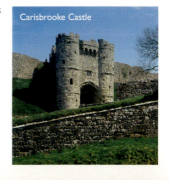
Carisbrooke Castle

www.english-heritage.org.uk/southeast

ABINGDON COUNTY HALL

OXFORDSHIRE – OX14 3HA

This 17th-century building housed the Assize Courts, which judged the more serious crimes such as murder. Today it is home to the Abingdon Museum and has great rooftop views.

Managed by Abingdon District Council.

OPENING TIMES

Daily	10.30am-4pm
Closed	25-26 Dec

and during exhibition changeovers

Please call for Christmas and public holiday opening. Roof-top visits – spring to autumn, Sats only. Adult £1.00, Child £0.50. Only children over 6 years admitted.

HOW TO FIND US

Direction: In Abingdon, 7 miles south of Oxford; in Market Place

Train: Radley 2½ miles

Bus: Oxford Bus 35/A/B from Oxford (passes ≷ Radley)

Tel: 01235 523703

🏛 ⚔

MAP	Page 258 (3C)
	OS Map 164 (ref SU 498971)

APPULDURCOMBE HOUSE

ISLE OF WIGHT – PO38 3EW

APPULDURCOMBE HOUSE

The shell of Appuldurcombe, once the grandest house on the Isle of Wight, stands in its own 'Capability' Brown-designed grounds. An exhibition of photographs and prints depicts the house and its history.

You can also visit the Freemantle Gate on the nearby public foot-path, and the adjacent Falconry Centre, a private attraction not owned by English Heritage.

Managed by Mr and Mrs Owen.

NON-MEMBERS

Adult	£2.50
Concession	£2.25
Child	£1.50
Family ticket	£7.00

Please note there is an additional charge for the Falconry Centre.

OPENING TIMES

19 Feb-30 Apr, daily	10am-3pm
(closes 5pm Easter weekend 2005)	
1 May-30 Sep, daily	10am-5pm
1-31 Oct, daily	10am-3pm
Last entry 1 hour before closing	

HOW TO FIND US

Direction: Wroxall ½ mile, off B3327

Train: Shanklin 3½ miles

Bus: Southern Vectis 3/A W Cowes – Ventnor; 7/A Ryde – Yarmouth

Ferry: Ryde 11 miles (Wightlink 0870 582 7744; Hovercraft 01983 811000); West Cowes 12 miles, East Cowes 12 miles (both Red Funnel – 0870 444 8898)

Tel: 01983 852484

P 🚶 ⛷ ♿ 🐕 📷

MAP	Page 258 (7C)
	OS Map 196 (ref SZ 543800)

1066 BATTLE OF HASTINGS, ABBEY AND BATTLEFIELD

EAST SUSSEX   GO TO PAGE 46

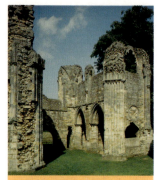

BAYHAM OLD ABBEY

KENT – TN3 8DE

The impressive ruins of an abbey of 'white canons' of the originally French Premonstratensian order. Includes the church, chapter house and a picturesque gate-house. Founded c.1208, the ruins are now set in an 18th-century landscape created by Earl Camden and Humphrey Repton, the famous landscape gardener who also designed the grounds of Kenwood House in London. Two rooms in the Georgian dower house are also open to the public.

NON-MEMBERS

Adult	£3.30
Concession	£2.50
Child	£1.70

OPENING TIMES

24 Mar-30 Sep, daily   11am-5pm

HOW TO FIND US

Direction: 1¾ miles W of Lamberhurst, off B2169

Train: Frant 4 miles

Bus: Coastal Coaches 256 Tunbridge Wells – Wadhurst (passes ≷ Tunbridge Wells)

Tel: 01892 890381

P 🚶 ⛷ 🪑 🐕 ♿ 📷 🏕 ♿ 🚻

Disabled access (grounds only).

MAP	Page 259 (5G)
	OS Map 188 (ref TQ 650365)

BISHOP'S WALTHAM PALACE

HAMPSHIRE – SO32 1DH

The ruins of a medieval palace (together with later additions) used by the senior clergy of Winchester when they travelled around their diocese. The Winchester diocese was the richest in England and its palaces were grandiose and extravagantly appointed. Other palaces of the Bishops of Winchester include Farnham Castle and Wolvesey Castle (Old Bishop's Palace).

Much of what can be seen today is the work of William Wykeham, who was bishop from 1367. There is an exhibition on the Winchester bishops on the first floor of the farmhouse.

NON-MEMBERS

Adult	£2.60
Concession	£2.00
Child	£1.30

Admission fee applies only on days when farmhouse is open

OPENING TIMES

Grounds only:
1 May-30 Sep, Mon-Fri 10am-5pm

Farmhouse & Grounds:
1 May-30 Sep, Sun and
Bank Hols   10am-5pm

HOW TO FIND US

Direction: In Bishop's Waltham

Train: Botley 3½ miles

Bus: Stagecoach in Hampshire 69 Winchester – Southsea (passes close to ⊞ Winchester and ⊞ Fareham); Solent Blue Line 8 from Eastleigh (passes ⊞ Botley)

Tel: 01489 892460

🅿 ♿ ⛺ 🎪 🐕 🚶 🚻 🖼 👁 ⚠

Disabled access (grounds only).
Dogs on leads (restricted areas only).
Toilets (nearby).

MAP   Page 258 (6C)
       OS Map 185 (ref SU 552174)

BOXGROVE PRIORY

WEST SUSSEX

The remains of a Benedictine priory built during the 12th century.

OPENING TIMES

Any reasonable time

HOW TO FIND US

Direction: N of Boxgrove; 4 miles E of Chichester, on minor road off A27

Train: Chichester 4 miles

Bus: Stagecoach in the South Downs 55 from ⊞ Chichester

🅿 🐕

MAP   Page 258 (6D)
       OS Map 197 (ref SU 908076)

BRAMBER CASTLE

WEST SUSSEX

A Norman motte and bailey castle, guarding the Adur Valley through the South Downs. The gatehouse stands almost to its full height, and the castle walls are still visible.

OPENING TIMES

Any reasonable time

HOW TO FIND US

Direction: On W side of Bramber village, off A283

Train: Shoreham-by-Sea 4½ miles

Bus: Brighton & Hove 2A Brighton – Steyning (passes ⊞ Shoreham-by-Sea)

🅿 🐕

Parking (limited).

MAP   Page 258 (6E)
       OS Map 198 (ref TQ 185107)

45

1066 BATTLE OF HASTINGS, ABBEY AND BATTLEFIELD EAST SUSSEX – TN33 0AD

Everyone knows at least one date in English history – 1066, the year the invading Normans defeated the Anglo-Saxons at the Battle of Hastings. In fact, the two armies did not fight at Hastings, but at a place north of the town now named Battle. In the ruins of Battle Abbey, which King William later built to commemorate the event, you can imagine you're standing on the very spot where the defeated King Harold fell.

The battlefield – later part of the abbey's Great Park – and the abbey were purchased for the nation in 1976.

A substantial portion of the abbey buildings remains, but little of the early Norman structure is left. Best preserved and most impressive is the Great Gatehouse, rebuilt c.1338 and arguably the finest of all surviving medieval abbey entrances. The west range of the monastic cloister, incorporating the medieval Great Hall of the abbots, was adapted as a country house by Tudor and Georgian owners after Henry VIII's Dissolution of the Monasteries.

The museum in the gatehouse takes a fascinating look at the monastic history of the site, and includes artefacts uncovered in excavations over the years. Visit the Discovery Centre, housing a fun, activity-based exhibition available to pre-booked school parties and open to families at weekends and throughout school holidays. Another display, *The Prelude to Battle*, provides more background information on the

Gatehouse Exhibition

Norman Conquest. There is also a themed children's outdoor play area, a gift shop and a battlefield and abbey audio tour.

The interactive audio tour re-creates the sounds of the battle as you stand where the Saxon army watched the Normans advancing towards them. The battle raged for some hours with neither side gaining an advantage, until the Normans pretended to flee, but then turned back to cut down the Saxons who had broken ranks in pursuit. Open battle raged until the death of Harold, perhaps struck in the eye by an arrow as depicted in the famous Bayeux Tapestry. The spot where he is thought to have fallen was marked by the high altar of the abbey, founded by William the Conqueror c.1070 to give thanks for his victory.

Why not while away a pleasant afternoon in Battle town: it has a Town Trail, plenty of antique shops, and hosts medieval fayres, events and farmers' markets. From Battle you can take the 1066 Walk to Pevensey Castle (one of Britain's oldest strong-holds) where William first landed before moving to Hastings (see page 62).

Find out about other places in the area by visiting the tourist information centre in the site shop, which is accessible from Battle High Street.

A re-enactment of the Battle of Hastings is the highlight of the year (15-16 Oct). For more details call 01424 775705 or visit **www.english-heritage.org.uk/events**

www.english-heritage.org.uk/battleabbey

Battle Re-enactment

NON-MEMBERS

Adult	£5.30
Concession	£4.00
Child	£2.70
Family ticket	£13.30

OPENING TIMES

24 Mar-30 Sep, daily	10am-6pm
1 Oct-31 Mar, daily	10am-4pm
Closed	24-26 Dec and 1 Jan

HOW TO FIND US

Direction: In Battle, at south end of High St. Take the A2100 off the A21

Train: Battle ½ mile. Inclusive rail and admission tickets package available; ask at any station

Bus: Arriva Kent & Sussex 4/5 Maidstone – Hastings

Tel: 01424 773792

Local Tourist Information: Battle (01424 773721) and Hastings (01424 781111)

Audio tours (interactive, also available for the visually impaired, those in wheelchairs or with learning difficulties, and in French, German and Japanese; braille guides in English only). Interactive tours will not be issued on special events days.

Disabled access (some steps).

Dogs on leads (restricted areas only).

Family learning resources available.

Parking (charge payable, free for EH members).

Toilets (managed by Rother District Council).

MAP	Page 259 (6G)
	OS Map 199 (ref TQ 749157)

CALSHOT CASTLE
HAMPSHIRE – SO4 1BR

This artillery fort, built by Henry VIII to defend the sea passage to Southampton, was recently used as a Navy and RAF base.

Managed by Hampshire County Council.

NON-MEMBERS

Adult	£2.50
Concession	£1.80
Child	£1.50
Family ticket	£6.00

OPENING TIMES

25 Mar-31 Oct, daily   10am-4pm

HOW TO FIND US

Direction: On spit, 2 miles SE of Fawley, off B3053

Bus: Solent Blue Line X9, 38 Southampton – Calshot (passes ⊋ Southampton), to within 1 mile

Tel: 02380 892023; when castle is closed, please call 02380 892077

🅿 ⛹ ♿ 🎫 ✂ 📷 ⚠

Disabled access (Keep: ground floor only; toilets).

MAP   Page 258 (6C)
       OS Map 196 (ref SU 489025)

CAMBER CASTLE
EAST SUSSEX – TN31 7RS

The ruins of an unusually original example of an artillery fort built by Henry VIII. There are monthly guided walks round Rye Harbour Nature Reserve, including the castle. Contact the Reserve Manager for further details.

Managed by Rye Harbour Nature Reserve

NON-MEMBERS

Adult	£2.00
Concession	£1.00
(Accompanied children free)	

OPENING TIMES

1 Jul-30 Sep, Sat-Sun   2pm-5pm
(last entry 4.30pm)

HOW TO FIND US

Direction: 1 mile walk across fields, off the A259; 1 mile S of Rye, off Harbour Road. No vehicle access.

Train: Rye 1¼ miles

Bus: From surrounding areas to Rye, then 1¼ miles

Tel: 01797 223862

✂

MAP   Page 259 (6H)
       OS Map 189 (ref TQ 922185)

CARISBROOKE CASTLE
ISLE OF WIGHT   GO TO PAGE 50

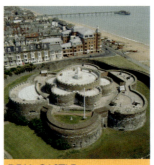

DEAL CASTLE
KENT – CT14 7BA

DEAL CASTLE

Deal Castle is one of the finest Tudor artillery works in England. It is among the earliest and most elaborate of a chain of coastal forts, which includes Calshot, Camber, Walmer and St. Mawes Castles. Most were built at great speed between 1539 and 1540, by order of King Henry VIII, who feared an invasion by the Catholic powers of Europe. Its squat, rounded turrets were designed to deflect incoming cannon fire and acted as platforms from which to launch barrages from increasingly sophisticated artillery pieces. It guarded the sheltered anchorage of 'the Downs' – the stretch of water between the shore and the infamous Goodwin Sands, which was considered a graveyard of ships. Today, you can explore the whole of the castle from the storerooms to the first-floor captain's residence. A pleasant cycle path links Deal and Walmer Castles along the beachfront.

🌂 Available for corporate and private hire.

🔔 Licensed for civil wedding ceremonies.

NON-MEMBERS

Adult	£3.70
Concession	£2.80
Child	£1.90

OPENING TIMES

24 Mar-30 Sep, daily   10am-6pm

HOW TO FIND US

Direction: SW of Deal town centre

Train: Deal ½ mile

Bus: From surrounding areas

Open for events during winter and October half term, please call 01304 211067 for details

DEAL CASTLE

Tel: 01304 372762

Audio tours (also available in French, German and Dutch).

Disabled access (courtyards and ground floor only, parking available).

| MAP | Page 259 (4J) |
| | OS Map 179 (ref TR 378522) |

DEDDINGTON CASTLE

OXFORDSHIRE

Extensive earthworks conceal the remains of this 12th-century castle.

Managed by Deddington Parish Council.

OPENING TIMES

Any reasonable time

HOW TO FIND US

Direction: S of B4031 on E side of Deddington; 17 miles N of Oxford

Train: King's Sutton 5 miles

Bus: Stagecoach in Banbury X59 Oxford – Banbury, to within ½ mile

| MAP | Page 258 (2C) |
| | OS Map 151 (ref SP 472316) |

DONNINGTON CASTLE

BERKSHIRE

The striking twin-towered 14th-century gatehouse of this castle, later the focus of a Civil War siege and battle, survives amid impressive earthworks.

OPENING TIMES

Any reasonable time; exterior viewing only

HOW TO FIND US

Direction: 1 mile N of Newbury, off B4494

DONNINGTON CASTLE

Train: Newbury 1¼ miles

Bus: Bennetts 130/4 from Newbury

Disabled access (steep slopes within grounds).

| MAP | Page 258 (4C) |
| | OS Map 174 (ref SU 461692) |

DOVER CASTLE AND THE SECRET WARTIME TUNNELS

KENT   GO TO PAGE 52

DOWN HOUSE – SEE THE HOME OF CHARLES DARWIN

KENT   GO TO PAGE 56

DYMCHURCH MARTELLO TOWER

KENT – TN29 0TJ

The best preserved of a chain of ingeniously-designed artillery towers, built at vulnerable points around the south-east coast to resist invasion by Napoleon.

NON-MEMBERS

Adult	£2.00
Concession	£1.50
Child	£1.00

OPENING TIMES

Open August Bank Hol and Heritage Open Days

HOW TO FIND US

Direction: In Dymchurch, from High St only

DYMCHURCH MARTELLO TOWER

Train: Sandling 7 miles; Dymchurch (Romney, Hythe and Dymchurch Railway) adjacent

Bus: Stagecoach in East Kent 11, 12/A and Stagecoach in Hastings 711 Dover – Hastings (passes close to Folkestone Central)

| MAP | Page 259 (5H) |
| | OS Map 189 (ref TR 102292) |

EYNSFORD CASTLE

KENT – DA44 0AA

One of the first stone castles to be built by the Normans. The moat and remains of the curtain wall and hall can still be seen.

OPENING TIMES

24 Mar-30 Sep, daily	10am-6pm
1 Oct-30 Nov, daily	10am-4pm
1 Dec-31 Jan, Wed-Sun	10am-4pm
1 Feb-31 Mar, daily	10am-4pm
Closed	24-26 Dec and 1 Jan

HOW TO FIND US

Direction: In Eynsford, off A225

Train: Eynsford 1 mile

Bus: Arriva G2, 413/5 Eynsford – Dartford

| MAP | Page 259 (4F) |
| | OS Map 177 (ref TQ 542658) |

Don't forget to check opening dates and times before you visit.

CARISBROOKE CASTLE

ISLE OF WIGHT – PO30 1XY

Crowning a hilltop south of Newport, Carisbrooke Castle held the dominant defensive position on the Isle of Wight for over 600 years.

The Gatehouse and Bridge

With its keep, battlements and working well house, Carisbrooke Castle is an exciting site for the whole family to explore. There has been a fortress here since Saxon times, but the present castle has existed on this site since 1100, when the island was granted to the de Redvers family.

When the Spanish Armada passed alarmingly close in 1588, Carisbrooke became enormously significant in the defence of the realm. It was suspected that the Spanish might attempt to seize the island, and in response the castle was transformed into an artillery fortress.

Charles I was imprisoned here in 1647. He was comfortably accommodated in the Constable's Lodging and a bowling green was constructed for his recreation. Nevertheless he made two attempts to escape: the first was foiled only when he became wedged in the window bars. Today, the Charles I room is furnished as a typical bedroom of the Stuart period.

The well house and tread wheel are still in working order and open to visitors. Prisoners may have originally worked the wheel, but from the late 17th century, donkeys were used. These hard-working animals can now be found happily giving demonstrations.

The on-site Isle of Wight Museum provides more historical information about the castle as well as memorabilia and artefacts relating to Charles I.

www.english-heritage.org.uk/carisbrooke

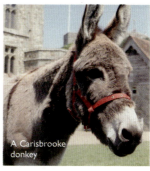

A Carisbrooke donkey

NON-MEMBERS

Adult	£5.30
Concession	£4.00
Child	£2.70
Family ticket	£13.30

OPENING TIMES

24 Mar-30 Sep, daily	10am-5pm
1 Oct-31 Mar, daily	10am-4pm
Closed	24-26 Dec and 1 Jan

HOW TO FIND US

Direction: 1¼ miles SW of Newport. Follow signs for Carisbrooke village and then the castle

Train: Ryde Esplanade 9 miles; Wootton (Isle of Wight Steam Railway) 5 miles

Bus: Southern Vectis 6, 7, 7A, 7B, 38 from Newport, West Wight and Ventnor, all to within ¼ mile

Ferry: West Cowes 5 miles, East Cowes 6 miles (Red Funnel – 0870 444 8898); Fishbourne 6 miles, Ryde 8 miles, Yarmouth 9 miles (Wightlink 0870 582 7744; Hovercraft Ryde 01983 811000)

Tel: 01983 522107

Local Tourist Information: 01983 813813

Disabled access (grounds and lower levels only).

Family learning resources available.

Tearooms (open Apr-Oct; call for details of winter arrangements).

MAP	Page 258 (7C)
	OS Map 196 (ref SZ 486878)

Bed in King Charles I room

DOVER CASTLE AND THE SECRET WARTIME TUNNELS KENT – CT16 1HU

Pivotal to the defence of England's shores right into the 20th century, Dover Castle tells the tale of the evolution of a fortress.

The impressive fortifications have withstood sieges and the ravages of time

No fortress in England boasts a longer history than Dover Castle. Commanding the shortest sea crossing between England and the continent, the site has served as a vital strategic centre during England's colourful history since Roman times.

William the Conqueror strengthened the existing Anglo-Saxon fortress in 1066, both Henry II and Henry VIII made their own additions, and Vice Admiral Ramsay famously oversaw the Dunkirk evacuations from the tunnels built into the cliffs beneath the castle.

Dover's wartime secret

The White Cliffs are one of England's most celebrated sights, yet hidden inside them is a fascinating and secret world. Deep underground lies an extensive network of tunnels – first dug during the Napoleonic Wars, but so strategically useful that they continued to be used right through to the 20th century.

There is good access for wheelchair users to the tunnels, although entry is down a steep slope. Mobility scooters, wheelchair routes and guides are available on site.

The Coastal Artillery Operations Room

Dunkirk evacuation – Operation Dynamo

In May 1940 these tunnels provided the nerve centre for Vice Admiral Ramsay to plan Operation Dynamo – the evacuation of the British and allied troops from the Dunkirk beaches of northern France.

This evacuation proved pivotal to saving the British army from total defeat and capture. The best estimate was that only 45,000 of the troops could be brought back, yet Sir Winston Churchill announced to the House of Commons on 4 June that 338,000 troops had been saved, despite the operation itself coming under fierce attack.

Today, you can take a tour of the Secret Wartime Tunnels and experience life as it was lived by the 700 personnel based here in the worst days ▶

www.english-heritage.org.uk/southeast

Telephone exchange in the Secret Wartime Tunnels

DOVER CASTLE

of World War II. You can see the Command Centre which Sir Winston Churchill visited to see the Battle of Britain, and relive the drama as a surgeon battles to save the life of an injured pilot in the underground hospital. Sounds, smells and film clips from the time create a realistic atmosphere of wartime Britain.

Outside, Admiralty Look-out stands on the edge of the cliff, offering a tremendous view of the White Cliffs and across to France. To the west of the look-out you can see a statue of Vice Admiral Ramsay and read about his key role in both the Dunkirk evacuations and the 1944 Normandy landings.

The key to medieval England

Under Henry II, the castle was rebuilt, including Avranches Tower, a polygonal structure built to control an angle in the eastern defences. There is a tremendous view from the tower along the outer moat and over the outer defences.

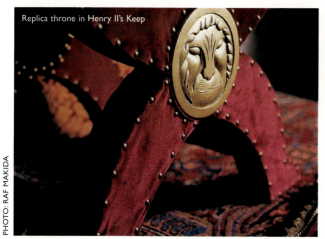
Replica throne in Henry II's Keep

PHOTO: RAF MAKIDA

Hellfire Corner

NON-MEMBERS

Adult	£8.95
Concession	£6.70
Child	£4.50
Family ticket	£22.40

This includes Secret Wartime Tunnels tour; the last tour begins one hour before the site closes. Additional charges for members and non-members may apply on event days.

The 1216 Siege Experience, a stunning presentation using light, film and sound technology, highlights the castle's key role in resisting invasion. It recounts the epic sieges of 1216-1217, when Dover Castle held out almost alone for King John against rebel barons and their French ally Prince Louis.

Henry VIII's visit

Following the annulment of his marriage to Catherine of Aragon, his excommunication by the Pope and the 1538 peace treaty between France and Spain, Henry VIII was isolated in Europe and a Catholic invasion of England seemed inevitable. The King commissioned a great chain of defensive coastal forts and came to Dover in 1539 to inspect the work personally. An exciting exhibition at the castle offers a tableau of the preparations for Henry VIII's visit. Very close to Dover you will find two of Henry's coastal defences, Deal Castle and Walmer Castle.

Also of interest at the site are the Princess of Wales' Royal Regiment Museum; one of the best-preserved Roman light-houses in Europe and the most complete Saxon church in Kent.

🍴 Dover Castle is available for corporate and private hire.

🎬 Zeffirelli's Hamlet, starring Mel Gibson, and To Kill a King, starring Dougray Scott.

www.english-heritage.org.uk/dovercastle

New for 2005

The Stone Hut, originally built in 1912 for the Royal Garrison Artillery, has been converted and is now being used as an archaeological store for the South East. On the first Friday of every month, visitors will be able to view treasures from across the region, including Roman coins and pots, as well as artefacts from both the Second World War and the Cold War.

Avranches Tower tours are available on a 'first come, first served' basis on the first Friday of every month This purpose-built archery tower was built in the 1180s to protect the castle from attack.

OPENING TIMES

24 Mar-30 Jun, daily	10am-6pm
1 Jul-31 Aug, daily	9.30am-6.30pm
1-30 Sep, daily	10am-6pm
1-31 Oct, daily	10am-5pm
1 Nov-31 Jan, Thu-Mon	10am-4pm
1 Feb-31 Mar, daily	10am-4pm
Closed	24-26 Dec and 1 Jan

Keep closes at 5pm on days of hospitality events. The site is open from noon on 12th April for the installation of the new Lord Warden, and closes at 4pm on 13th-15th May for 'Pop in the Castle' event.

HOW TO FIND US

Direction: E of Dover town centre

Train: Dover Priory 1½ miles

Bus: Stagecoach in East Kent 90, 90C, 91 and 113 from 🚉 Dover Priory

Tel: 01304 211067

Local Tourist Information Dover 01304 205108

Audio tours (small charge – separate tour for battlement walk and Medieval Underground Works – available in English, French and German).

Disabled access (courtyard, grounds and basement. Some very steep slopes).

Dogs on leads (restricted areas only).

Family learning resources available.

MAP	Page 259 (5J)
	OS Map 179 (ref TR 325419)

THE HOME OF CHARLES DARWIN, DOWN HOUSE

KENT – BR6 7JT

It was at Down House that Charles Darwin worked on his scientific theories and *On the Origin of Species by Means of Natural Selection* – the book that both scandalised and re-volutionised the Victorian world when it was published in 1859.

The house, built in the early 18th century, remains much as it was when Darwin lived here. The rooms on the ground floor have been furnished to reflect the domestic life of the family, while the study holds his writing desk,

chair and numerous objects connected with his work. The first floor offers an interactive exhibition on his life, his research and his discoveries.

English Heritage has recently restored the gardens to how they would have looked during Darwin's time. Some of Darwin's experiments on natural selection are recreated in the garden, and visitors can stroll around the famous Sandwalk, the path Darwin paced as he worked out his ideas.

You can discover more about Darwin and his family from our inclusive audio tour, which is narrated by Sir David Attenborough.

New for 2005

From Feb-May 2005: Thinking Path. A photographic exploration of the Sandwalk at Down House, Darwin's 'thinking path'; by artist Shirley Chubb

From June 2005: Emma – from Wedgwood to Darwin. An exhibition about the early life of Darwin's wife, Emma.

The Old Study

NON-MEMBERS

Adult	£6.60
Concession	£5.00
Child	£3.30
Family ticket	£16.50

OPENING TIMES

24 Mar-30 Sep, Wed-Sun and Bank Hols	10am-6pm
1-31 Oct, Wed-Sun	10am-5pm
1 Nov-31 Mar, Wed-Sun	10am-4pm
Closed	19 Dec-31 Jan
Last entry 30 mins before closing	

HOW TO FIND US

Direction: Luxted Rd, Downe; off A21 or A233

Train: Orpington 3¾ miles

Bus: 146 from Bromley North and South railway station; R8 from ⊕ Orpington

Tel: 01689 859119

Audio tours (English by David Attenborough; also in French, German and Japanese, and for those with sight or hearing impairment).

Parking (plus space for one coach).

MAP	Page 259 (4F) OS Map 177 (ref TQ 431611)

FARNHAM CASTLE KEEP

SURREY – GU6 0AG

This motte-and-bailey castle has been continuously occupied since the 12th century, and was once one of the seats of the Bishop of Winchester.

There are market stalls and a shopping area in Farnham, and Waverley Abbey is a short car journey away.

NON-MEMBERS

Adult	£2.60
Concession	£2.00
Child	£1.30

OPENING TIMES

24 Mar-30 Sep, Fri-Sun and Bank Hols   12pm-5pm

HOW TO FIND US

Direction: ½ mile N of Farnham town centre, on A287

Train: Farnham ¾ mile

Bus: From surrounding areas

Tel: 01252 713393

FAVERSHAM STONE CHAPEL

KENT

This ruined chapel is all that remains of a small medieval church. It incorporates visible remnants of a 4th-century Romano-British pagan mausoleum, suggesting continuity of worship here.

Managed by The Faversham Society.

OPENING TIMES

Any reasonable time

HOW TO FIND US

Direction: 1¼ miles W of Faversham on A2

Train: Faversham 1½ miles

Bus: Arriva 333, Jaycrest 335 Maidstone – Faversham (passes ☰ Faversham)

Tel: 01795 534542

MAP   Page 259 (4H)
OS Map 178 (ref TQ 992613)

FLOWERDOWN BARROWS

HAMPSHIRE

These barrows are part of a Bronze Age burial site and were part of a larger group.

OPENING TIMES

Any reasonable time

HOW TO FIND US

Direction: Off B3049, out of Winchester to Littleton; at crossroads in centre of village

Train: Winchester 2 miles

Bus: Stagecoach in Hampshire 86 from Winchester (passes ☰ Winchester)

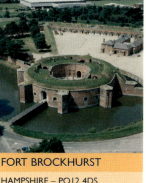

FORT BROCKHURST

HAMPSHIRE – PO12 4DS

One of a number of forts built in the 1850s to protect Portsmouth and its vital harbour. Largely unaltered, the parade ground, gun ramps and moated keep can all be viewed. The fort opens occasionally for pre-booked guided tours only and is also available for private hire.

The historic dockyards of Portsmouth are nearby, where you can see the Mary Rose, HMS Warrior and HMS Victory.

OPENING TIMES

The fort opens occasionally for pre-booked tours and Heritage Open Days; please call 01424 775705

HOW TO FIND US

Direction: Off A32, in Gunner's Way, Elson; on N side of Gosport

Train: Fareham 3 miles

Bus: First 81-7 Fareham – Gosport Ferry (passes ☰) Fareham also Gosport Ferry links with ☰ Portsmouth & Southsea)

Disabled access (grounds and ground floor only).
Dogs on leads (restricted areas only).

FORT CUMBERLAND

HAMPSHIRE – PO4 9LD

Perhaps England's most impressive piece of 18th-century defensive architecture, Fort Cumberland was reconstructed into a pentagonal shape by the Duke of Cumberland from 1785-1810, and designed to protect Langstone Harbour. Southsea beach is nearby.

OPENING TIMES

The fort opens occasionally for pre-booked guided tours and Heritage Open Days; please call 01424 775705

HOW TO FIND US

Direction: In Portsmouth's Eastney district on the estuary approach, via Henderson Rd off Eastney Rd, or from the Esplanade

Train: Fratton 2 miles

Bus: First 15, 16/A 🚉 Portsmouth Harbour – Hayling Ferry

⚠

| MAP | Page 258 (6C) |
| | OS Map 196 (ref SZ 683993) |

THE HOME OF CHARLES DARWIN (DOWN HOUSE)

KENT   GO TO PAGE 56

HORNE'S PLACE CHAPEL

KENT

This 14th-century domestic chapel was once attached to the manor house. The house and chapel are privately owned.

HORNE'S PLACE CHAPEL

OPENING TIMES

By arrangement; please call 01304 211067

HOW TO FIND US

Direction: 1½ miles N of Appledore

Train: Appledore 2½ miles

🅿 🏛
Parking (nearby).

| MAP | Page 259 (5H) |
| | OS Map 189 (ref TQ 958309) |

HURST CASTLE

HAMPSHIRE – SO41 0TP

One of the most sophisticated fortresses built by Henry VIII, and later strengthened in the 19th and 20th centuries, it commands the narrow entrance to the Solent.

Managed by Hurst Castle Services.

NON-MEMBERS

Adult	£3.00
Concession	£2.70
Child	£1.80

OPENING TIMES

| 25 Mar-31 Oct, daily | |
| | 10.30am-5.30pm |

HOW TO FIND US

Direction: On Pebble Spit S of Keyhaven; best approached by ferry from Keyhaven – call 01590 642500 for ferry details

HURST CASTLE

Train: Lymington Town 4½ miles to Keyhaven, 6½ miles to site

Bus: Wilts & Dorset 123/4 Bournemouth – Lymington (passes 🚉 New Milton), to within 2½ miles, or 1 mile to ferry

Tel: 01590 642344

🚶 🚻 💼 🏛 ⚠

Dogs on leads (restricted areas only).

Tearoom/restaurant (Castle Café, not managed by EH. Open Apr-May weekends only, Jun-Sep daily).

| MAP | Page 258 (7B) |
| | OS Map 196 (ref SZ 318897) |

ITCHEN ABBAS ROMAN VILLA

ITCHEN, HAMPSHIRE

The remains of a prehistoric settlement consisting of a Roman villa, enclosures, ditches and trackways visible in the form of cropmarks. Pottery dating from the Iron Age and a hypocaust system for underfloor heating have been found here.

OPENING TIMES

No public access. For more information call 01424 775705

| MAP | Page 258 (5C) |
| | OS Map 185 (ref SU 528343) |

KING JAMES'S AND LANDPORT GATES

HAMPSHIRE – PO1 2EJ

Both of these gates were important elements of Portsmouth's 17th-century defences. Landport Gate is the only Portsmouth town gate still in its original position.

OPENING TIMES

Any reasonable time; exterior viewing only

KING JAMES'S AND LANDPORT GATES

HOW TO FIND US

Direction: King James's Gate forms the entrance to United Services Recreation Ground (officers), Burnaby Rd; Landport Gate as above, men's entrance on St George's Road

Train: Portsmouth Harbour ¼ mile

Bus: From surrounding areas

MAP	Page 258 (6C) OS Map 196 (King James's Gate ref SZ 636999, Landport Gate ref SZ 634998)

KIT'S COTY HOUSE AND LITTLE KIT'S COTY HOUSE

KENT

The remains of two impressive prehistoric burial chambers.

OPENING TIMES

Any reasonable time

HOW TO FIND US

Direction: W of A229 2 miles N of Maidstone.

Train: Aylesford 2½ miles

Bus: Arriva 101 ⇌ Maidstone East – Gillingham.

MAP	Page 259 (4G) OS Map 188 (Kit Coty's House ref TQ 745608, Little Kit Coty's House ref TQ 744604)

KNIGHTS TEMPLAR CHURCH, DOVER

KENT

The foundations of a small medieval church, traditionally the site of King John's submission to the Papal Legate in 1213.

OPENING TIMES

Any reasonable time

KNIGHTS TEMPLAR CHURCH, DOVER

HOW TO FIND US

Direction: On the Western Heights above Dover

Train: Dover Priory ¾ mile

Tel: 01304 211067

Dogs on leads (restricted areas only).

MAP	Page 259 (5J) OS Map 179 (ref TR 313407)

LULLINGSTONE ROMAN VILLA

KENT – DA4 0JA

This is one of the most exciting archaeological finds in all of England. It was built c. AD100, but extended during 300 years of Roman occupation; much is still visible today. View the superb mosaic-tiled floors, wall paintings and the display of skeletal remains uncovered on site. Marvel at the extensive 4th-century bath complex, built when the villa was at its most prosperous.

NON-MEMBERS

Adult	£3.70
Concession	£2.80
Child	£1.90

OPENING TIMES

24 Mar-30 Sep, daily	10am-6pm
1 Oct-30 Nov, daily	10am-4pm
1 Dec-31 Jan, Wed-Sun	10am-4pm
1 Feb-31 Mar, daily	10am-4pm
Closed	24-26 Dec and 1 Jan

HOW TO FIND US

Direction: ½ mile SW of Eynsford; off A225; off junction 3 of M25

LULLINGSTONE ROMAN VILLA

Train: Eynsford ¾ mile

Tel: 01322 863467

Local Tourist Information: Clacketts La 01959 565063

Audio tours (also available for the visually impaired and for those with learning difficulties, and in French and German).

Family learning resources available.

MAP	Page 259 (4F) OS Map 177 (ref TQ 530651)

MAISON DIEU

KENT – ME13 8NS

This medieval building, forming part of a hospital, royal lodging and almshouse, houses Roman artefacts from nearby sites.

Managed by The Faversham Society.

NON-MEMBERS

Adult	£1.00
Concession	£0.80
Child	£0.50

OPENING TIMES

24 Mar-31 Oct, Sat-Sun, Good Friday and Bank Hols 2pm-5pm

Please call for further details

HOW TO FIND US

Direction: In Ospringe on A2; ½ mile W of Faversham

Train: Faversham ¾ mile

Bus: Arriva 333, Jaycrest 335 Maidstone – Faversham (passes ⇌ Faversham)

Tel: 01795 534542

MAP	Page 259 (4H) OS Map 179 (ref TR 313407)

MEDIEVAL MERCHANT'S HOUSE

HAMPSHIRE – SO1 0AT

60

John Fortin, a merchant who traded with Bordeaux, started building this house c.1290. A residence and place of business, it stood on one of the busiest streets in medieval Southampton. It has now been restored to its mid-14th-century appearance by the removal of later additions. The house stands near the medieval town wall, built to defend Southampton against seaborne attacks. Netley Abbey, Calshot Castle and Hurst Castle are all within reasonable travelling distance.

NON-MEMBERS

Adult	£3.30
Concession	£2.50
Child	£1.70

OPENING TIMES

24 Mar-30 Sep, Sat-Sun, Good Friday and Bank Hols   10am-5pm

HOW TO FIND US

Direction: 58 French St, ¼ mile S of city centre, just off Castle Way (between High St and Bugle St)

Train: Southampton ¾ mile

Bus: First 17/A from 🚉 Southampton

MEDIEVAL MERCHANT'S HOUSE

Tel: 02380 221503

🚶 🚻 🎧 ♿ 🖥 ✖

Audio tours (also available for the visually impaired and those with learning difficulties).

Disabled access (one step).

MAP	Page 258 (6B)
	OS Map 196 (ref SU 419112)

MILTON CHANTRY

KENT – DA12 2BH

This small 14th-century building housed the chapel of a leper hospital and a family chantry. Dissolved during the Reformation, it later became a tavern and, in 1780, part of a fort.

Managed by Gravesham Borough Council.

NON-MEMBERS

Adult	£1.00
Concession	£0.50
Child	£0.50

OPENING TIMES

1 Apr-30 Sep, Wed-Sat	12pm-5pm
Sun and Bank Hols	10am-5pm
1 Oct-23 Dec and 1-31 Mar:	
Sat	12pm-4pm
Sun	10am-4pm
Closed	Jan and Feb

HOW TO FIND US

Direction: In New Tavern Fort Gardens; E of central Gravesend, off A226

Train: Gravesend ¾ mile

Bus: From surrounding areas

Tel: 01474 321520

✖ ⚠

MAP	Page 259 (4G)
	OS Map 177 (ref TQ 653743)

MINSTER LOVELL HALL AND DOVECOTE

OXFORDSHIRE

The picturesque ruins of a 15th-century manor house, home of Richard III's henchman Lord Lovell.

OPENING TIMES

Any reasonable time.
Dovecote – exterior only

HOW TO FIND US

Direction: Adjacent to Minster Lovell church; 3 miles W of Witney, off A40

Train: Charlbury 7 miles

Bus: Stagecoach in Oxford 102/3 Witney – Carterton with connections from 🚉 Oxford

✖

MAP	Page 258 (2B)
	OS Map 164 (ref SP 325113)

NETLEY ABBEY

HAMPSHIRE

NETLEY ABBEY

The Cistercian abbey at Netley was founded by Peter de Roches, Bishop of Winchester from 1204-1238. The first monks entered in 1239, but it is probable that little building took place until it received the patronage of Henry III a few years later. Few major alterations were made to the monastic buildings, so most of those still visible are of 13th-century origin.

OPENING TIMES

Any reasonable time

HOW TO FIND US

Direction: In Netley; 4 miles SE of Southampton, facing Southampton Water

Train: Netley 1 mile

Bus: First 16 ⊠ Southampton – Hamble; Solent Blue Line 9A Winchester – Hamble

Tel: 02392 378291

🅿 ♿ 🚻 🚻 🐕 ⚠

Toilets (nearby, across the road near the estuary).

MAP	Page 258 (6C)
	OS Map 196 (ref SU 453090)

NORTH HINKSEY CONDUIT HOUSE

OXFORDSHIRE

Roofed conduit for Oxford's first water mains, constructed during the early 17th century.

OPENING TIMES

Exterior viewing only 10am-4pm

HOW TO FIND US

Direction: In North Hinksey off A34; 1½ miles W of Oxford. Located off track leading from Harcourt Hill; use the footpath from Ferry Hinksey Lane (near railway station).

NORTH HINKSEY CONDUIT HOUSE

Train: Oxford 1 mile

MAP	Page 258 (3C)
	OS Map 164 (ref SP 495050)

NORTH LEIGH ROMAN VILLA

OXFORDSHIRE

These are the remains of a large, well-built Roman courtyard villa. The most important feature is a near complete mosaic tile floor, patterned in reds and browns.

OPENING TIMES

Grounds – any reasonable time. There is a viewing window for the mosaic tile floor. Pedestrian access only from main road – 550 metres (600 yards)

HOW TO FIND US

Direction: 2 miles N of North Leigh; 10 miles W of Oxford, off A4095

Train: Hanborough 3½ miles

Bus: Stagecoach in Oxford 11 Oxford – Witney, to within 1½ miles

🅿 🐕

Parking (lay-by, not in access lane).

MAP	Page 258 (2B)
	OS Map 164 (ref SP 397154)

NORTHINGTON GRANGE

HAMPSHIRE

NORTHINGTON GRANGE

Northington Grange lies at the centre of a landscaped park. The house was remodelled in 1809 by William Wilkins, and is one of the earlier Greek revival houses in Europe. It provides a stunning setting for the opera evenings which take place here in the summer; call 01962 868600 for details.

🎬 The 1999 film, *Onegin*, with Ralph Fiennes, was filmed here.

OPENING TIMES

Exterior only:
24 Mar-31 May, daily	10am-6pm
1 Jun-31 Jul, daily	10am-3pm
1 Aug-30 Sep, daily	10am-6pm
1 Nov-31 Mar, daily	10pm-4pm

Closes 3pm June and July for opera evenings

Closed 24-26 Dec and 1 Jan

HOW TO FIND US

Direction: Located 4 miles N of New Alresford, off B3046 along a farm track – 450 metres (493 yards)

Train: Winchester 8 miles

Bus: Stagecoach in Hampshire 309 Basingstoke – Alresford (passes close to ⊠ Basingstoke), to within ½ mile

Tel: 01424 775705

🅿 ♿ 🐕 🏛 ⚠

Disabled access (with assistance, steep steps to terrace).

MAP	Page 258 (5C)
	OS Map 185 (ref SU 562362)

ℹ Check Heritage Today for news and information on forthcoming events and exclusive members' offers.

OLD SOAR MANOR

KENT – TN15 0QX

The solar block of a late 13th-century knight's manor house, possibly owned by the Culpepper family.

Maintained, managed and owned by the National Trust.

OPENING TIMES

2 Apr-29 Sep, Sat-Thu
& Bank Hols   10am-6pm

HOW TO FIND US

Direction: 1 mile E of Plaxtol

Train: Borough Green and Wrotham 2½ miles

Bus: New Enterprise 222 🚲 Tunbridge Wells – 🚆 Borough Green (passing 🚆 Tonbridge); Kent Passenger Services 404 from 🚆 Sevenoaks. On both, alight at the E end of Plaxtol, then ¾ mile by footpath

Tel: 01732 810378

🅿 ⊠
Parking (limited).

MAP	Page 259 (5G)
	OS Map 179 (ref TR 228693)

OSBORNE HOUSE

ISLE OF WIGHT   GO TO PAGE 64

PEVENSEY CASTLE

EAST SUSSEX – BN24 5LE

This is one of Britain's oldest and most important strongholds, with fortifications surviving from three distinct periods: Roman, medieval and World War II.

New For 2005

A new exhibition opens in the medieval North Tower in 2005, which describes Pevensey's importance as part of a coastal chain of Roman 'Saxon Shore' fortresses, as well as the sieges that took place here during medieval times.

PEVENSEY CASTLE

The exhibition also shows how the coastline here has changed during the last 2,000 years.

Many important historic characters are associated with the castle, including William the Conqueror who landed at Pevensey in September 1066. He may have used the old fort as a shelter for his troops on the way to the Battle of Hastings.

An audio tour is available. The castle is within easy reach of Eastbourne as well as beaches at Pevensey Bay and Norman's Bay.

NON-MEMBERS

Adult	£3.70
Concession	£2.80
Child	£1.90

OPENING TIMES

24 Mar-30 Sep, daily	10am-6pm
1 Oct-31 Mar, Sat-Sun	10am-4pm
Closed	24-26 Dec and 1 Jan

HOW TO FIND US

Direction: In Pevensey off A259

Train: Pevensey & Westham or Pevensey Bay, both ½ mile

Bus: Stagecoach in Hastings 710 from Eastbourne

Tel: 01323 762604

🅿 ♿ 🧍 🧍 🐾 🎧 💷 📷 🖼
🚻 ⚠
Dogs on leads (restricted areas only).
Parking (charge payable).
Tearooms (call 01424 775705 for opening arrangements).
Toilets (nearby).

MAP	Page 259 (6G)
	OS Map 199 (ref TQ 645048)

PORTCHESTER CASTLE

HAMPSHIRE   GO TO PAGE 68

RECULVER TOWERS AND ROMAN FORT

KENT

An imposing landmark, the twin 12th-century towers of the ruined church stand amid the remains of an important Roman shore fort. Richborough Roman Fort is nearby.

OPENING TIMES

Any reasonable time; external viewing only

HOW TO FIND US

Direction: At Reculver; 3 miles E of Herne Bay

Train: Herne Bay 4 miles

Bus: Regents 634, 635; Stagecoach in East Kent 26 from Herne Bay

Tel: 01227 740676

🅿 🧍 🧍 🐾 ♿
Disabled access (grounds only – long slope up from car park).

MAP	Page 259 (4J)
	OS Map 179 (ref TR 228693)

RICHBOROUGH ROMAN FORT AND AMPHITHEATRE

KENT – CT13 9JW

RICHBOROUGH ROMAN FORT AND AMPHITHEATRE

The Romans' main entry port into Britain is now over two miles from the sea, with remains dating back to the Claudian invasion of AD43. Archaeological finds from the entire period of the Roman occupation are on display, including an early Christian baptismal font.

It is possible to reach the fort as the Romans would have done, by boat, from Sandwich. However, boats do not sail every day, so you should contact the site to check on times.

The remains of a Roman amphitheatre associated with the fort, built in the 3rd century, can be seen nearby.

NON-MEMBERS

Adult	£3.70
Concession	£2.80
Child	£1.90

OPENING TIMES

Fort:
24 Mar-30 Sep, daily   10am-6pm

Amphitheatre: Any reasonable time, access across grazed land from footpath; please call 01304 612013 for details

HOW TO FIND US

Direction: At the A256/A257 roundabout, take the road for Sandwich and then turn left at the fire station

Train: Sandwich 2 miles

Tel: 01304 612013

🅿 ♿ 🏠 🖼 🎁 🍴 🛒 ⚠
Dogs on leads (restricted areas only).

MAP   Page 259 (4J)
       OS Map 179 (ref TR 324602)

ROCHESTER CASTLE

KENT – MEI ISW

An ancient castle besieged and rebuilt over centuries.

Guarding an important crossing of the River Medway, Rochester Castle was one of the first English castles to be rebuilt in stone during the late 11th century. Today, the castle stands as a proud reminder of the history surrounding the old town of Rochester, along with the cathedral, the cobbled streets and the Dickensian associations.

Strategically placed astride the London Road, this imposing fortress has a complex history of destruction and rebuilding. Its mighty Norman tower-keep of Kentish ragstone was built c.1127 by William of Corbeil, Archbishop of Canterbury, with the encouragement of Henry I. Consisting of three floors above a basement, it still stands 113 feet high.

On the second floor of the keep, and above the castle entrance, was the chapel. Some measure of the chapel's original splendour is still apparent in the surviving vaulting and the beautifully decorated windows.

ROCHESTER CASTLE

In 1215 Rochester Castle, garrisoned by rebel barons, endured an epic siege by King John. Having first undermined the outer wall, John used the fat of 40 pigs to fire a mine under the keep, bringing its southern corner crashing down. Even then the defenders held out within the building, until they were eventually starved out after a resistance of nearly two months.

Rebuilt under Henry III and Edward I, the castle remained a viable fortress in the 15th century. By the 17th century it was neglected, and in 1870 the grounds became a public park.

Managed by Medway Council.

NON-MEMBERS

Adult	£4.00
Concession	£3.00
Child	£3.00
Family ticket	£11.00

OPENING TIMES

1 Apr-30 Sep, daily	10am-6pm
1 Oct-31 Mar, daily	10am-4pm
Closed	24-26 Dec and 1 Jan

HOW TO FIND US

Direction: By Rochester Bridge (A2); junction 1 of M2 and junction 2 of M25

Train: Rochester ½ mile

Bus: From surrounding areas

Tel: 01634 402276

🏠 🏛 🖼 📷 🅴 ♿ 🛒 ⚠
Audio tours (small charge).
Toilets (in castle grounds).

MAP   Page 259 (4G)
       OS Map 178 (ref TQ 741686)

www.english-heritage.org.uk/southeast

OSBORNE HOUSE ISLE OF WIGHT – PO32 6JY

After her marriage to Prince Albert in 1840, Queen Victoria felt the need for a family residence in the country. To use her words, 'a place of one's own – quiet and retired'.

The Drawing Room

Queen Victoria knew and liked the Isle of Wight after visiting as a child, and both Queen Victoria and the Prince Consort were determined to buy a property there.

'It is impossible to imagine a prettier spot,' wrote the Queen after a visit to Osborne House. In 1845 the royal couple purchased the property with an estate of 342 acres, plus the adjacent Barton Manor to house equerries and grooms and to serve as the home farm.

Before the deeds had even changed hands, architect Thomas Cubitt had been approached – firstly to build a new wing and then to demolish the old house and add further wings. Once all the work was complete, an exquisite pair of Italianate towers dominated the landscape and looked out over passing ships in the nearby Solent.

Artistic interiors

The interiors of Osborne House abound with opulence in both architectural design and decoration. Marble sculptures, commissioned by Victoria and Albert, line the classically designed Grand Corridor of the house and recall the royal couple's love of the arts. Portraits and frescos adorn the walls and serve as a reminder of the family's links to the crowned heads of Europe, and of the unrivalled supremacy of the British Empire. Family photographs on the desks of Queen Victoria and Prince Albert offer a further insight into the way they lived.

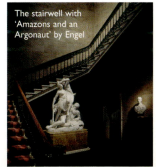

The stairwell with 'Amazons and an Argonaut' by Engel

The Walled Garden

OSBORNE HOUSE

Queen Victoria's role as Empress of India is celebrated in the richly decorated Durbar Room. Constructed from 1890-91, the room served as an elaborate banqueting hall and every surface, from floor to ceiling, is ornately embellished.

The walls are decorated with symbols of Ganesh – the elephant god of good fortune – and the deeply coffered ceiling is composed of fibrous plaster. The completion of the room coincided with the introduction of electricity, so the Indian-influenced lamp stands were designed to take full advantage of this emerging technology.

Italianate gardens

Prince Albert worked with Cubitt on the Italianate designs for the terraced formal gardens which complement the house. Visitors can now enjoy the Walled Garden much as Victoria and Albert did, as English Heritage has restored it as part of the Contemporary Heritage Gardens Scheme.

The Swiss Cottage

The grounds also contain a summerhouse, a museum, a miniature fort and barracks as well as the Swiss Cottage, which was originally built for the royal children to play in. There is a beautiful wild flower meadow near the Swiss Cottage, and red squirrels can be seen throughout the gardens. There is a courtesy minibus, with wheelchair access, to Swiss Cottage. Queen Victoria loved to stroll through the gardens and the primroses in the woods were her particular favourites.

Most of the gardens are accessible on tarmac and compacted gravel paths.

A new restaurant has recently opened at Osborne House within the former Orangery and Victoria Hall. It serves lunches and teas, including the substantial Victoria Hall afternoon tea – well worth missing lunch for! (Please note, for non-members a minimum grounds charge applies).

There is also a children's play area, horse and carriage rides (extra charge) and a display of Queen Victoria's Indian gifts.

Please note: Osborne House can be very busy during July and August. Between November and March, entry is by guided tour only – pre-booking is essential.

⊤ Available for corporate and private hire.

www.english-heritage.org.uk/ osbornehouse

NON-MEMBERS HOUSE AND GROUNDS	
Adult	£8.95
Concession	£6.70
Child	£4.50
Family ticket	£22.40

NON-MEMBERS GROUNDS ONLY	
Adult	£5.30
Concession	£4.00
Child	£2.70
Family ticket	£13.30

OPENING TIMES

24 Mar-30 Sep, daily   10am-6pm
1-31 Oct, Sun-Thu   10am-4pm
1 Nov-31 Mar, Sun-Thu 10am-4pm
(guided house tours only – pre-booking essential. Last tour 2.30pm)
Closed   24-26 Dec and 1 Jan

HOW TO FIND US

Direction: 1 mile SE of East Cowes

Bus: Southern Vectis 4, Ryde – E Cowes; 5 Newport – E Cowes

Train: Ryde Esplanade 7 miles; Wootton (Isle of Wight Steam Railway) 3 miles

Ferry: East Cowes 1½ mile (Red Funnel – 0870 4448898); Fishbourne 4 miles; Ryde 7 miles (Wightlink 0870 5827744; Hovercraft: Ryde 01983 811000)

Tel: 01983 200022

Local Tourist Information: Cowes and Newport 01983 813818

Disabled access (During 2005, Osborne House will be trialling access for wheelchair users to the first floor, by an existing lift. Whilst we endeavour to provide this service whenever the house is open, there will be occasions when wheelchair access to the first floor is not available).

Family learning resources available.

MAP	Page 258 (7C) OS Map 196 (ref SZ 516948)

PORTCHESTER CASTLE
HAMPSHIRE – PO16 9QW

There are impressive views from Portchester Castle, and on a clear day you can see across to Portsmouth, Southsea and Hayling Island. It is this incredible location which has made Portchester Castle a major player in the Solent's coastal defences for hundreds of years.

The most impressive and best-preserved of Roman 'Saxon Shore' forts, Portchester Castle is the only Roman stronghold in northern Europe whose multi-towered walls still mainly stand to their full original height. Subsequently housing a Saxon settlement, the huge waterside fortress became a Norman castle in the 12th century, when a formidable tower-keep was built in one corner.

A brief history
During the 12th century, Henry I used the castle as a secure lodging and a safe depository for treasury bullion. The French captured the castle in 1215 during the barons' rebellion against King John, and its demolition was ordered by his successor, Henry III. It was retained, however, and used to store munitions for wars against France.

The castle was in the front line throughout the Hundred Years War, serving as a staging-post for expeditions and repelling raids from across the Channel. When Richard II made temporary peace with France in 1396, he transformed part of the castle into a palace: but when war was renewed, Henry V used it as a departure point for the Agincourt campaign in 1415. Thereafter it was superseded by Portsmouth and saw little action. It was used to house troops in the Civil War and prisoners of war during the Napoleonic Wars; graffiti from the late 18th and early 19th centuries can still be seen.

www.english-heritage.org.uk/portchester

New for 2005
Inside the keep there is a new exhibition that describes the history of the castle, as well as the extensive archaeological finds excavated on site. Themes in the exhibition include the Roman and Saxon occupation, the development of Portchester Manor and village, and the use of Portchester Castle as a prison.

NON-MEMBERS

Adult	£3.70
Concession	£2.80
Child	£1.90

OPENING TIMES

24 Mar-30 Sep, daily	10am-6pm
1 Oct-31 Mar, daily	10am-4pm
Closed	24-26 Dec and 1 Jan

HOW TO FIND US

Direction: On the S side of Portchester off A27; Junction 11 on M27

Train: Portchester 1 mile

Bus: First 1/A/B, 5 Fareham – Southsea to within ¼ mile

Tel: 02392 378291

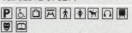

Disabled access (grounds and lower levels only).
Dogs on leads (restricted areas only).
Family learning resources available.
Toilets (facilities are in the car park).

MAP   Page 258 (6C)
       OS Map 196 (ref SU 625046)

ROLLRIGHT STONES

OXFORDSHIRE

The Rollright Stones consist of three groups of stones; The King's Men, The Whispering Knights and The King Stone. They span nearly 2,000 years of history of the Neolithic and Bronze Ages. During 2005, stone repair specialists will be hard at work cleaning the stones, which were damaged when yellow paint was thrown at them by vandals in April 2004.

Managed by The Rollright Trust

OPENING TIMES

All the stones are accessible sunrise to sunset, 'The Whispering Knights' and 'The King Stone' via a footpath; entry to 'The King's Men' is courtesy of the owner, who may levy a charge (Adult 50p, Child 25p).

HOW TO FIND US

Direction: Off unclassified road between A44 and A3400; 3 miles NW of Chipping Norton, near villages of Little Rollright and Long Compton

Train: Moreton-in-Marsh 6½ miles

Tel: 01553 631330

P ⌘
Parking (in lay-by).

MAP   Page 258 (2B)
       OS Map 151 (ref SP 297309)

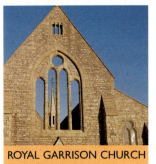

ROYAL GARRISON CHURCH

HAMPSHIRE – PO1 2NJ

ROYAL GARRISON CHURCH

Royal Garrison Church was constructed around 1212 as a hospital. Although the church was badly damaged in a 1941 fire-bomb raid on Portsmouth, the chancel was saved.

OPENING TIMES

1 Apr-30 Sep, Mon-Sat 11am-4pm (contact the key keeper in winter 02392 378291)

HOW TO FIND US

Direction: In Portsmouth; on Grand Parade S of High St

Train: Portsmouth Harbour ¾ mile

Bus: From surrounding areas

Tel: 02392 378291

P ⌖ ⌘
Parking (nearby).

MAP   Page 258 (6C)
       OS Map 196 (ref SZ 633992)

ST AUGUSTINE'S ABBEY

KENT – CT1 1TF

This great abbey, marking the rebirth of Christianity in southern England, was founded in AD597 by St Augustine. Originally created as a burial place for the Anglo-Saxon kings of Kent, it is part of the Canterbury World Heritage site, along with the cathedral and St Martin's Church.

ST AUGUSTINE'S ABBEY

The impressive abbey is situated outside the city walls and is sometimes missed by visitors. At the abbey, you can also enjoy the museum and free interactive audio tour.

NON-MEMBERS

Adult	£3.70
Concession	£2.80
Child	£1.90

OPENING TIMES

24 Mar-30 Sep, daily	10am-6pm
1 Oct-31 Mar, Wed-Sun 10am-4pm	
Closed	24-26 Dec and 1 Jan

HOW TO FIND US

Direction: In Canterbury, ¼ mile E of Cathedral Close

Train: Canterbury East and West, both ¾ mile

Bus: From surrounding area

Tel: 01227 767345

Local Tourist Information: Canterbury 01227 766567

P ⌖ ⌂ E ⌘ ⌸ ⌑ ◻ ⚠
Audio tours (interactive).
Disabled access (some steps).
Parking (nearby).

MAP   Page 259 (4J)
       OS Map 179 (ref TR 155578)

ST AUGUSTINE'S ABBEY CONDUIT HOUSE

KENT

The Conduit House is part of the monastic waterworks that supplied nearby St Augustine's Abbey.

OPENING TIMES

Any reasonable time; exterior viewing only

ST AUGUSTINE'S ABBEY CONDUIT HOUSE

HOW TO FIND US

Direction: In Canterbury, from ring road turn right into Havelock St, right into North Holmes Rd, left into St Martin's Rd, right into King's Park. Approximately 5-10 min walk from St Augustine's Abbey

Train: Canterbury East or West, both 1½ miles

MAP   Page 259 (4J)
         OS Map 179 (ref TR 159580)

ST AUGUSTINE'S CROSS
KENT

This 19th-century cross of Saxon design marks what is traditionally thought to have been the site of St Augustine's landing on the shores of England in AD597. Accompanied by 30 followers, Augustine is said to have held a mass here before moving on.

OPENING TIMES
Any reasonable time

HOW TO FIND US
Direction: 2 miles E of Minster off B29048

Train: Minster 2 miles

Bus: Stagecoach in East Kent 33, 94 from Ramsgate

MAP   Page 259 (4J)
         OS Map 179 (ref TR 340642)

ST CATHERINE'S ORATORY
ISLE OF WIGHT

A lighthouse was first built here in the 14th century. Affectionately known as the Pepperpot, this lighthouse stands on one of the highest parts of the Isle of Wight.

ST CATHERINE'S ORATORY

It is part of the Tennyson Heritage Coast, which is a series of linked cliff-top monuments. Another lighthouse and several monuments can be seen nearby.

Maintained and managed by the National Trust.

OPENING TIMES
Any reasonable time

HOW TO FIND US
Direction: E of Blackgang roundabout, off A3055

Train: Shanklin 9 miles

Bus: Southern Vectis 6 Ventnor – Newport; 7/A Yarmouth – Ryde, to within 1 mile

Ferry: West Cowes 14 miles, East Cowes 14 miles (both Red Funnel – 0870 444 8898); Yarmouth 15 miles (Wightlink – 0870 582 7744)

MAP   Page 258 (7C)
         OS Map 196 (ref SZ 494773)

ST JOHN'S COMMANDERY
KENT

This medieval chapel was converted into a farmhouse during the 16th century. It has a fine moulded-plaster ceiling and a remarkable timber roof.

OPENING TIMES
Any reasonable time for exterior viewing. Internal viewing by appointment only; please call 01304 211067 for details

HOW TO FIND US
Direction: 2 miles NE of Densole, off A260

Train: Kearsney 4 miles

ST JOHN'S COMMANDERY

Bus: Stagecoach in East Kent 16/A
Folkestone Central – Canterbury, to within 1 mile
Tel: 01553 631330

MAP   Page 259 (5J)
         OS Map 179 (ref TR 232440)

ST LEONARD'S TOWER
KENT

This early example of a Norman tower keep was probably built c.1080 by Gundulf, Bishop of Rochester. The tower stands almost to its original height and takes its name from a chapel dedicated to St Leonard which once stood nearby.

Managed by West Malling Parish Council.

OPENING TIMES
Any reasonable time for exterior viewing. Internal viewing by appointment only; please call 01732 870872.

HOW TO FIND US
Direction: Nr West Malling, on unclassified road W of A228

Train: West Malling 1 mile

Bus: Arriva 70 from Maidstone, 151 from Chatham

Disabled access (grounds only).

MAP   Page 259 (4G)
         OS Map 188 (ref TQ 676571)

SOUTH EAST

72

SILCHESTER ROMAN CITY WALLS AND AMPHITHEATRE

HAMPSHIRE

In the Iron Age, the region in which modern Silchester is located was part of the tribal territory of the Atrebates. During the Roman period, their tribal centre became known as Calleva Atrebatum and grew into a substantial settlement of over 400,000 square metres (100 acres). Though none of the ancient buildings are visible today, archaeological investigations have given us an idea of the town's overall layout and how this would have changed over time. On the edge of the Roman town, outside the stone walls, are the remains of a rural amphitheatre built AD50-75 and able to seat about 3,000 people.

OPENING TIMES

Any reasonable time

HOW TO FIND US

Direction: On a minor road, 1 mile E of Silchester

Train: Bramley or Mortimer, both 2¾ miles

Bus: Stagecoach in Hampshire 44A from Basingstoke (passes ⮑ Bramley), to within 1 mile

MAP   Page 258 (4C)
      OS Map 175 (ref SU 639624)

SOUTHWICK PRIORY

HAMPSHIRE

Ruins of a house of Austin Canons, who moved to this site from Portchester Castle in 1133.

OPENING TIMES

No public access. For more information call 01424 775705

MAP   Page 258 (6C)
      OS Map 196 (ref SU 628084)

SUTTON VALENCE CASTLE

KENT

The ruins of a 12th-century stone keep.

OPENING TIMES

Any reasonable time

HOW TO FIND US

Direction: 5 miles SE of Maidstone; in Sutton Valence village, on A274

Train: Headcorn 4 miles, Hollingbourne 5 miles

Bus: Arriva 12 Maidstone – Tenterden (passes ⮑ Headcorn)

MAP   Page 259 (5G)
      OS Map 188 (ref TQ 815491)

TEMPLE MANOR

KENT

A manor house of the Knights Templar, constructed during the 13th century.

Managed by Medway Council.

OPENING TIMES

Easter Sun 2005	10am-4pm
1 Apr-30 Sep, Sun only	10am-6pm
1-31 Oct, Sun only	10am-4pm

(By prior arrangement, please call 01634 338110).

HOW TO FIND US

Direction: Located in Strood (Rochester), off A228

Train: Strood ¾ mile

Bus: From surrounding areas

Disabled access (grounds only).

MAP   Page 259 (4G)
      OS Map 178 (ref TQ 733685)

TITCHFIELD ABBEY

HAMPSHIRE – PO15 5RA

The remains of a 13th-century abbey, its church converted into a grand Tudor gatehouse.

Managed by The Titchfield Abbey Association.

OPENING TIMES

1 Apr-30 Sep, daily	10am-6pm
1-31 Oct, daily	10am-5pm
1 Nov-31 Mar, daily	10am-4pm
Closed	25 Dec

HOW TO FIND US

Direction: Located ½ mile N of Titchfield, off A27

Train: Fareham 2 miles

Bus: Solent Blue Line 26/A Fareham – Southampton

Tel: 01329 842133

MAP   Page 258 (6C)
      OS Map 196 (ref SU 542067)

UFFINGTON CASTLE, WHITE HORSE AND DRAGON HILL

OXFORDSHIRE

These atmospheric sites lie along the Ridgeway. Uffington 'Castle' is a large Iron Age hillfort, Dragon Hill a natural mound associated in legend with St George. The famous and enigmatic White Horse is the oldest chalk-cut hill figure in Britain, and may be more than 2,500 years old.

Owned and managed by the National Trust.

UFFINGTON CASTLE, WHITE HORSE AND DRAGON HILL

OPENING TIMES

Any reasonable time

HOW TO FIND US

Direction: S of B4507, 7 miles W of Wantage

MAP	Page 258 (3B)
	OS Map 174 (ref SU 301866)

UPNOR CASTLE

KENT – ME2 4XG

Upnor Castle was built in the 1540s to protect the Royal Navy anchorage in the Medway. It saw action in 1667 when the Dutch navy sailed up the Medway to attack the dockyard at Chatham.

Managed by Medway Council.

NON-MEMBERS

Adult	£4.00
Concession	£3.00
Child	£3.00
Family ticket	£11.00

OPENING TIMES

25-31 Mar, daily	10am-4pm
1 Apr-30 Sep, daily	10am-6pm
1-31 Oct, daily	10am-4pm

HOW TO FIND US

Direction: At Upnor, on unclassified road off A228

Train: Strood 2 miles

Bus: ASD 197 from ⊠ Chatham; Arriva 191-4 Chatham – Hoo, alight Wainscott, then 1 mile

UPNOR CASTLE

Tel: 01634 718742 or 01634 338110 when castle is closed

Disabled access (grounds only).

Dogs on leads (restricted areas only).

Parking (at a slight distance from castle – park before village).

MAP	Page 259 (4G)
	OS Map 178 (ref TQ 759706)

WALMER CASTLE AND GARDENS

KENT   GO TO PAGE 74

WAVERLEY ABBEY

SURREY

Waverley was the first Cistercian abbey to be established in England in 1128, by William Gifford, Bishop of Winchester.

OPENING TIMES

Any reasonable time

HOW TO FIND US

Direction: 2 miles SE of Farnham, off B3001; off Junction 10 of M25

Train: Farnham 2 miles

Bus: Stagecoach in Hants & Surrey 46 Guildford – Aldershot (passing ⊠ Farnham)

Parking (limited).

MAP	Page 258 (5D)
	OS Map 186 (ref SU 868453)

WAYLAND'S SMITHY

OXFORDSHIRE

Near the Uffington White Horse lies this evocative Neolithic burial site, surrounded by a small circle of trees.

Managed by the National Trust.

OPENING TIMES

Any reasonable time

HOW TO FIND US

Direction: On the Ridgeway; ¾ mile NE of B4000, Ashbury – Lambourn Road

Parking (may be a charge).

MAP	Page 258 (3B)
	OS Map 178 (ref TQ 759706)

WESTERN HEIGHTS

KENT

A huge fortification begun during the Napoleonic Wars and completed in the 1860s, designed to protect Dover from French invasion. Only the moat can be visited. Part of the White Cliffs Countryside Project.

OPENING TIMES

Any reasonable time

HOW TO FIND US

Direction: Above Dover town on W side of harbour

Train: Dover Priory ¾ mile

Tel: 01304 211067

MAP	Page 259 (5J)
	OS Map 179 (ref TR 312408)

WALMER CASTLE AND GARDENS
KENT – CT14 7LJ

Originally built during the reign of Henry VIII as part of a string of coastal defences against Catholic attack from across the channel, Walmer Castle has evolved over time into a comfortable residence.

Queen Mother's Garden

View across the Broadwalk to the castle

Walmer became the official residence of the Lord Warden of the Cinque Ports in 1708.

When visiting, it is easy to imagine why the Duke of Wellington, who held the post of Lord Warden for 23 years, enjoyed his time here so much.

The spirit of Napoleon's nemesis and the victor of Waterloo still lives on at Walmer, and the yellow chintz armchair in which he died on 14 September 1852 can still be seen here. Wellington preferred unsophisticated surroundings, and his campaign bed – with its original horsehair mattress and bedding – remains on display as a testament to his spartan tastes. A pair of original

'Wellington boots' can also be seen alongside a great many personal effects in the fascinating on-site Wellington museum.

The honorary title of Lord Warden of the Cinque Ports – the ancient 'five ports' of the south-east coast – is the oldest military honour England can give, and is still awarded today. Admiral Sir Michael Boyce GCB was appointed the Lord Warden in 2004.

Successive Lords Warden have left their mark on Walmer's buildings and gardens. Thus Lady Hester Stanhope used local militia to create new landscaping as a surprise for her uncle William Pitt, Lord Warden and

Prime Minister: while Lord Warden W.H.Smith – founder of the famous stationers – saved many of the valuable furnishings now on display throughout the site.

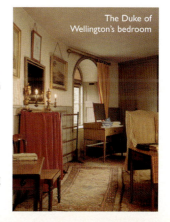

The Duke of Wellington's bedroom

www.english-heritage.org.uk/southeast

WALMER CASTLE

In recent years, Lords Warden of the Cinque Ports have been provided with private apartments above the gatehouse and, although these were never used by Sir Winston Churchill during his tenure, both Sir Robert Menzies (former Australian Prime Minister) and Her Majesty Queen Elizabeth the Queen Mother made regular visits and stopovers at the castle. Some of the rooms used by the Queen Mother are open to visitors, as is her magnificent garden, designed by Penelope Hobhouse and given to Her Majesty on her 95th birthday.

There are beautiful gardens surrounding the house, including a commemorative lawn, woodland walk, croquet lawn and a working kitchen garden, as well as a double herbaceous border flanked by mature yew hedges. The remainder of the grounds are mostly wildlife gardens and are a great place to spot birds.

When you need a break, homemade lunches and teas are available at the Lord Warden's Tearoom, and the well-stocked gift shop is well worth a visit. An interactive audio tour is available at the site and, for those inspired by the magnificent gardens, plants are on sale.

There is a pleasant cycle path between Deal and Walmer castles along the beachfront.

Duke of Wellington enthusiasts may also be interested in two other properties managed by English Heritage. Apsley House (page 26) was the Duke's impressive London residence, and the spectacular Wellington Arch (page 35), situated opposite Apsley House, originally had a large statue of the Duke of Wellington erected on the top.

🍴 Available for corporate and private hire.

🔔 Licensed for civil wedding ceremonies.

www.english-heritage.org.uk/walmercastle

NON-MEMBERS

Adult	£5.95
Concession	£4.50
Child	£3.00
Family ticket	£14.90

OPENING TIMES

24 Mar-30 Sep, daily (closes at 4pm Sat)	10am-6pm
1-31 Oct, Wed-Sun	10am-4pm
1-31 Mar, daily	10am-4pm
Closed when Lord Warden in residence	

HOW TO FIND US

Direction: On coast S of Walmer, on A258; Junction 13 of M20 or from M2 to Deal

Train: Walmer 1 mile

Bus: From surrounding areas

Tel: 01304 364288

Local Tourist Information Deal 01304 369576 and Dover 01304 205108

Audio tours (also in French, Dutch and German).

Disabled access (courtyard and garden only; parking available).

Parking (near approach to castle).

MAP	Page 259 (5J) OS Map 179 (ref TR 378501)

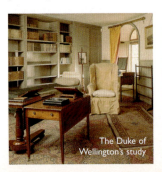

The Duke of Wellington's study

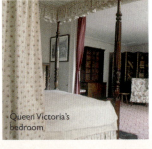

Queen Victoria's bedroom

WOLVESEY CASTLE (OLD BISHOP'S PALACE)

HAMPSHIRE

Once one of the greatest medieval buildings in England, the palace was the chief residence of the Bishops of Winchester. Situated in Winchester, next to the Cathedral, its extensive ruins reflect their importance and wealth. The last great occasion at Wolvesey was on 25 July 1554, when Queen Mary and Philip of Spain held their wedding breakfast in the East Hall.

OPENING TIMES

1 Apr-30 Sep, daily   10am-5pm

HOW TO FIND US

Direction: ¾ mile SE of Winchester Cathedral, next to the Bishop's Palace; access from College St

Train: Winchester ¾ mile

Bus: From surrounding areas

Tel: 01424 775705

MAP   Page 258 (5C)
       OS Map 185 (ref SU 484291)

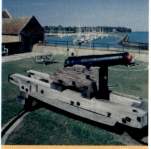

YARMOUTH CASTLE

ISLE OF WIGHT – PO41 0PB

This last addition to Henry VIII's coastal defences was completed after his death in 1547. It houses exhibitions of paintings of the Isle of Wight and photographs of old Yarmouth. The site also provides a magnificent picnic spot, with views over the Solent. Other defensive forts built by Henry VIII include Walmer Castle, Deal Castle, Hurst Castle and St Mawes Castle.

There is a waterbus link to Hurst Castle. Contact site for further information.

NON-MEMBERS

Adult	£2.60
Concession	£2.00
Child	£1.30

OPENING TIMES

24 Mar-30 Sep, Sun-Thu 11am-4pm

HOW TO FIND US

Direction: In Yarmouth, adjacent to car ferry terminal

Bus: Southern Vectis 7, 7A, 7B from Newport

Ferry: Yarmouth (Wightlink – 0870 582 7744)

Tel: 01983 760678

Disabled access (ground floor only).

Parking (coaches and cars 200 metres (200 yards) limited to 1 hour only).

MAP   Page 258 (7B)
       OS Map 196 (ref SZ 354898)

Check *Heritage Today* for news and information on forthcoming events and exclusive members' offers.

If you would like more information on properties, events and membership please call 0870 333 1181 or email **customers@ english-heritage.org.uk**

English Heritage members can take up to 6 children, as part of a family group, into our properties at no extra cost (see page 6).

OTHER HISTORIC ATTRACTIONS

DISCOUNTED ENTRY TO OUR MEMBERS (DISCOUNTS MAY NOT APPLY ON EVENT DAYS)

ANNE OF CLEVES HOUSE
LEWES, EAST SUSSEX

This 16th-century timber framed Wealden hall-house was given to Anne as part of her divorce settlement from Henry VIII.

Managed by Sussex Past.

ENTRY

Adult	£3.00
Concession	£2.70
Child	£1.50

Half price for EH members

OPENING TIMES

Please call site for details

Tel: 01273 474610

www.sussexpast.co.uk

MAP   Page 259 (6F)
OS Map 198 (ref TQ 411096)

DOVER MUSEUM & BRONZE AGE BOAT GALLERY
DOVER, KENT

This modern museum tells the story of Dover's rich history and is home to the world's oldest seagoing boat.

Managed by Dover District Council and Heritage Projects Ltd.

ENTRY

Adult	£2.00
Concession	£1.25
Child	£1.25

Half price for EH members.
Prices subject to change.

OPENING TIMES

Please call site for details

Tel: 01304 201066

www.dovermuseum.co.uk

MAP   Page 259 (5J)
OS Map 179 (ref TR 319414)

FISHBOURNE ROMAN PALACE
CHICHESTER, WEST SUSSEX

The remains of a military supply base, built at the time of the Roman invasion in AD43, and a sumptuous palace, constructed AD75, with 20 spectacular mosaic floors in various states of completeness.

Managed by Sussex Past.

ENTRY

Adult	£5.40
Concession	£4.60
Child	£2.80

Half price for EH members

OPENING TIMES

Please call site for details

Tel: 01243 785859

www.sussexpast.co.uk

MAP   Page 258 (6D)
OS Map 197 (ref SU 839048)

LEEDS CASTLE
Nr MAIDSTONE, KENT

Listed in the Domesday Book, Leeds Castle has been a Norman stronghold, a royal residence for six of England's medieval queens and a palace of Henry VIII. Other attractions at the site include a spectacular aviary and a maze with an underground grotto, plus regular special events.

Managed by Leeds Castle Enterprises Ltd.

LEEDS CASTLE

ENTRY

Adult	£13.00
Concession	£11.00
Child	£9.00

20% reduction for EH members

OPENING TIMES

Please call site for details

Tel: 01622 765400

www.leeds-castle.com

MAP   Page 259 (5G)
OS Map 188 (ref TQ 837533)

HISTORIC DOCKYARD
CHATHAM, KENT

The only virtually complete dockyard surviving from the Trafalgar era, Chatham's Historic Dockyard is among the world's most significant and fascinating maritime heritage sites. The 80-acre site displays both spectacular architecture and exciting naval exhibits.

Managed by Chatham Historic Dockyard Trust.

ENTRY

Adult	£10.00
Concession	£7.50
Child	£6.50
Family ticket	£26.50

20% reduction for EH members.
Prices subject to change.

OPENING TIMES

12 Feb-30 Oct, daily   10am-6pm
Closes 6pm or dusk if earlier
Weekends only in November
Last entry: Nov-March,   3pm
Apr-Oct,   4pm
Tel: 01634 823807

www.chdt.org.uk

MAP   Page 259 (4G)
OS Map 178 (ref TQ 75969)

LEWES CASTLE AND BARBICAN HOUSE MUSEUM

LEWES, EAST SUSSEX

Begun in the 1070s, this castle was finally completed 300 years later. Its history is told in 'The Story of Lewes Town' at the Barbican House Museum.

Managed by Sussex Past.

ENTRY

Adult	£4.40
Concession	£3.90
Child	£2.20

Half price for EH members

OPENING TIMES

Please call site for details

Tel: 01273 486290

www.sussexpast.co.uk

MAP	Page 259 (6F)
	OS Map 198 (ref TQ 413101)

MARLIPINS MUSEUM

SHOREHAM-BY-SEA, WEST SUSSEX

A c.14th-century building with a knapped Caen stone chequer-work façade, containing a fully accessible museum with many exhibits of local interest.

Managed by Sussex Past.

ENTRY

Adult	£2.00
Concession	£1.50
Child	£1.00

Half price for EH members

OPENING TIMES

Please call site for details

Tel: 01273 462994

www.sussexpast.co.uk

MAP	Page 258 (6E)
	OS Map 198 (ref TQ 215050)

MICHELHAM PRIORY

EAST SUSSEX   GO TO PAGE 80

ROYAL PAVILION

BRIGHTON, EAST SUSSEX

This Regency Palace was the magnificent seaside residence of King George IV. The exterior, which was inspired by Indian architecture, contrasts with interiors decorated in Chinese taste.

Managed by Brighton and Hove City Council.

Prices subject to change April 2005

ENTRY

Adult	£5.95
Concession	£4.20
Child	£3.50

Adult EH members are entitled to a group discount rate.

OPENING TIMES

Apr-Sep, daily	9.30-5.45pm
Oct-Mar, daily	10am-5.15pm

Last admission 45 mins before closing.

Closed	25/26 Dec

Tel: 01273 290900

www.royalpavilion.org.uk

MAP	Page 259 (6F)
	OS Map 198 (ref TQ 313042)

RYCOTE CHAPEL

OXFORDSHIRE

This 15th-century chapel has original furniture, including exquisitely carved and painted woodwork.

Owned by Mr and Mrs Bernard Taylor and managed by the Rycote Buildings Charitable Foundation.

Prices subject to change

ENTRY

Adult	£3.50
Concession	£2.50
Child	£1.50

OPENING TIMES

1 Apr-30 Sep, Fri-Sun   2pm-6pm
Times may change at short notice – please ring for details

Directions: 3 miles SW of Thame off A329

Bus: Arriva the Shires 260, 280 Oxford – Aylesbury (passes ⊛ Haddenham and Thame Parkway), to within ½ mile

Train: Haddenham and Thame Parkway 5 miles

Tel: 01424 775705

MAP	Page 258 (3C)
	OS Map 187 (ref TQ 362325)

MICHELHAM PRIORY

Nr HAILSHAM, EAST SUSSEX

Part of a 13th-century priory — later converted into a Tudor mansion — surrounded by seven acres of wonderful gardens and England's longest water-filled medieval moat.

Managed by Sussex Past.

ENTRY

Adult	£5.40
Concession	£4.60
Child	£2.80

Half price for EH members

OPENING TIMES

Please call site for details

Tel: 01323 844224

www.sussexpast.co.uk

MAP	Page 259 (6F)
	OS Map 199 (ref TQ 559093)

THE PRIEST HOUSE

WEST HOATHLY, WEST SUSSEX

Standing in the beautiful surroundings of a traditional cottage garden on the edge of Ashdown Forest, the Priest House is an early 15th-century timber-framed hall-house with a dramatic roof of Horsham stone. Inside the house are many interesting exhibits, while outside is a delightful formal herb garden.

Managed by Sussex Past

THE PRIEST HOUSE

ENTRY

Adult	£2.70
Concession	£2.40
Child	£1.35

Half price for EH members

OPENING TIMES

Please call site for details

Tel: 01342 810479

www.sussexpast.co.uk

MAP	Page 259 (5F)
	OS Map 187 (ref TQ 362325)

WEALD AND DOWNLAND OPEN AIR MUSEUM

Nr CHICHESTER, WEST SUSSEX

England's leading museum of historic buildings, set in 50 acres of beautiful Sussex countryside.

ENTRY

Adult	£7.70
Concession	£6.70
Child	£4.10

Reduction for EH members, please call site for details

Managed by the Weald and Downland Open Air Museum

OPENING TIMES

March-Oct, daily	10.30am-6pm
Nov-Feb, weekends, Wed and Feb half term	10.30am-4pm

Tel: 01243 811348

www.wealddown.co.uk

MAP	Page 258 (6D)
	OS Map 197 (ref SU 874128)

Sign-up on-line for our email Members' Newsletter at www.english-heritage.org.uk

Don't forget your membership card when you visit any of the properties listed in this handbook.

Looking for a unique present?

Why not browse our online shop at www.english-heritage.org.uk/shopping

You can find out more about the work of English Heritage at www.english-heritage.org.uk

Fairytale castles
for magical weddings

English Heritage now have 3 magical castles in Kent
available for hire.

For more information, please contact the
Hospitality Manager on **01304 209889** or visit the
website **www.english-heritage.org.uk/hospitality**

Merlin's Cave –
Tintagel Castle

SOUTH WEST

The South West is England's leading holiday destination, offering unparalleled diversity in the counties it encompasses. From the sheltered harbours of Cornwall to the mysteries of Stonehenge, there is plenty to explore.

www.english-heritage.org.uk/southwest

PROPERTIES

SEE INDIVIDUAL LISTINGS FOR DETAILS

BRISTOL & surrounding area
Kingswood Abbey Gatehouse, Stanton Drew Circles and Cove, Stoney Littleton Long Barrow, Temple Church

CORNWALL
Ballowall Barrow, Carn Euny Ancient Village, Chysauster Ancient Village, Dupath Well, Halliggye Fogou, Hurlers Stone Circles, King Doniert's Stone, Launceston Castle, Pendennis Castle, Penhallam, Restormel Castle, St Breock Downs Monolith, St Catherine's Castle, St Mawes Castle, Tintagel Castle, Tregiffian Burial Chamber, Trethevy Quoit

DEVON
Bayard's Cove Fort, Berry Pomeroy Castle, Blackbury Camp, Coldharbour Mill, Dartmouth Castle, Grimspound, Hound Tor Deserted Medieval Village, Kirkham House, Lydford Castle and Saxon Town, Merrivale Prehistoric Settlement, Okehampton Castle, Royal Citadel (Plymouth), Totnes Castle, Upper Plym Valley

DORSET
Abbotsbury Abbey Remains, Christchurch Castle and Norman House, Fiddleford Manor, Jordan Hill Roman Temple, Kingston Russell Stone Circle, Knowlton Church and Earthworks, Lulworth Castle, Maiden Castle, The Nine Stones, Portland Castle, St Catherine's Chapel, Sherborne Old Castle, Winterbourne Poor Lot Barrows

GLOUCESTERSHIRE
Belas Knap Long Barrow, Blackfriars, Cirencester Amphitheatre, Great Witcombe Roman Villa, Greyfriars, Hailes Abbey, Notgrove Long Barrow, Nympsfield Long Barrow, Odda's Chapel, Offa's Dyke, Over Bridge, St Briavel's Castle, St Mary's Church, Uley Long Barrow (Hetty Pegler's Tump), Windmill Tump Long Barrow

ISLES OF SCILLY
Bant's Carn Burial Chamber and Halangy Down Ancient Village, Cromwell's Castle, Garrison Walls, Harry's Walls, Innisidgen Lower and Upper Burial Chambers, King Charles's Castle, Old Blockhouse, Porth Hellick Down Burial Chamber

SOMERSET
Butter Cross, Cleeve Abbey, Farleigh Hungerford Castle, Gallox Bridge, Glastonbury Tribunal, Meare Fish House, Muchelney Abbey, Nunney Castle, Sir Bevil Grenville's Monument, Yarn Market

WILTSHIRE
Alexander Keiller Museum, Avebury, Avebury Stone Circles, Bradford-on-Avon Tithe Barn, Bratton Camp and White Horse, Chisbury Chapel, Hatfield Earthworks, Ludgershall Castle and Cross, Netheravon Dovecote, Old Sarum, Old Wardour Castle, The Sanctuary, Silbury Hill, Stonehenge, West Kennet Avenue, West Kennet Long Barrow, Windmill Hill, Woodhenge

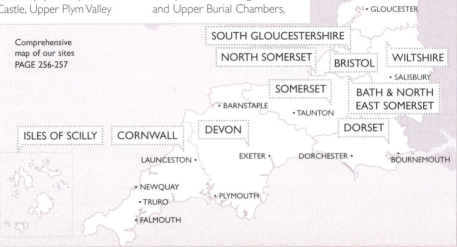

Comprehensive map of our sites
PAGE 256-257

GLOUCESTERSHIRE
• CHELTENHAM
• GLOUCESTER
SOUTH GLOUCESTERSHIRE
NORTH SOMERSET
BRISTOL
WILTSHIRE
• SALISBURY
SOMERSET
BATH & NORTH EAST SOMERSET
• BARNSTAPLE
• TAUNTON
ISLES OF SCILLY
CORNWALL
DEVON
DORSET
LAUNCESTON
EXETER •
DORCHESTER •
BOURNEMOUTH
• NEWQUAY
• TRURO
• PLYMOUTH
• FALMOUTH

Portland Castle

HISTORY, MYTH AND LEGEND UNITE IN THE SOUTH WEST

The 630-mile long South West Coast Path borders the picturesque sea coast of the region, taking in the outstanding natural beauty of Cornwall, Devon and Dorset. Magnificent castles like Dartmouth, Portland, Pendennis and St Mawes defend the southern coastline and evoke the real dangers of invasion, while to the north the mystical Tintagel Castle has inspired legends and myths, most famously that it is the birthplace of King Arthur. Offshore the unique and beautiful Isles of Scilly, warmed by the Gulf Stream, are an archaeological treasure trove.

Inland the dramatic landscapes of the Dartmoor and Exmoor National Parks contrast with the quintessentially English rolling Cotswold countryside of Gloucestershire and the peaceful Somerset levels. Everywhere the rich inheritance of the people who have inhabited the South West is there to be explored in the prehistoric monuments, Iron Age settlements, castles, great centres of pilgrimage, and grand homes of this wonderful region.

English Heritage protects our rich past, and also seeks to use the historic environment as a positive force in cultural regeneration. An example of this is Tintagel Castle, where the new visitor facilities, castle shop and introductory visual presentation are just part of the wider Tintagel village regeneration scheme. This project brings together local, county and European partners to improve the environment and provide better experiences for visitors and locals alike, now and in the future.

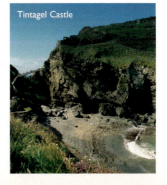
Tintagel Castle

ABBOTSBURY ABBEY REMAINS

DORSET

The remains of a cloister building of the Benedictine Abbotsbury Abbey, founded in the 11th century and suppressed in 1539.

OPENING TIMES

Any reasonable time

HOW TO FIND US

Direction: Located in Abbotsbury, off B3157, near a churchyard

Train: Upwey 7½ miles

Bus: First X53 Poole – Exeter (passes close to 🚉 Weymouth)

P 🏠

Parking (charged).

MAP	Page 257 (5H)
	OS Map 194 (ref SY 578852)

ALEXANDER KEILLER MUSEUM, AVEBURY

WILTSHIRE – SN8 1RF

One of the most important prehistoric archaeological collections in Britain. The admission fee includes access to the National Trust's Barn Gallery – an interpretation gallery using interactive exhibits and CD-ROMs to tell the story of the landscape and its people over the past 6,000 years.

Part of the Avebury World Heritage Site.

The museum collection is managed by the National Trust.

NON-MEMBERS

Adult	£4.20
Child	£2.10

OPENING TIMES

1 Apr-31 Oct	10am-6pm
1 Nov-31 Mar	10am-4pm
Closed	24-25 Dec

ALEXANDER KEILLER MUSEUM

HOW TO FIND US

Direction: In Avebury, 7 miles W of Marlborough

Train: Pewsey 10 miles; Swindon 11 miles

Bus: Stagecoach in Swindon/ First 49 Swindon – Trowbridge; Thamesdown 48A, 49/A from Marlborough; Wilts & Dorset 5/6 Salisbury – Swindon (all services pass close to 🚉 Swindon)

P 🏠 🚻 ♿ E ♿ 🏠

Parking (visitor car park free to EH members. S of Avebury off A4361. Free disabled visitors' parking in village car park).

MAP	Page 257 (3J)
	OS Map 173 (ref SU 099700)

AVEBURY

WILTSHIRE

A World Heritage Site, the landscape around Avebury has, like Stonehenge, achieved international recognition as a valuable prehistoric location.

Managed by the National Trust.

AVEBURY STONE CIRCLES

WILTSHIRE

AVEBURY STONE CIRCLES

Originally erected 4,500 years ago, many of the stones were located and re-erected in the 1930s by Alexander Keiller. The Circles and Henge encircle part of the village.

Part of the Avebury World Heritage Site.

Owned and managed by the National Trust.

OPENING TIMES

Any reasonable time

Usual facilities may not be available around the Summer Solstice 20-22 June. Please check before you visit

HOW TO FIND US

Direction: 7 miles W of Marlborough

Train: Pewsey 10 miles; Swindon 11 miles

Bus: Stagecoach in Swindon/ First 49 Swindon – Trowbridge; Thamesdown 48A, 49/A from Marlborough; Wilts & Dorset 5/6 Salisbury – Swindon (all services pass close to 🚉 Swindon)

P ♿ ♿

Parking (Visitor car park free to EH members. S of Avebury off A4361. Free disabled visitors' parking in village car park).

MAP	Page 257 (3J)
	OS Map 173 (ref SU 099700)

BALLOWALL BARROW

CORNWALL

In a spectacular position, this is an unusual Bronze Age chambered tomb with a complex layout. It includes an entrance grave and a series of cists (burial chambers).

Managed by the National Trust.

OPENING TIMES

Any reasonable time

BALLOWALL BARROW

HOW TO FIND US

Direction: 1 mile W of St Just, near Carn Gloose

Train: Penzance 8 miles

Bus: First 17/A Penzance – St Just, then 1 mile

MAP	Page 256 (7A)
	OS Map 203 (ref SW 355312)

BAYARD'S COVE FORT

DEVON

This is a small artillery fort, built c.1529 to defend Dartmouth harbour entrance.

OPENING TIMES

Any reasonable time

HOW TO FIND US

Direction: Located in Dartmouth, on the riverside

Train: Paignton, 7 miles; Kingswear (Paignton & Dartmouth Railway) few minutes walk, both by ferry

Bus: Stagecoach in Devon 120 Paignton – Kingswear, then ferry to Dartmouth; First 111 Torquay – Dartmouth

MAP	Page 257 (6F)
	OS Map 202 (ref SX 879509)

BELAS KNAP LONG BARROW

GLOUCESTERSHIRE

This is a good example of a Neolithic long barrow, with the mound still intact and surrounded by a stone wall. The tomb chambers, where the remains of 31 Stone Age people were found, have been opened up so that visitors can see inside.

Managed by Gloucestershire County Council.

BELAS KNAP LONG BARROW

OPENING TIMES

Any reasonable time

HOW TO FIND US

Direction: Near Charlton Abbots; ½ mile on Cotswold Way

Train: Cheltenham 9 miles

Bus: Castleways from Cheltenham, to within 1¾ miles of site

MAP	Page 257 (1J)
	OS Map 163 (ref SP 021254)

BERRY POMEROY CASTLE

DEVON – TQ9 6NJ

This romantic ruined castle is situated in a picturesque Devon valley and is steeped in local folklore and legend.

The gatehouse and defensive curtain wall date from the late 15th century, and behind them are the remains of an Elizabethan country house built c.1560-1600 by the Seymour family. Edward Seymour, first Duke of Somerset – the uncle and governor of the boy-king, Edward VI – acquired the castle in 1547. On the wall of the gatehouse chamber is a 15th-century painting of the Three Kings bearing gifts to Christ. A fascinating audio tour is also available.

BERRY POMEROY CASTLE

NON-MEMBERS

Adult	£3.30
Concession	£2.50
Child	£1.70

OPENING TIMES

24 Mar-30 Jun, daily	10am-5pm
1 Jul-31 Aug, daily	10am-6pm
1-30 Sep, daily	10am-5pm
1-31 Oct, daily	10am-4pm

HOW TO FIND US

Direction: 2½ miles E of Totnes off A385

Train: Totnes 3½ miles

Bus: First 111 Torquay – Dartmouth (passes Totnes)

Tel: 01803 866618

Disabled access (grounds and ground floor only).
Parking (no coach access).
Tearoom (not managed by EH).

MAP	Page 257 (6F)
	OS Map 202 (ref SX 839623)

BLACKBURY CAMP

DEVON

The site of an Iron Age hillfort, defended by a bank and ditch.

OPENING TIMES

Any reasonable time

HOW TO FIND US

Direction: Off B3174/A3052

Train: Honiton 6½ miles

MAP	Page 257 (5G)
	OS Map 192 (ref SY 187924)

Sign-up on-line for our email Members' Newsletter at **www.english-heritage.org.uk**

BLACKFRIARS, GLOUCESTER

GLOUCESTERSHIRE

This Dominican friary survives largely as it was built in the 13th century, despite conversion into a Tudor house and cloth factory. Notable features include the church and fine scissor-braced roof.

ENTRY

Non-Member	£3.50
EH Members and Children	£3.00

OPENING TIMES

Access by guided tour only	
Jul-Aug, Sun	3pm
Heritage Open Days (Free), 10-11 Sep	1pm & 3pm

HOW TO FIND US

Direction: In Blackfriars Lane, off Ladybellegate St, off Southgate St, Gloucester

Train: Gloucester ½ mile

Bus: From surrounding areas

Parking (adjacent. Charge applies, not managed by EH).

MAP   Page 257 (2J)
OS Map 163 (ref SP 021254)

i

English Heritage members can take up to 6 children, as part of a family group, into our properties at no extra cost (see page 6).

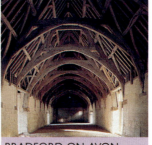

BRADFORD-ON-AVON TITHE BARN

WILTSHIRE

A spectacular medieval monastic barn with slate roof and wooden-beamed interior.

OPENING TIMES

Daily	10.30am-4pm
Closed	25 Dec

HOW TO FIND US

Direction: Located ½ mile S of town centre off B3109

Train: Bradford-on-Avon ¼ mile

Bus: First/Wilts & Dorset X4/5 Bath – Salisbury

Parking (charged).

MAP   Page 257 (3H)
OS Map 173 (ref ST 823604)

BRATTON CAMP AND WHITE HORSE

WILTSHIRE

An Iron Age hillfort, and white horse carved into the hillside; the horse is at least 300 years old, although its shape has altered.

BRATTON CAMP AND WHITE HORSE

OPENING TIMES

Any reasonable time

HOW TO FIND US

Direction: 2 miles E of Westbury off B3098, 1 mile SW of Bratton

Train: Westbury 3 miles

Bus: First 87 Trowbridge – Devizes (passes ⇌ Westbury)

MAP   Page 257 (3J)
OS Map 173 (ref ST 823604)

BUTTER CROSS

SOMERSET

The plinth of a rare medieval stone cross.

Managed by the National Trust

OPENING TIMES

Any reasonable time

HOW TO FIND US

Direction: Beside minor road to Alcombe, 350 metres (400 yards) NW of Dunster parish church

Train: Dunster (West Somerset Railway) 1 mile

Bus: First 28, 928 ⇌ Taunton – Minehead; 38/9 from Minehead to within ½ mile

MAP   Page 257 (4F)
OS Map 173 (ref ST 823604)

CARN EUNY ANCIENT VILLAGE

CORNWALL

CARN EUNY
ANCIENT VILLAGE

Surviving features of this Iron Age settlement include the foundations of stone huts and an intriguing curved under-ground passage and chamber, or 'fogou'.

Managed by the Cornwall Heritage Trust.

OPENING TIMES

Any reasonable time

HOW TO FIND US

Direction: 1¼ miles SW of Sancreed off A30

Train: Penzance 6 miles

Bus: First 17/A Penzance – St Just, to within 2 miles of the site

Parking (600 metres (660 yards) away in Brane).

MAP	Page 256 (7A)
	OS Map 2033 (ref SW 402288)

CHISBURY CHAPEL

WILTSHIRE

This thatched chapel, dating from the 13th century, was once used as a farm building.

OPENING TIMES

Any reasonable time

HOW TO FIND US

Direction: On unclassified road, ¼ mile E of Chisbury, off A4; 6 miles E of Marlborough

Train: Bedwyn 1 mile

MAP	Page 257 (3K)
	OS Map 174 (ref SU 280660)

CHRISTCHURCH CASTLE AND NORMAN HOUSE

DORSET

Set on the riverbank, the ruins of this Norman keep and constable's house date back to the 12th century. The latter site features one of only five Norman chimneys still surviving in England.

OPENING TIMES

Any reasonable time

HOW TO FIND US

Direction: Located in Christchurch, near the Priory

Train: Christchurch ¾ mile

Bus: From surrounding areas

MAP	Page 257 (5K)
	OS Map 195 (ref SZ 160927)

CHYSAUSTER ANCIENT VILLAGE

CORNWALL – TR20 8XA

This Celtic settlement was originally occupied almost 2,000 years ago. The 'village' consisted of eight stone-walled home-steads known as 'courtyard houses', which are only found on the Land's End peninsula and the Isles of Scilly. Each house had an open central courtyard surrounded by a number of thatched rooms. The houses form one of the oldest village streets in the country.

NON-MEMBERS

Adult	£2.30
Concession	£1.70
Child	£1.20

CHYSAUSTER ANCIENT VILLAGE

OPENING TIMES

24 Mar-30 Jun, daily	10am-5pm
1 Jul-31 Aug, daily	10am-6pm
1-30 Sep, daily	10am-5pm
1-31 Oct, daily	10am-4pm

HOW TO FIND US

Direction: Located 2½ miles NW of Gulval, off B3311

Train: Penzance 3½ miles

Bus: First 16 Penzance – St Ives, to within 1½ miles

Tel: 07831 757934

MAP	Page 256 (7B)
	OS Map 203 (ref SW 472350)

CIRENCESTER AMPHITHEATRE

GLOUCESTERSHIRE

Cirencester (Roman Corinium) was an important Roman city and administrative centre. Its amphitheatre is situated 200 metres south-west of the ancient city's Bath Gate and would have accommodated audiences of up to 9,000 people. The earthwork remains still survive on the edge of the modern town.

OPENING TIMES

Any reasonable time

HOW TO FIND US

Direction: Located W of Cirencester, next to the bypass. Access from the town, or along Chesterton Lane from the W end of bypass, on to Cotswold Ave

Train: Kemble 4 miles

Bus: Alex Cars/Beaumont 55 from Kemble; Beaumont 55 from Moreton-in-Marsh

MAP	Page 257 (2J)
	OS Map 163 (ref SP 020014)

CLEEVE ABBEY

SOMERSET – TA23 0PS

90

This is one of the few 13th-century monastic sites left with such a complete set of cloister buildings, together with rare Cistercian wall paintings and a medieval painted chamber (viewing may be limited). The magnificent false hammer-beam roof is one of the best in the country, and one of the three tiled pavements is of international importance.

NON-MEMBERS

Adult	£3.30
Concession	£2.50
Child	£1.70

OPENING TIMES

24 Mar-30 Jun, daily	10am-5pm
1 Jul-31 Aug, daily	10am-6pm
1-30 Sep, daily	10am-5pm
1-31 Oct, daily	10am-4pm
Closed	1 Nov-31 Mar

HOW TO FIND US

Direction: Located in Washford, ¼ mile S of A39

Train: Washford ½ mile (West Somerset Railway)

Bus: First 28, 928 ⬛ Taunton – Minehead; 38 from Minehead

Tel: 01984 640377

Disabled access (grounds & ground floor only, plus toilet).

Dogs on leads (restricted areas only).

MAP   Page 257 (4F)
          OS Map 181 (ref ST 047407)

NEW FOR 2005

COLDHARBOUR MILL MUSEUM

DEVON – EX15 3EE

This 200 year old woollen mill still produces knitting yarns and woven tartans and tells the story of the once flourishing West Country woollen industry. In addition to the recently restored waterwheel, there are steam-powered mill engines and a 1910 Lancashire boiler still steamed on special steam-up days.

Owned and managed by the Coldharbour Mill Trust.

NON-MEMBERS

Adult	£5.95
Concession	£5.50
Child	£2.95
Family	£16.00

For tour times and special events details please call 01884 840960. www.coldharbourmill.org.uk.

Discount does not extend to English Heritage Corporate Partners

OPENING TIMES

Mar-Oct, daily (last tour 3:30pm)	10:30am-5pm
Nov-Feb, Sun only	10.30am-5pm

HOW TO FIND US

Direction: Located just off B3440 as it enters Uffculme from Willand. 2 miles south-east of J27 on M5.

Train: Tiverton Parkway 2½ miles

Bus: First 92/92A Taunton – Exeter/Tiverton; Stagecoach 373 Cullompton – Tiverton

---

COLDHARBOUR MILL MUSEUM

Tel: 01884 840960

Disabled access (partial).

Dogs on leads (grounds only).

MAP   Page 257 (5F)
          OS Map 181 (ref ST 062122)

DARTMOUTH CASTLE

DEVON   SEE OPPOSITE PAGE

DUPATH WELL

CORNWALL

This charming and almost complete well-house of c.1500 stands over an ancient holy well. Built of granite blocks, it houses the remains of an immersion bath for cure-seekers.

Managed by the Cornwall Heritage Trust.

OPENING TIMES

Any reasonable time

HOW TO FIND US

Direction: 1 mile E of Callington off A388

Train: Gunnislake 4½ miles

Bus: First 76 Plymouth – Launceston, then 1 mile

MAP   Page 256 (6D)
          OS Map 201 (ref SX 375692)

Dartmouth Castle

DARTMOUTH CASTLE

DEVON – TQ6 0JN

This beautifully positioned defensive castle juts out into the narrow entrance of the Dart Estuary.

Begun in the late 14th century, the 'fortalice' was intended to protect the homes of Dartmouth merchants from shipborne attack. By 1491 it had been reinforced by a gun tower, the very first fortification in England purpose-built to mount heavy cannon.

It is said that Chaucer based *The Shipman* character in his *Canterbury Tales* on John Hawley – the colourful merchant and Mayor of Dartmouth who began the first castle on this site. Today, you can enjoy other tales of the castle as you journey through time from the Tudor period and the Civil War to World War II. Displays on the castle's 600-year history add to the experience.

Make it a full day out. Why not take a boat trip from the quayside at Dartmouth, which lands you just a short walk from the castle entrance.

www.english-heritage.org.uk/dartmouth

NON-MEMBERS

Adult	£3.60
Concession	£2.70
Child	£1.80

OPENING TIMES

24 Mar-30 Jun, daily	10am-5pm
1 Jul-31 Aug, daily	10am-6pm
1-30 Sep, daily	10am-5pm
1-31 Oct, daily	10am-4pm
1 Nov-31 Mar, Sat-Sun	10am-4pm
Closed	24-26 Dec and 1 Jan

HOW TO FIND US

Direction: 1 mile SE of Dartmouth off B3205, narrow approach road

Train: Paignton 8 miles via ferry
Bus: Stagecoach in Devon 120 Paignton – Kingswear, then a ferry to Dartmouth; First 111 Torquay – Dartmouth (🚆 passing Totnes). On both, alight Dartmouth, then 1 mile walk or ferry to site

Tel: 01803 833588

Local Tourist Information
Dartmouth Tel: 01803 834224

Parking (not owned by EH, small charge).
Family learning resources available.
Tearooms (not managed by EH).
Toilets (not managed by EH).

MAP	Page 257 (6F)
	OS Map 202 (ref SX 887503)

FARLEIGH HUNGERFORD CASTLE

SOMERSET – BA2 7RS

Sir Thomas Hungerford acquired and fortified Farleigh manor in 1370 and, over time, it became Farleigh Hungerford Castle. Of the original castle, the two south towers, parts of the curtain wall, the outer gatehouse, the 14th-century chapel and the crypt remain. Following major conservation works, the chapel is open, displaying splendid Hungerford tombs, and a unique wall painting of St George on foot, slaying the dragon.

New displays for 2005.

NON-MEMBERS

Adult	£3.30
Concession	£2.50
Child	£1.70

OPENING TIMES

24 Mar-30 Jun, daily	10am-5pm
1 Jul-31 Aug, daily	10am-6pm
1-30 Sep, daily	10am-5pm
1 Oct-31 Mar, Sat-Sun	10am-4pm
Closed	24-26 Dec and 1 Jan

HOW TO FIND US

Direction: In Farleigh Hungerford, 9 miles SE of Bath; 3½ miles W of Trowbridge on A366

Train: Avoncliff 2 miles; Trowbridge 3½ miles

Bus: Bodmans 96 from Trowbridge (passes close to Trowbridge ⇄) then 1½ mile

---

FARLEIGH HUNGERFORD CASTLE

Tel: 01225 754026

Disabled access (grounds only. Toilet not presently adapted).

Family learning resources available.

MAP	Page 257 (3H)
	OS Map 173 (ref ST 801576)

FIDDLEFORD MANOR

DORSET

Part of a medieval manor house, featuring a remarkable interior. The 600-year-old roofs of the hall and upper living room boast collar-beam trusses and timber-work of great complexity.

Please note
The adjoining building is a private residence and is not open to visitors.

OPENING TIMES

1 Apr-30 Sep, daily	10am-6pm
1 Oct-31 Mar, daily	10am-4pm
Closed	24-26 Dec and 1 Jan

HOW TO FIND US

Direction: 1 mile E of Sturminster Newton off A357

Bus: Damory 310 from Blandford

Disabled access (ground floor only – with 1 step).

Parking (no coach access).

MAP	Page 257 (4H)
	OS Map 162 (ref ST 801136)

GALLOX BRIDGE

SOMERSET

This ancient stone packhorse bridge, featuring two ribbed arches, spans the old mill stream, part of the River Avill.

Managed by the National Trust

OPENING TIMES

Any reasonable time

GALLOX BRIDGE

HOW TO FIND US

Direction: Located off A396 at the S end of Dunster village

Train: Dunster ¾ mile (West Somerset Railway)

Bus: First 28, 928 ⇄ Taunton – Minehead, also 38/9 from Minehead, to within ¼ mile of site

MAP	Page 257 (4F)
	OS Map 181 (ref SS 989432)

GLASTONBURY TRIBUNAL

SOMERSET – BA6 9DP

This 14th-century town house, with a stone façade of the 16th century, was most likely used by a merchant for commercial purposes. It is now a tourist information centre.

Managed by Glastonbury Tribunal Ltd.

NON-MEMBERS
Non-members will be charged for museum entry

Adult	£2.00
Child	£1.50

OPENING TIMES

1 Apr-30 Sep, Sun-Thu	10am-5pm
1 Apr-30 Sep, Fri-Sat	10am-5.30pm
1 Oct-31 Mar, Sun-Thu	10am-4pm
1 Oct-31 Mar, Fri-Sat	10am-4.30pm
Closed	25-26 Dec and 1 Jan

HOW TO FIND US

Direction: In Glastonbury High St

Train: Avoncliff 2 miles; Trowbridge 3½ miles

Bus: First 376/7, 976/7 ⇄ Bristol Temple Meads – Street

Tel: 01458 832954

Disabled access (ground floor – 2 steps).
Parking (charged).

MAP	Page 257 (4H)
	OS Map 182 (ref ST 499389)

GREAT WITCOMBE ROMAN VILLA

GLOUCESTERSHIRE

These remains of a large villa, built round three sides of a courtyard, originally had a luxurious bathhouse complex.

OPENING TIMES

Exterior: Reasonable daylight hours

HOW TO FIND US

Direction: Located 5 miles SE of Gloucester off A46; ½ mile S of reservoir in Witcombe Park; 400 metres (440 yards) from Cotswold Way National Trail

Train: Gloucester 6 miles

Bus: Stagecoach in Gloucester 10 from ⬛ Gloucester, to within 1½ miles of site

🐕 P ⚠

Parking (no access for coaches. No parking permitted in the lane to or beyond the car park).

MAP Page 257 (2J)
     OS Map 163 (ref SO 899142)

GREYFRIARS, GLOUCESTER

GLOUCESTERSHIRE

Remains of a late 15th/early 16th-century Franciscan friary church.

OPENING TIMES

Any reasonable time

HOW TO FIND US

Direction: On Greyfriars Walk

Train: Gloucester ½ mile

Bus: From surrounding areas

♿ 🐕

MAP Page 257 (2J)
     OS Map 162 (ref SO 832184)

GRIMSPOUND

DEVON

Late Bronze Age settlement featuring the remains of 24 huts within an area of over 6,000 sq metres (4 acres), enclosed by a stone wall.

Managed by Dartmoor National Park Authority.

OPENING TIMES

Any reasonable time

HOW TO FIND US

Direction: 6 miles SW of Moretonhampstead, off B3212

Bus: First 82 ⬛ Exeter St David's – Plymouth, to within 2 miles of the site

MAP Page 256 (5E)
     OS Map 191 (ref SX 701809)

HAILES ABBEY

GLOUCESTERSHIRE – GL54 5PB

The Cistercian abbey of Hailes was founded in 1246 by Richard of Cornwall, in thanksgiving for deliverance from shipwreck, and dissolved on Christmas Eve 1539.

HAILES ABBEY

Though never housing large numbers of monks, it had extensive and elaborate buildings, financed by pilgrims visiting its renowned relic, 'the Holy Blood of Hailes' – allegedly a phial of Christ's own blood.

Sculptures, stonework and other finds from the site can be viewed in the museum and an audio tour allows you to learn even more about the site.

New for 2005

Plant sales throughout the season.

Owned by National Trust, maintained and managed by English Heritage.

NON-MEMBERS

Adult	£3.30
Concession	£2.50
Child	£1.70

National Trust members admitted free, but charged for audio tours (£1.50) and special events

OPENING TIMES

24 Mar-30 Jun, daily	10am-5pm
1 Jul-31 Aug, daily	10am-6pm
1-30 Sep, daily	10am-5pm
1-31 Oct, daily	10am-4pm

HOW TO FIND US

Direction: 2 miles NE of Winchcombe off B4632

Train: Cheltenham 10 miles

Bus: Castleways from Cheltenham, to within 1½ miles of site

Tel: 01242 602398

P 🐕 🚻 ♿ 🏛 ⬛ E 🛍 📖 🍴

Audio tours (also for visually impaired and those with learning difficulties).

Disabled access (ramp to museum).

MAP Page 257 (1J)
     OS Map 150 (ref SP 050300)

HALLIGGYE FOGOU

CORNWALL

One of several fascinating underground tunnels associated with Iron Age villages. It consists of a long, narrow tunnel leading to a two-section chamber. Its function has yet to be discovered.

Fogou is a word derived from Cornish – meaning chamber or cave – and is one of the few Cornish words still used in English.

Free entry to the fogou. Entry to the rest of the Trelowarren Estate is charged.

Managed by the Trelowarren Estate.

OPENING TIMES

Reasonable daylight hours Apr-Oct, but completely blocked Nov-Mar, inclusive

HOW TO FIND US

Direction: 5 miles SE of Helston off B3293. E of Garras on Trelowarren Estate

Bus: Truronian T2/3 from Truro

Parking (free to members producing a membership card).

Visitors are advised to bring a torch.

MAP	Page 256 (7B)
	OS Map 203 (ref SW 713239)

HATFIELD EARTHWORKS

WILTSHIRE

These earthworks are part of a 3,500-year-old Neolithic enclosure complex.

OPENING TIMES

Any reasonable time

HOW TO FIND US

Direction: 5½ miles SE of Devizes, off A342; NE of village of Marden

---

HATFIELD EARTHWORKS

Train: Pewsey 5 miles

MAP	Page 257 (3J)
	OS Map 173 (ref SU 092583)

HOUND TOR DESERTED MEDIEVAL VILLAGE

DEVON

The remains of three or four medieval farmsteads. The village was first occupied during the Bronze Age and abandoned in the Middle Ages.

Managed by the Dartmoor National Park Authority.

OPENING TIMES

Any reasonable time

HOW TO FIND US

Direction: 1½ miles S of Manaton, ½ mile from the Ashburton road

Parking (¼ mile walk across moor to monument).

MAP	Page 256 (5E)
	OS Map 191 (ref SX 746788)

HURLERS STONE CIRCLES

CORNWALL

These three Bronze Age stone circles, arranged in a line, are among the best examples of ceremonial standing stones in the whole of the south west.

Managed by the Cornwall Heritage Trust.

OPENING TIMES

Any reasonable time

HOW TO FIND US

Direction: Located ½ mile NW of Minions, off B3254

Train: Liskeard 7 miles

MAP	Page 256 (6D)
	OS Map 201 (ref SX 258714)

JORDAN HILL ROMAN TEMPLE

DORSET

The foundations of a Romano-Celtic temple.

OPENING TIMES

Any reasonable time

HOW TO FIND US

Direction: Located 2 miles NE of Weymouth, off A353

Train: Upwey or Weymouth, both 2 miles

Bus: First 4/A, 31, 500/3, from Weymouth

MAP	Page 257 (5H)
	OS Map 194 (ref SY 699821)

KING DONIERT'S STONE

CORNWALL

Two decorated pieces of a 9th-century cross, with an inscription believed to commemorate Durngarth, King of Cornwall, who drowned c. AD 875.

Managed by the Cornwall Heritage Trust.

OPENING TIMES

Any reasonable time

HOW TO FIND US

Direction: 1 mile NW of St Cleer, off B3254

Train: Liskeard 7 miles

Bus: Western Greyhound 573 Callington-Looe (passing Liskeard) to within ½ mile

Parking (in lay-by).

MAP	Page 256 (6D)
	OS Map 201 (ref SX 236688)

KINGSTON RUSSELL STONE CIRCLE

DORSET

A Bronze Age stone circle consisting of 18 stones, thought to have been built about 4,000 years ago.

OPENING TIMES

Any reasonable time

HOW TO FIND US

Direction: Located 2 miles N of Abbotsbury; 1 mile along a footpath off a minor road to Hardy Monument

Train: Dorchester South or West, both 8 miles

Parking (on verge at entrance to Gorwell Farm).

MAP   Page 257 (5H)
        OS Map 194 (ref SY 578878)

KINGSWOOD ABBEY GATEHOUSE

SOUTH GLOUCESTERSHIRE

This 16th-century gatehouse, one of the latest monastic buildings in England, displays a richly carved mullioned window. It is the sole survivor of this Cistercian abbey.

OPENING TIMES

Exterior: any reasonable time
Interior: key available from 3 Wotton Road, Abbey St 10am-3.30pm weekdays only

HOW TO FIND US

Direction: In Kingswood, off B4060; 1 mile SW of Wotton-under-Edge

Train: Yate 8 miles

Bus: First 309 Bristol – Dursley

Toilets (adjacent to monument).

MAP   Page 257 (2H)
        OS Map 162 (ref ST 747920)

KIRKHAM HOUSE

DEVON

This well-preserved medieval stone residence has undergone considerable work, and provides an insight into life in a town house during the 15th century.

Managed in association with the Paignton Preservation & Local History Society.

OPENING TIMES

25 Mar, 28 Mar, 2 May, 20 May, 29 Aug and every Sun in Jul-Aug:
                            2pm-5pm
Heritage Open Days
10-11 Sep   11am-4pm

HOW TO FIND US

Direction: Located in Kirkham St, off Cecil Rd, Paignton

Train: Paignton ½ mile

Bus: From surrounding areas

MAP   Page 257 (6F)
        OS Map 202 (ref SX 885610)

KNOWLTON CHURCH AND EARTHWORKS

DORSET

The setting of this Norman church among Neolithic earthworks symbolises the transition from pagan to Christian worship.

OPENING TIMES

Any reasonable time

HOW TO FIND US

Direction: SW of Cranborne on B3078

MAP   Page 257 (4J)
        OS Map 195 (ref SU 024103)

LAUNCESTON CASTLE

CORNWALL – PL15 7DR

Launceston Castle is set on the high motte of a stronghold built soon after the Norman Conquest. It was famously used as a jail for George Fox during the reign of Charles II. As the venue for the county assizes and gaol, the castle witnessed the trials and hangings of numerous criminals. The last execution was in 1821. A hands-on display at the castle traces 1,000 years of history, with finds from site excavations.

NON-MEMBERS

Adult	£2.30
Concession	£1.70
Child	£1.20

OPENING TIMES

24 Mar-30 Jun, daily	10am-5pm
1 Jul-31 Aug, daily	10am-6pm
1-30 Sep, daily	10am-5pm
1-31 Oct, daily	10am-4pm
Closed	1 Nov-31 Mar

HOW TO FIND US

Direction: In Launceston

Bus: First X8, 76 ⬛ Plymouth – Bude

Tel: 01566 772365

Disabled access (outer bailey).

MAP   Page 256 (5D)
        OS Map 201 (ref SX 331846)

LUDGERSHALL CASTLE AND CROSS

WILTSHIRE

Following conservation works, the ruins and earthworks of a 12th/13th-century royal hunting lodge are now open. The medieval cross is located in the centre of the village.

OPENING TIMES

Any reasonable time

HOW TO FIND US

Direction: Located on the N side of Ludgershall, off A342

Train: Andover 7 miles

Bus: Stagecoach in Hampshire/ Wilts & Dorset 7-9 ⇌ Andover – Salisbury

P ✗ ⚠

Disabled access (part of site only and village cross).
Parking (limited).

MAP   Page 257 (3K)
      OS Map 184 (ref SU 264512)

LULWORTH CASTLE

DORSET – BH20 5QS

An early 17th-century hunting lodge, the castle later became a country house set in beautiful parkland. After it was gutted by fire in 1929, the exterior was restored. The interior displays trace its history.

Owned and managed by the Lulworth Estate.

LULWORTH CASTLE

ENTRY

Adult	£7.00 (£8.50)*	
Concession	£5.00 (£7.00)*	
Child	£4.00 (£4.50)*	

(Children under 5 go free)

(* Bracketed figures indicates entry fee for jousting season: 24 Jul-29 Aug inclusive)

Family ticket
(2 adults and 3 children)   £21.00
(1 adult and 3 children)   £15.00

Only the castle is free to members. Half-price admission to the Chapel, Woodland Walk, Play Area, Childrens' Summer Farm and Park.

Members will be charged full entry price for special event days : 27/28 Mar, 7/8 May, 30/31 Jul. During the jousting season (24 Jul-29 Aug), half-price admission is on offer to members for the whole estate and joust.

Free access to the castle only is also available during this time, except 30/31 Jul.

OPENING TIMES

25 Mar-30 Sep, Sun-Fri	10.30am-6pm
2 Oct-30 Dec, Sun-Fri	10.30am-4pm
2-7 Jan, Sun-Fri	10.30am-4pm
23 Jan-24 Mar, Sun-Fri	10.30am-4pm
Closed	24-25 Dec and 8-22 Jan

Closed on Saturdays throughout the year, except over Easter weekend.

HOW TO FIND US

Direction: Located in E Lulworth off B3070; 3 miles NE of Lulworth Cove

Train: Wool 4 miles

Bus: First 103 ⇌ Wool – Dorchester

Tel: 0845 450 1054

🚶 ♿ P 🏕 ✗ ♿ 📷 💻 🖕

Disabled access (limited).
Tearooms (not managed by EH).

MAP   Page 257 (5J)
      OS Map 194 (ref SY 853822)

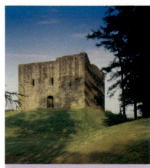

LYDFORD CASTLE AND SAXON TOWN

DEVON

Standing above the gorge of the River Lyd, this 12th-century tower-keep became a courthouse and prison notorious for harsh punishments. The earthworks of an earlier fortress lie to the south.

Managed by the National Trust

OPENING TIMES

Any reasonable time

HOW TO FIND US

Direction: In Lydford off A386; 8 miles S of Okehampton

Bus: First 86 Plymouth – Barnstaple (passes ⇌ Plymouth)

✗ P

MAP   Page 256 (5E)
      OS Map 201 (SX 509848)

MAIDEN CASTLE

DORSET

MAIDEN CASTLE

This is one of the finest and largest Iron Age hillforts in Europe. Its banks enclose an area the size of 50 football pitches, which would have been home to about 200 families. When the site was excavated in the 1930s and 1980s, it provided important details about life in these communities, as well as dramatic proof of British resistance to the Roman invasion in AD44. It also supports theories suggesting that long-term tribal rivalries prevented the Britons from uniting in their own defence.

OPENING TIMES

Any reasonable time

HOW TO FIND US

Direction: 2 miles S of Dorchester, off A354, N of bypass

Train: Dorchester South or West, both 2 miles

MAP Page 257 (5H)
OS Map 194 (ref SY 669884)

MEARE FISH HOUSE

SOMERSET

A simple and well-preserved stone dwelling, probably once the house of the Abbot of Glastonbury's water bailiff.

OPENING TIMES

Any reasonable time

The key for the house is available from Manor House farm

HOW TO FIND US

Direction: In Meare village, on B3151

Train: First 668 Cheddar – Street

MAP Page 257 (4G)
OS Map 182 (ref ST 458417)

MERRIVALE PREHISTORIC SETTLEMENT

DEVON

These Bronze Age village remains feature two double rows of stones, each with a standing stone at the uphill end. There are also cists (burial chambers) and a stone circle at the site.

Managed by Dartmoor National Park Authority.

OPENING TIMES

Any reasonable time

HOW TO FIND US

Direction: 1 mile E of Merrivale

Train: Gunnislake 10 miles

Bus: Plymouth Citybus 98 Yelverton – Tavistock (with connections from Plymouth)

MAP Page 256 (6E)
OS Map 191(ref SX 554748)

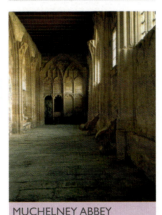

MUCHELNEY ABBEY

SOMERSET – TA10 0DG

Muchelney Abbey was one of the earliest in Somerset, probably founded by the Saxon King Ine c. 693. It was subsequently rebuilt by the Normans as a Benedictine monastery, with a church, cloisters and dependent buildings.

Little remains above ground of the Saxon or Norman buildings, but they have been excavated and their outlines can be traced.

What remains magnificently visible are the monks' kitchen and latrine, part of the fan-vaulted cloister, and the superb great chamber of the abbot's lodging, all rebuilt in the early 16th century.

This had not long been completed when the abbey was swept away by Henry VIII's agents during the suppression of the monasteries. The lodging survived because it converted so easily into a gentry house.

Take time to look out for the remarkable kitchen roof and the curious wallpainting in imitation of rich hangings.

New for 2005

Improved access to the grounds and building. Plant sales throughout the season. New guidebook.

NON-MEMBERS

Adult	£3.00
Concession	£2.30
Child	£1.50

OPENING TIMES

24 Mar-30 Jun, daily	10am-5pm
1 Jul-31 Aug, daily	10am-6pm
1-30 Sep, daily	10am-5pm
1-31 Oct, daily	10am-4pm

HOW TO FIND US

Direction: In Muchelney, 2 miles S of Langport via Huish Episcopi

Bus: First 54 Taunton – Yeovil (passes close to ⛭ Taunton), to within 1 mile of site

Tel: 01458 250664

Disabled access (grounds and most of ground floor only).

MAP Page 257 (4G)
OS Map 193 (ref ST 429249)

NETHERAVON DOVECOTE

WILTSHIRE

A charming 18th-century brick dovecote, still with most of its 700 or more nesting boxes.

OPENING TIMES

Exterior viewing only

HOW TO FIND US

Direction: In Netheravon, 4½ miles N of Amesbury on A345

Train: Pewsey 9 miles, Grateley 11 miles

Bus: Wilts & Dorset 5/6 Salisbury – Swindon (passes close to ⬛ Salisbury and Swindon)

🐕

MAP   Page 257 (3J)
        OS Map 184 (ref SU 147484)

THE NINE STONES

DORSET

The remains of a prehistoric circle of nine standing stones of varying heights and sizes, constructed approximately 4,000 years ago, are now surrounded by trees.

OPENING TIMES

Any reasonable time

THE NINE STONES

HOW TO FIND US

Direction: 1½ miles SW of Winterbourne Abbas, on A35

Train: Weymouth 4½ miles

Bus: First 31 Weymouth – ⬛ Axminster (passing ⬛ Dorchester South)

🅿 🐕 ⚠
Parking (in small lay-by opposite, next to barn).
Warning (cross road with care).

MAP   Page 257 (5H)
        OS Map 194 (ref SY 611904)

NOTGROVE LONG BARROW

GLOUCESTERSHIRE

A Neolithic burial mound, the long barrow contains chambers for human remains opening off a stone-built central passage.

Managed by Gloucestershire County Council

OPENING TIMES

Any reasonable time

HOW TO FIND US

Direction: Located 1½ miles NW of Notgrove, on A436

Bus: Pulham's Moreton-in-Marsh – Cheltenham (passes close to ⬛ Moreton-in-Marsh)

🅿 🐕

MAP   Page 257 (1J)
        OS Map 163 (ref SP 096212)

NUNNEY CASTLE

SOMERSET

NUNNEY CASTLE

The striking and picturesque moated castle of Nunney was built in the 1370s by Sir John de la Mere, who had seemingly served in the French wars. Certainly it was designed in the latest French style, resembling a miniature version of the famous Paris Bastille.

Held for the King during the Civil War, it was quickly reduced by Parliamentarian cannon in 1645: but not until Christmas Day 1910 did the gun-damaged portion of the wall collapse.

OPENING TIMES

Any reasonable time

HOW TO FIND US

Direction: Located in Nunney, 3½ miles SW of Frome, off A361 (no coach access)

Train: Frome 3½ miles

Bus: First 161/2, 960 Frome – Wells

🐕 ♿ ⚠
Disabled access (exterior only).

MAP   Page 257 (3H)
        OS Map 183 (ref ST 737457)

NYMPSFIELD LONG BARROW

GLOUCESTERSHIRE

Neolithic chambered mound 30 metres long.

Managed by Gloucestershire County Council

OPENING TIMES

Any reasonable time

HOW TO FIND US

Direction: Located 1 mile NW of Nympsfield on B4066

Train: Stroud 5 miles

🅿 🐕

MAP   Page 257 (2H)
        OS Map 162 (ref SO 794013)

ODDA'S CHAPEL
GLOUCESTERSHIRE

Anglo-Saxon chapel attached to a late 16th-century half-timbered farmhouse.

Managed by Deerhurst Parish Council

OPENING TIMES

I Apr-31 Oct, daily	10am-6pm
I Nov-31 Mar, daily	10am-4pm
Closed	24-26 Dec and I Jan

HOW TO FIND US

Direction: Located in Deerhurst off B4213, at Abbots Court; SW of parish church

Train: Cheltenham 8 miles

Bus: Swanbrook 351 Gloucester-Upton-upon-Severn (passing close to ⊋ Gloucester)

P ⊠
Parking (charged).

MAP	Page 257 (1J)
	OS Map 150 (ref SO 869298)

OFFA'S DYKE
GLOUCESTERSHIRE

Three-mile section of the great defensive earthwork built by Offa, King of Mercia from AD757 to AD796; the dyke ran from the Severn Estuary to the North Wales coast.

OFFA'S DYKE

OPENING TIMES

Any reasonable time

HOW TO FIND US

Direction: Located 3 miles NE of Chepstow, off B4228. Via Forest Enterprise Tidenham car park, I mile walk (waymarked) down to The Devil's Pulpit on Offa's Dyke (access is suitable only for those wearing proper walking shoes and is not suitable for the very young, old or infirm)

Train: Chepstow 7 miles

Bus: Stagecoach in South Wales; Welcome 69 Chepstow – Monmouth, to within ½ mile

⊠

MAP	Page 257 (2H)
	OS Map 162 (ref SO 546011-ST 549975)

OKEHAMPTON CASTLE
DEVON – EX20 1JB

The ruins of the largest castle in Devon, in a stunning setting on the foothills of Dartmoor. Only the shattered remains of the castle can be seen today. Laid waste by Henry VIII, the ruins include a gatehouse, Norman Keep and the remains of the 14th-century great hall, buttery and kitchens. It was the medieval home of the earls of Devon and there have been sightings of Lady Howard's ghost. There is a riverside picnic area of exceptional beauty and some enchanting woodland walks nearby.

OKEHAMPTON CASTLE

NON-MEMBERS

Adult	£3.00
Concession	£2.30
Child	£1.50

OPENING TIMES

24 Mar-30 Jun, daily	10am-5pm
I Jul-31 Aug, daily	10am-6pm
1-30 Sep, daily	10am-5pm
Closed	I Oct-31 Mar

HOW TO FIND US

Direction: Located I mile SW of Okehampton town centre

Train: Okehampton (summer Sundays only) ½ mile

Bus: First X9/10 Exeter – Bude; 86 Plymouth – Barnstaple

Tel: 01837 52844

P ⅋ ♿ ⌖ ⊠ ◉ ⬚ ⬚ ◎ ⬚ ⚠
Audio tours (also available for the visually impaired and those with learning difficulties).

MAP	Page 256 (5E)
	OS Map 191 (ref SX 583942)

OLD SARUM
WILTSHIRE   GO TO PAGE 100

OLD WARDOUR CASTLE
WILTSHIRE   GO TO PAGE 101

English Heritage properties turn any private or corporate function into a truly historic occasion. See page 16 for a list of properties which are available for hire.

View from the north east

OLD SARUM

WILTSHIRE – SP1 3SD

This great earthwork, with its huge banks and ditch, lies near Salisbury on the edge of Wiltshire's chalk plains. Occupied from Neolithic times, the present structure was built by Iron Age peoples c. 500BC. It was later occupied by the Romans, the Saxons and, most importantly, the Normans. It has long been known as Old Sarum.

In 1070, William the Conqueror paid off his army here and, in 1085, demanded loyalty from his nobles. A castle, palace and cathedral were built inside the earthwork, but disputes between soldiers and priests, plus inadequate water supplies, proved to be huge obstacles to life.

With the founding of New Sarum (the city we know as Salisbury) in 1226, this settlement began to fade away.

However, although the old cathedral was dismantled and a magnificent new one built in the valley, the castle at Old Sarum remained in use until Tudor times.

Today, the remains of the prehistoric fortress and of the Norman palace, castle and cathedral evoke memories of thousands of years of history.

Discover Old Sarum's momentous past from graphic panels as you move around the site.

Contact the site for details of our special events for 2005.

www.english-heritage.org.uk/oldsarum

NON-MEMBERS

Adult	£2.90
Concession	£2.20
Child	£1.50

OPENING TIMES

24 Mar-30 Jun, daily	10am-5pm
1 Jul-31 Aug, daily	9am-6pm
1-30 Sep, daily	10am-5pm
1-31 Oct, daily	10am-4pm
1 Nov-28 Feb, daily	11am-3pm
1-31 Mar, daily	10am-4pm
Closed	24-26 Dec and 1 Jan

HOW TO FIND US

Direction: 2 miles N of Salisbury, Wiltshire off A345

Train: Salisbury 2 miles

Bus: Wilts & Dorset/Stagecoach in Hampshire 3, 5-9 from Salisbury

Tel: 01722 335398

Local Tourist Information Salisbury: 01722 334956

Disabled access (outer bailey and grounds only).
Family learning resources available.

MAP	Page 257 (4J)
	OS Map 184 (ref SU 138327)

OLD WARDOUR CASTLE

WILTSHIRE – SP3 6RR

This romantic ruin, set beside a lake, was originally built in the late 14th century for John, fifth Lord Lovel. The unusual six-sided castle was unique in medieval English architecture, and Old Wardour was intended to impress visitors and guests with its builder's wealth, taste and power. It was also a luxurious residence, with multiple rooms for guests.

Badly damaged in the English Civil War, it was restored to the Arundell family, who integrated it into the landscaped grounds of nearby Wardour New Castle (not managed by EH), which they built in 1776. Its setting makes it one of England's most romantic ruins, and it is the only Registered Landscape (on the Register of Parks and Gardens) in the South West.

It may be familiar to many visitors as a setting for the film *Robin Hood Prince of Thieves* starring Kevin Costner.

An audio tour brings the long history of this fascinating castle to life. Please contact the site for details of special events at the castle.

⊤ Available for corporate and private hire.

www.english-heritage.org.uk/oldwardour

NON-MEMBERS

Adult	£3.00
Concession	£2.30
Child	£1.50

OPENING TIMES

24 Mar-30 Jun, daily	10am-5pm
1 Jul-31 Aug, daily	10am-6pm
1-30 Sep, daily	10am-5pm
1-31 Oct, daily	10am-4pm
1 Nov-31 Mar, Sat-Sun	10am-4pm
Closed	24-26 Dec and 1 Jan

HOW TO FIND US

Direction: Located off A30 2 miles SW of Tisbury. Also accessible from A350

Train: Tisbury 2½ miles

Bus: Wilts & Dorset 26 Salisbury – Shaftesbury (passes ≋ Tisbury)

Tel: 01747 870487

P 🚶 🚹 ♿ 🎁 🎧 ♿ ⊤ 🖼
🎫 ⚠
Disabled access (grounds and ground floor only).

MAP	Page 257 (4J)
	OS Map 184 (ref ST 939263)

OVER BRIDGE

GLOUCESTERSHIRE

A single-arch stone bridge spanning the River Severn, built by Thomas Telford between 1825 and 1827.

OPENING TIMES

Any reasonable time

HOW TO FIND US

Direction: 1 mile NW of Gloucester, at junction of A40 (Ross) and A417 (Ledbury)

Train: Gloucester 2 miles

Bus: From 🚆 Gloucester

🅿 🐕
Parking (in lay-by).

MAP	Page 257 (1H)
	OS Map 162 (ref SO 816196)

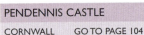

PENDENNIS CASTLE

CORNWALL   GO TO PAGE 104

PENHALLAM

CORNWALL

The low, grass-covered ruins of a medieval manor house, surrounded by a protective moat in a delightful woodland setting.

OPENING TIMES

Any reasonable time

HOW TO FIND US

Direction: Signposted from Week St Mary, off a minor road off A39 from Treskinnick Cross (10 minutes' walk from the car park on the forest track)

🅿 🐕
Parking (limited).

MAP	Page 256 (5D)
	OS Map 190 (ref SX 224974)

PORTLAND CASTLE

DORSET   GO TO PAGE 106

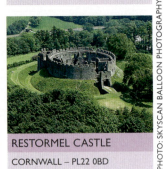

RESTORMEL CASTLE

CORNWALL – PL22 0BD

Surrounded by a deep, dry moat and perched on a high mound, the huge circular keep of this castle, built in the 13th century, survives in good condition. Built as a symbol of wealth and status and once a possession of Edward the Black Prince, it offers splendid views over the surrounding countryside. It's also a marvellous picnic spot.

NON-MEMBERS

Adult	£2.30
Concession	£1.70
Child	£1.20

OPENING TIMES

24 Mar-30 Jun, daily	10am-5pm
1 Jul-31 Aug, daily	10am-6pm
1-30 Sep, daily	10am-5pm
1-31 Oct, daily	10am-4pm

HOW TO FIND US

Direction: Located 1½ miles N of Lostwithiel, off A390

Train: Lostwithiel 1½ miles

Tel: 01208 872687

🅿 🚶 🚻 ⛺ 🐕 📷 🏪 ⚠

Access (via a stock grazing area so appropriate footwear must be worn. There are three steps on the entrance path, so disabled visitors may want to call the site in advance to arrange alternative access).

MAP	Page 256 (6C)
	OS Map 200 (ref SX 104614)

ℹ

English Heritage membership makes a lovely gift.

Call 0870 333 1181 or visit **www.english-heritage.org.uk/gift** for more details.

ROYAL CITADEL, PLYMOUTH
DEVON

A dramatic 17th-century fortress built to defend the coastline from the Dutch, and still in use by the military today. Viewing is only by weekly tours led by Blue Badge Guides.

ENTRY

Non-member	£3.50
EH members and children	£3.00

OPENING TIMES

By guided tour only, May-Sep:
Tue & Thu only   2.30pm

HOW TO FIND US

Direction: At E end of Plymouth Hoe

Train: Plymouth 1 mile

Bus: From surrounding areas

plymouthukbbg@hotmail.com

MAP	Page 256 (6E)
	OS Map 201 (ref SX 480538)

ST BREOCK DOWNS MONOLITH
CORNWALL

A prehistoric standing stone, originally 5 metres (16 ft) high and weighing some 16.75 tonnes, this is Cornwall's heaviest monolith. The stone is set in beautiful countryside.

Managed by the Cornwall Heritage Trust

OPENING TIMES

Any reasonable time

HOW TO FIND US

Direction: Located on St Breock Downs; 3½ miles SW of Wadebridge off unclassified road to Rosenannon

Train: Roche 5½ miles

MAP	Page 256 (6C)
	OS Map 200 (ref SW 968683)

ST BRIAVELS CASTLE
GLOUCESTERSHIRE

This splendid 13th-century castle, set in marvellous walking country, is now a youth hostel.

The grounds are available for public use.

OPENING TIMES

Exterior: any reasonable time

Bailey: 1 Apr-30 Sep, daily 1pm-4pm

HOW TO FIND US

Direction: In St Briavels; 7 miles NE of Chepstow off B4228

Train: Chepstow 8 miles

Tel: 01594 530272

MAP	Page 257 (2H)
	OS Map 162 (ref SO 559046)

ST CATHERINE'S CASTLE
CORNWALL

A small fort built by Henry VIII in the 16th century to defend Fowey Harbour, consisting of two storeys with gun ports at ground level.

OPENING TIMES

Any reasonable time

HOW TO FIND US

Direction: 1½ miles SW of Fowey, along a woodland footpath off A3082

Train: Par 4 miles

Parking (Ready Money Cove Car Park, Fowey ¾ mile walk).

MAP	Page 256 (6C)
	OS Map 200 (ref SX 119509)

ST CATHERINE'S CHAPEL
DORSET

This small stone chapel, set on a hilltop above the village of Abbotsbury and previously used as a lighthouse, has an unusual roof and small turret.

OPENING TIMES

Any reasonable time

HOW TO FIND US

Direction: ½ mile S of Abbotsbury; by path from village, off B3157

Train: Upwey 7 miles

Bus: First X53 Poole – Bridport

MAP	Page 257 (5H)
	OS Map 194 (ref SY 573848)

ST MARY'S CHURCH, KEMPLEY
GLOUCESTERSHIRE

A delightful Norman church, displaying one of the most outstandingly complete and well-preserved sets of medieval wall paintings in England, dating from the 12th and 14th centuries.

Managed by the Friends of Kempley Church

OPENING TIMES

1 Mar-31 Oct, daily	10am-6pm

Telephone for appointment in winter.

HOW TO FIND US

Direction: 1 mile N of Kempley off B4024; 6 miles NE of Ross-on-Wye

Train: Ledbury 8 miles

Tel: 01531 660214

MAP	Page 257 (1H)
	OS Map 149 (ref SO 670313)

PENDENNIS CASTLE CORNWALL – TR11 4LP

Pendennis Castle has seen a great deal of active service, and was continually adapted over 400 years to meet new enemies, from the French and Spanish in the 16th century, through to World War 11.

Constructed between 1540-1545, Pendennis and its sister, St Mawes Castle, form the Cornish end of a chain of castles built by Henry VIII on the south coast.

In 1598, during Elizabeth I's reign, a new type of defensive wall was added around the original fort. The castle was strengthened again prior to the Civil War (1642-1651) and in fact Pendennis played host to the future Charles II in 1646, before he sailed to the Isles of Scilly. The castle then withstood five months of siege before becoming the penultimate Royalist garrison on the English mainland to surrender.

Pendennis continued to play a vital role in the country's defences throughout the late 19th and early 20th centuries, and saw significant action during World War II.

Evidence of the castle's fascinating history is on show throughout the site; the Noonday Gun is fired every day during July and August, and the Guardhouse has been returned to its World War I appearance. You can also visit the underground magazines and tunnels, including the World War II Half Moon Battery, as well as the original 16th-century Keep complete with recreated Tudor gun deck.

The on-site museum, tearooms and tactile exhibits in the Discovery Centre make the Pendennis experience a great day out for all the family.

New for 2005
From mid July the Barrack Block will open with family orientated displays about the site.

🍷 Available for corporate and private hire.

💒 Licensed for civil wedding ceremonies.

www.english-heritage.org.uk/pendennis

Barrack Block

NON-MEMBERS

Adult	£4.60
Concession	£3.50
Child	£2.30
Family ticket	£11.50

OPENING TIMES

24 Mar-30 Jun, daily	10am-5pm
1 Jul-31 Aug, daily	10am-6pm
1-30 Sep, daily	10am-5pm
24 Mar-30 Sep, Sat	closes at 4pm
1 Oct-31 Mar, daily	10am-4pm
Closed	24-26 Dec and 1 Jan.

The keep will close for 1 hour at lunch on Saturdays when events are booked.

HOW TO FIND US

Direction: On Pendennis Headland, 1 mile SE of Falmouth. The Falmouth Land Train stops in Castle Car Park (summer only)

Train: Falmouth Docks ½ mile

Bus: First 309 (Summer Service)

Tel: 01326 316594

Local Tourist Information: 01326 313457

Disabled access (wheelchair access to the grounds, there are steep steps or drops in places).

Dogs on leads (grounds only).

Family learning resources available.

Tearooms (open Apr-Oct).

MAP	Page 256 (7C)
	OS Map 204 (ref SW 824318)

The Battery Observation Post

Portland Castle and gun platform

PORTLAND CASTLE

DORSET – DT5 1AZ

The history of this fortress, which overlooks Portland harbour, is diverse and fascinating. Built by Henry VIII to defend Weymouth against possible French and Spanish invasion, its squat appearance is typical of the artillery forts built in the early 1540s.

Unusually for a fortress of this period, the castle has survived largely unaltered. It first witnessed serious fighting during the Civil War, when it was seized by both Parliamentarians and Royalists.

It became a Seaplane Station during World War I, and was in the forefront of the D-Day preparations which helped to end World War II.

The Governor's Garden, designed by Christopher Bradley-Hole as part of the Contemporary Heritage Garden series, contains an impressive circular amphitheatre made from local Portland stone, with two-level seating for about 200 people. This perfectly sheltered spot is a great place to relax and enjoy the dramatic sea and harbour views.

Portland Castle offers accessibility for all – there are audio tours and a Touch Tour for the visually impaired. You can even come face-to-face with Henry VIII in the Great Hall. When you need a break, the recently refurbished tearoom is the ideal place for a light lunch or a cup of tea.

Contact the site for details of special summer 2005 events.

⚊ Available for corporate and private hire

⚊ Licensed for civil wedding ceremonies.

www.english-heritage.org.uk/portland

NON-MEMBERS

Adult	£3.60
Concession	£2.70
Child	£1.80

OPENING TIMES

24 Mar-30 Jun, daily	10am-5pm
1 Jul-31 Aug, daily	10am-6pm
1-30 Sep, daily	10am-5pm
1-31 Oct, daily	10am-4pm
Closed	1 Nov-31 Mar

HOW TO FIND US

Direction: Overlooking Portland Harbour in Castletown, Isle of Portland

Train: Weymouth 4½ miles

Bus: First 1/A, 7/A from Weymouth (passing close to ⮂ Weymouth)

Ferry: From Weymouth Harbour, Good Fri-end Sep (weather permitting). Call the castle for details.

Tel: 01305 820539

Disabled access (Captain's House, ground floor of the castle and Governor's Garden).

Captain's House Tearooms (table service & outdoor servery).

Family learning resources available.

MAP	Page 257 (6H) OS Map 194 (ref SY 685744)

ST MAWES CASTLE

CORNWALL – TR2 3AA

This, the best preserved of Henry VIII's coastal fortresses, was built to counter the invasion threat from France and Spain, in partnership with its twin, Pendennis, on the other side of the Fal Estuary. It fell to landward attack from Parliamentarian forces in 1646 and was not properly refortified until the late 19th and early 20th centuries. Other forts built as part of Henry VIII's coastal defences include Portland, Deal and Walmer.

⊤ Available for corporate and private hire.

⊡ Licensed for civil wedding ceremonies.

NON-MEMBERS

Adult	£3.60
Concession	£2.70
Child	£1.80

OPENING TIMES

24 Mar-30 Jun, daily	10am-5pm
1 Jul-31 Aug, daily	10am-6pm
1-30 Sep, daily	10am-5pm
24 Mar-30 Sep, Sat closes at 1pm	
Fri & Sun, 4.30pm if events booked.	
1-31 Oct, daily	10am-4pm
1 Nov-31 Mar, Fri-Mon	10am-4pm
Closed	24-26 Dec and 1 Jan

ST MAWES CASTLE

HOW TO FIND US

Direction: In St Mawes on A3078

Train: Penmere, 4 miles via Prince of Wales Pier and ferry

Bus: First 50 Truro – St Mawes to within ½ mile

Tel: 01326 270526

Dogs on leads (grounds only).
Family learning resources available.

MAP   Page 256 (7C)
      OS Map 204 (ref SW 841328)

THE SANCTUARY

WILTSHIRE

Probably 5,000 years old, the Sanctuary consists of two concentric circles of stone and six of timber uprights, now indicated by concrete posts.

Managed by the National Trust.
Part of the Avebury World Heritage Site.

OPENING TIMES

Any reasonable time.
Usual facilities may not be available around the Summer Solstice June 20-22. Please check before you visit.

HOW TO FIND US

Train: Pewsey 9 miles, Bedwyn 12 miles

Bus: Wilts and Dorset 5/6 Salisbury – Swindon (passes close to 🚉 Swindon)

Parking (in lay-by).

MAP   Page 257 (3J)
      OS Map 173 (ref SU 118680)

SHERBORNE OLD CASTLE

DORSET – DT9 3SA

Built by Bishop Roger of Salisbury in the 12th century as a strongly defended palace, Sherborne Old Castle became a powerful Royalist base during the Civil War. Described as 'malicious and mischievous' by Cromwell, it fell in 1645 after a fierce eleven-day siege.

NON-MEMBERS

Adult	£2.30
Concession	£1.70
Child	£1.20

Joint ticket for Sherborne Castle grounds £5.00, members' discounts see page 119

OPENING TIMES

24 Mar-30 Jun, Tue-Thu & Sat-Sun	10am-5pm
1 Jul-31 Aug, Tue-Thu & Sat-Sun	10am-6pm
1-30 Sep, Tue-Thu & Sat-Sun	10am-5pm
1-31 Oct, Tue-Thu & Sat-Sun	10am-4pm
Open on Bank Holidays 24 Mar-31 Aug	
Closed	1 Nov-31 Mar

HOW TO FIND US

Direction: Located ½ mile E of Sherborne, off B3145

Train: Sherborne ¾ mile

Tel: 01935 812730

MAP   Page 257 (4H)
      OS Map 183 (ref ST 648168)

STONEHENGE WILTSHIRE – SP4 7DE

The great and ancient stone circle of Stonehenge is one of the wonders of the world. What visitors see today are the substantial remnants of the last in a sequence of such monuments erected between c. 3000BC and 1600BC. Each monument was a circular structure, aligned with the rising of the sun at the solstice.

Sarsen circle bluestones and one trilithon

Stones silhouette at sunset

There has always been intense debate over quite what purpose Stonehenge served. Certainly it was the focal point in a landscape filled with prehistoric ceremonial structures. It also represented an enormous investment of labour and time. A huge effort and great organisation was needed to carry the stones tens, and sometimes hundreds, of miles by land and water, and then to shape and raise them. Only a sophisticated society could have mustered so large a workforce, and the design and construction skills necessary to produce Stonehenge and its surrounding monuments.

Aerial view in the snow

Stonehenge's orientation in relation to the rising and setting sun has always been one of its most remarkable features. Whether this was because its builders came from a sun-worshipping culture or because – as some scholars have asserted – the circle and its banks were part of a huge astronomical calendar, remains a mystery.

What cannot be denied is the ingenuity of the builders of Stonehenge. With only very basic tools at their disposal, they shaped the stones and formed the mortises and tenons that linked uprights to lintels.

Using antlers and bones, they dug the pits to hold the stones and made the banks and ditches that enclosed them.

There are direct links with the people who built Stonehenge in their tools, artefacts, pottery and even the contents of their graves. Some of these are displayed in the museums at Salisbury and Devizes.

The first monument in the Stonehenge landscape consisted of a circular bank and ditch with a ring of 56 wooden posts, the pits for which are now known as Aubrey Holes. Later monuments all used and reused the great stones we see today, many of which were brought from some distance away. The final phase comprised the construction of an outer circle of huge standing stones – super-hard sarsens, from the Marlborough Downs. These were topped by lintels, forming a ring. Inside this stood a horseshoe of five still-larger constructions, known as trilithons: pairs of uprights with a lintel across each. All the stones were connected using mortise-and-tenon joints.

Smaller bluestones, from the Preseli Mountains in South Wales, were arranged in a ring and a horseshoe, within the great circle and horseshoe of sarsen stones. In an earlier phase, these bluestones had been erected in a different arrangement.

STONEHENGE

Burial mounds, possibly containing the graves of ruling families, are also integral to the landscape. Neolithic long barrows and the various types of circular barrows which came later are still visible. So too are other earthworks and monuments. Some remain enigmatic, such as the long oval earthwork to the north, the Cursus – once thought to be a chariot racecourse. You can visit the Cursus and other parts of the Stonehenge landscape.

Woodhenge, two miles to the north east, was a wooden oval-post structure, also aligned with the solstice sunrise.

It is believed to be contemporary with the first phase of Stonehenge.

Now a World Heritage Site, Stonehenge and all its surroundings remain powerful witnesses to the once great civilisations of the Stone and Bronze Ages, between 5,000 and 3,000 years ago.

Stonehenge is surrounded by 1,500 acres of land owned by the National Trust, with excellent walks.

Stone Circle Access by advanced booking only.

New for 2005
New guidebook

For the latest information, visit **www.english-heritage.org.uk/ stonehenge or www.the stonehengeproject.org**

NON-MEMBERS

Adult	£5.50
Concession	£4.10
Child	£2.80
Family ticket	£13.80

National Trust members admitted free.

OPENING TIMES

16 Mar-31 May, daily 9.30am-6pm
1 Jun-31 Aug, daily 9am-7pm
1 Sep-15 Oct, daily 9.30am-6pm
16 Oct-15 Mar, daily 9.30am-4pm
Closed 24-26 Dec and 1 Jan
Opening times from 20 to 22 June may be subject to change due to Summer Solstice. Please check with Customer Services before your visit.
Recommended last admission time no later than 30 minutes before the advertised closing time. Stonehenge will close promptly 20 minutes after the advertised closing time.
When weather conditions are bad, access may be restricted and visitors may not be able to use the walkway around the stone circle.

HOW TO FIND US

Direction: 2 miles W of Amesbury on junction of A303 and A344/A360

Train: Salisbury 9½ miles

Bus: Wilts & Dorset 3 from 🚆 Salisbury

Tel: 0870 333 1181 (Customer Services)

Local Tourist Information Amesbury: 01980 622833; and Salisbury: 01722 334956

Stone Circle Access Line: 01980 626267, advance booking only

🅿 🚶 ♿ 📷 💷 📺 🔁 ✖

Audio tours (complimentary – available in nine languages & hearing loop: subject to availability).

Catering (Stonehenge Kitchen, open all year).

Family learning resources available.

Guidebooks (also available in French, German and Japanese; large print and braille guides in English only).

No dogs allowed (except guide and hearing dogs).

Parking (seasonal charge for non-members, refundable on entry).

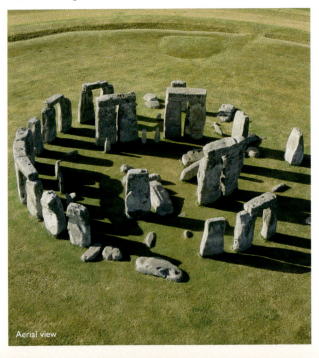
Aerial view

MAP   Page 257 (4J)
        OS Map 184 (ref SU 122422)

SILBURY HILL

WILTSHIRE

The largest Neolithic construction of its type in Europe – an extraordinary artificial prehistoric mound.

Part of the Avebury World Heritage Site.

OPENING TIMES

Viewing area at any reasonable time. Strictly no access to the hill itself

Usual facilities may not be available around the Summer Solstice 20-22 June. Please check before you visit.

HOW TO FIND US

Direction: 1 mile W of West Kennet on A4

Train: Pewsey 9 miles, Swindon 13 miles

Bus: Stagecoach in Swindon/First 49 Swindon – Trowbridge; Thamesdown 48/A, 49/A from Marlborough; Wilts & Dorset 5/6 Salisbury – Swindon (all pass within ¾ mile and pass close to ⇌ Swindon)

P 🚻 🐕
Disabled access (viewing area).

MAP	Page 257 (3J)
	OS Map 173 (ref SU 100685)

SIR BEVIL GRENVILLE'S MONUMENT

SOMERSET

Erected to commemorate the heroism of a Royalist commander and his Cornish pikemen at the Battle of Lansdown, 1643.

OPENING TIMES

Any reasonable time

HOW TO FIND US

Direction: Located 4 miles NW of Bath on the N edge of Lansdown Hill, near the road to Wick

Train: Bath Spa 4½ miles

Bus: South Gloucestershire 620 ⇌ Bath Spa – Tetbury

P 🐕
Parking (in lay-by).

MAP	Page 257 (3H)
	OS Map 172 (ref ST 722703)

STANTON DREW CIRCLES AND COVE

BATH & NE SOMERSET

Recent research at this assembly of stone circles, avenues and a 'cove' of three standing stones has revealed that there was once a huge timber structure within the Great Circle. The complex dates from around 3000BC.

STANTON DREW CIRCLES AND COVE

OPENING TIMES

Cove: any reasonable time. Two main stone circles; access at the discretion of the landowner, who may levy a charge.

HOW TO FIND US

Direction: Cove: located in the garden of the Druid's Arms public house. Circles: located E of Stanton Drew village

Train: Bristol Temple Meads 7 miles

Bus: First 672 ⇌ Bristol Temple Meads – Cheddar

🐕

MAP	Page 257 (3H)
	OS Map 172 (cove ref ST 597631, circles ref ST 601633)

STONEHENGE

WILTSHIRE   GO TO PAGE 108

STONEY LITTLETON LONG BARROW

BATH & NE SOMERSET

This Neolithic burial mound is about 30 metres long, and features multiple axial chambers where human remains once lay.

OPENING TIMES

Any reasonable daylight hours

HOW TO FIND US

Direction: 1 mile S of Wellow off A367

Train: Bath Spa 6 miles

P
Parking (limited).

Note: visitors are advised to bring a torch, and that there may be mud on approach and interior floor.

MAP	Page 257 (3H)
	OS Map 172 (ref ST 735572)

TEMPLE CHURCH

BRISTOL

The tower and walls of this 15th-century church defied the bombs of the Second World War. The graveyard now serves as a public garden.

OPENING TIMES

Exterior only: any reasonable time

HOW TO FIND US

Direction: Located in Temple St, off Victoria St

Train: Bristol Temple Meads ¼ mile

Bus: From surrounding areas

🐕

MAP	Page 257 (3H)
	OS Map 172 (ref ST 593727)

TINTAGEL CASTLE

CORNWALL   GO TO PAGE 114

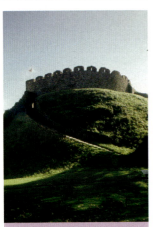

TOTNES CASTLE

DEVON –TQ9 5NU

One of the best-preserved Norman shell keeps, this motte and bailey castle offers splendid views over the River Dart. The once great ditch which surrounded the structure is now filled with cottages and gardens.

TOTNES CASTLE

NON-MEMBERS

Adult	£2.30
Concession	£1.70
Child	£1.20

OPENING TIMES

24 Mar-30 Jun, daily	10am-5pm
1 Jul-31 Aug, daily	10am-6pm
1-30 Sep, daily	10am-5pm
1-31 Oct, daily	10am-4pm

HOW TO FIND US

Direction: In Totnes, on a hill overlooking the town

Train: Totnes ¼ mile

Tel: 01803 864406

🅿️ 📷 🐕 🎒 🏕️ ⚠️

Parking (charged, 64 metres (70 yards); cars only, narrow approach roads). Family learning resources available.

MAP	Page 256 (6E)
	OS Map 202 (ref SX 800605)

TREGIFFIAN BURIAL CHAMBER

CORNWALL

A Neolithic or early Bronze Age chambered tomb with an entrance passage, walled and roofed with stone slabs, leading into the central chamber.

Managed by the Cornwall Heritage Trust.

OPENING TIMES

Any reasonable time

HOW TO FIND US

Direction: Located 2 miles SE of St Buryan, on B3315

Train: Penzance 5½ miles

🐕

MAP	Page 256 (7B)
	OS Map 203 (ref SW 431244)

TRETHEVY QUOIT

CORNWALL

This well-preserved and impressive Neolithic burial chamber stands 2.7 metres (8.9 ft) high. There are five standing stones, surmounted by a huge capstone.

Managed by Cornwall Heritage Trust.

OPENING TIMES

Any reasonable time

HOW TO FIND US

Direction: 1 mile NE of St Cleer, near Darite; off B3254

Train: Liskeard 3½ miles

Bus: Western Greyhound 573 Callington – Looe (passes 🚆 Liskeard) within ½ mile

🐕

MAP	Page 256 (6D)
	OS Map 201 (ref SX 259688)

ULEY LONG BARROW (HETTY PEGLER'S TUMP)

GLOUCESTERSHIRE

Dating from about 3000BC, this 55-metre (180 ft) Neolithic chambered burial mound is unusual in that its mound is still intact.

Managed by Gloucestershire County Council.

OPENING TIMES

Any reasonable time

HOW TO FIND US

Direction: Located 3½ miles NE of Dursley, on B4066

Train: Stroud 6 miles

Bus: Stagecoach in the Cotswolds 20 Stroud – Uley (passes close to 🚆 Stroud), then 1 mile

🐕

MAP	Page 257 (2H)
	OS Map 162 (ref SO 790000)

UPPER PLYM VALLEY
DEVON

Scores of prehistoric and medieval sites covering 15.5 square kilometres (six square miles) of ancient English landscape.

Managed by the National Trust.

OPENING TIMES
Any reasonable time

HOW TO FIND US
Direction: 4 miles E of Yelverton

MAP   Page 256 (6E)
       OS Map 202 (ref SX 580660)

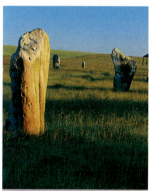

WEST KENNET AVENUE
WILTSHIRE

This is one of two known avenues of standing stones which once ran from the Avebury Stone Circles and Henge. This avenue ends at The Sanctuary (see page 107).

Part of the Avebury World Heritage Site.

Owned and managed by the National Trust.

OPENING TIMES
Any reasonable time.

Usual facilities may not be available around the Summer Solstice June 20-22. Please check before you visit.

WEST KENNET AVENUE

HOW TO FIND US
Direction: Runs alongside B4003

Train: Pewsey 9 miles, Swindon 12 miles

Bus: Stagecoach in Swindon/ First 49 Swindon – Trowbridge; Thamesdown 48/A, 49/A from Marlborough; Wilts and Dorset 5/6 Salisbury – Swindon (all pass close to 🚉 Swindon)

🐕 ♿
Disabled access (on roadway).

MAP   Page 257 (3J)
       OS Map 173 (ref SU 105695)

WEST KENNET LONG BARROW
WILTSHIRE

A Neolithic chambered tomb, consisting of a long earthen mound containing a passage with side chambers.

Part of the Avebury World Heritage Site.

Managed by the National Trust.

WEST KENNET LONG BARROW

OPENING TIMES
Any reasonable time.

Usual facilities may not be available around the Summer Solstice June 20-22. Please check before you visit.

HOW TO FIND US
Direction: ¾ mile SW of West Kennet, along footpath off A4

Train: Pewsey 9 miles, Swindon 13 miles

Bus: Stagecoach in Swindon/ First 49 Swindon – Trowbridge; Thamesdown 48/A, 49/A from Marlborough; Wilts and Dorset 5/6 Salisbury – Swindon (all pass close to 🚉 Swindon)

🅿 🐕
Parking (in lay-by).

MAP   Page 257 (3J)
       OS Map (ref SU 105677)

WINDMILL HILL
WILTSHIRE

Neolithic remains of three concentric rings of ditches, enclosing an area of almost 5,000 square metres (21 acres).

Part of the Avebury World Heritage Site.

Managed by the National Trust.

OPENING TIMES
Any reasonable time

HOW TO FIND US
Direction: 1¼ mile NW of Avebury

Train: Swindon 11 miles

Bus: Stagecoach in Swindon/ First 49 Swindon – Trowbridge; Thamesdown 48/A, 49/A from Marlborough; Wilts and Dorset 5/6 Salisbury – Swindon (all pass close to 🚉 Swindon)

MAP   Page 257 (3J)
       OS Map 173 (ref SU 087714)

TINTAGEL CASTLE CORNWALL – PL34 0HE

With its spectacular location on one of England's most dramatic coastlines, Tintagel is an awe-inspiring and romantic spot, a place of legends.

The bridge giving access to the 'The Island Ward'

Joined to the mainland by a narrow neck of land, Tintagel Island faces the full force of the Atlantic. On the mainland itself, the gaunt remains of the medieval castle represent only one phase in a long history of occupation. Even before Richard, Earl of Cornwall, built his castle, Tintagel had come to be associated with the conception of King Arthur. The connection was later renewed by Alfred, Lord Tennyson, in his 'Idylls of the King'.

After a period as a Roman settlement and military outpost, Tintagel is thought to have been a trading settlement of Celtic kings during the 5th and 6th centuries. Legend has it that one of these was King Mark, whose nephew Tristan fell in love with Yseult (or Isolde). Their doomed romance is part of Tintagel's story.

The remains of the 13th-century castle are breathtaking. Steep stone steps, stout walls and rugged windswept cliff edges encircle the Great Hall, where Richard, Earl of Cornwall, once feasted.

The emphasis here is always on the word 'may', as there are so many unanswered questions and legends surrounding Tintagel. The castle has an amazing capacity to surprise us, even after years of investigation.

In June 1998, excavations were undertaken under the direction of Professor Chris Morris of the University of Glasgow, on a relatively sheltered and small site on the eastern side of the island, first excavated in the 1930s. Pottery from the 5th and 6th centuries was found, as well as some fine glass fragments believed to be from 6th or 7th-century Málaga in Spain. Even more remarkable was a 1,500-year-old piece of slate on which remain two Latin inscriptions. The second inscription reads: 'Artognou, father of a descendant of Coll, has had [this] made.' Who exactly Artognou was continues to be a subject for lively speculation.

Searching for King Arthur, an audio visual presentation introduces visitors to the castle, its legends and history. During the summer you can also enjoy a special introductory talk.

Access to the castle is difficult for disabled visitors (via over 100 steep steps). The Land Rover service from the village can take visually impaired and ambulant disabled people to the exhibition and shop (Apr-Oct only). Contact the site for service information.

www.english-heritage.org.uk/tintagel

NON-MEMBERS

Adult	£3.90
Concession	£2.90
Child	£2.00

OPENING TIMES

24 Mar-30 Sep, daily	10am-6pm
1-31 Oct, daily	10am-5pm
1 Nov-31 Mar, daily	10am-4pm
Closed	24-26 Dec and 1 Jan

HOW TO FIND US

Direction: On Tintagel Head, ½ mile along uneven track from Tintagel; no vehicles except Land Rover Service

Bus: Western Greyhound 524 Bude – Wadebridge, 594 Bude – Truro (with connections on 555 at Wadebridge to 🚆 Bodmin Parkway)

Tel: 01840 770328

Local Tourist Information
Tintagel Visitors' Centre:
01840 779084;
Camelford (summer only):
01840 212954
Padstow: 01841 533449

🅿 🚶 ♿ 🏞 🍴 ♿ 🚻 ⚠

Disabled access (limited via Land Rover service to castle Apr-Oct, extra charge).

Family learning resources available.

Parking (600 metres (660 yards) in the village).

MAP   Page 256 (5C)
OS Map 200 (ref SX 049891)

WINDMILL TUMP LONG BARROW, RODMARTON

GLOUCESTERSHIRE

A Neolithic long barrow with two porthole entrances.

Managed by Gloucestershire County Council.

OPENING TIMES

Any reasonable time

HOW TO FIND US

Direction: 1 mile SW of Rodmarton

Train: Kemble 5 miles

Bus: Alex Cars from ⇌ Kemble

MAP	Page 257 (2J)
	OS Map 163 (ref ST 933973)

WINTERBOURNE POOR LOT BARROWS

DORSET

Part of an extensive, 4,000-year-old Bronze Age cemetery.

OPENING TIMES

Any reasonable time

HOW TO FIND US

Direction: 2 miles W of Winterbourne Abbas, S of junction of A35 with a minor road to Compton Valence. Access via Wellbottom Lodge – 180 metres (200 yards) E along A35 from junction

Train: Dorchester West or South, both 7 miles

Bus: First 31 Weymouth – ⇌ Axminster (passes ⇌ Dorchester South)

No adjacent parking.
Warning; cross road with care.

MAP	Page 257 (5H)
	OS Map 194 (ref SY 590907)

WOODHENGE

WILTSHIRE

Neolithic monument, dating from about 2300BC, with concrete markers replacing timbers originally aligned in six concentric rings to the solstice sunrise.

Part of the Stonehenge World Heritage Site.

OPENING TIMES

Any reasonable time.

Usual facilities may not be available around the Summer Solstice June 20-22. Please check before you visit.

HOW TO FIND US

Direction: 1½ miles N of Amesbury, off A345, just S of Durrington

Train: Salisbury 9 miles

Bus: Wilts & Dorset 5/6 Salisbury – Swindon (passes close to ⇌ Salisbury and Swindon); 16 from Amesbury

MAP	Page 257 (4J)
	OS Map 184 (ref SU 151434)

YARN MARKET

SOMERSET

A 17th-century octagonal market hall.

Managed by the National Trust.

OPENING TIMES

Any reasonable time

HOW TO FIND US

Direction: In Dunster High St

Train: Dunster (West Somerset Railway) ½ mile

Bus: First 28, 928 ⇌ Taunton – Minehead, to within ¼ mile; 38/9 from Minehead

MAP	Page 257 (4F)
	OS Map 181 (ref SS 992438)

Cromwell's Castle, Tresco

THE HERITAGE OF SCILLY

ISLES OF SCILLY

The stunningly beautiful Isles of Scilly hold vast arrays of archaeological riches both above and below the sea. English Heritage recognises the importance of promoting this unique cultural landscape, and provides expert advice and significant funding to regeneration and conservation projects throughout the Isles.

This compact archipelago of about 100 islands lies around 28 miles to the south-west of Land's End. None of them is any bigger than three miles across and only five are inhabited. Despite their landmass of only 16 square kilometres (10 sq miles), these islands contain a remarkable number of historic sites.

These range from traditional farmhouses and dwellings to ritual burial monuments, cist grave cemeteries and Romano-Celtic shrines. Early settlements provide evidence of a distinctive Scillonian culture which thrived in the island group 2,000 years ago.

More recently, defensive monuments constructed during the Civil War and World War II stand as testament to the strategic importance of the islands. The Gulf Stream keeps the climate warm, enabling exotic plants and wildlife to thrive.

Bant's Carn Burial Chamber

OPENING TIMES

All EH properties on the Scillies are open at any reasonable time

HOW TO FIND US

Direction: See individual property entries on page 118 for access details

Tel: 0117 9750700 (Regional office)

www.english-heritage.org.uk/southwest

BANT'S CARN BURIAL CHAMBER AND HALANGY DOWN ANCIENT VILLAGE

ST MARY'S, ISLES OF SCILLY

In a wonderfully scenic location, on a hill above the site of the ancient Iron Age village, stands this Bronze Age burial mound with entrance passage and inner chamber.

OPENING TIMES

Any reasonable time

HOW TO FIND US

Direction: 1 mile N of Hugh Town

MAP   Page 256 (5B)
         OS Map 203 (ref SV 910123)

CROMWELL'S CASTLE

TRESCO, ISLES OF SCILLY

Standing tall on a rocky promontory guarding the lovely anchorage between Bryher and Tresco, this 17th-century round tower was built to command the haven of New Grimsby.

OPENING TIMES

Any reasonable time

HOW TO FIND US

Direction: On the shoreline, approach with care, ¾ mile NW of New Grimsby

MAP   Page 256 (4A)
         OS Map 203 (ref SV 882159)

GARRISON WALLS

ST MARY'S, ISLES OF SCILLY

You can enjoy a two-hour walk alongside the ramparts of these defensive walls and earthworks, dating from the 17th century.

OPENING TIMES

Any reasonable time

GARRISON WALLS

HOW TO FIND US

Direction: Around the headland W of Hugh Town

MAP   Page 256 (5A)
         OS Map 203 (ref SV 898104)

HARRY'S WALLS

ST MARY'S, ISLES OF SCILLY

A 16th-century fort built above St Mary's Pool harbour, but never finished.

OPENING TIMES

Any reasonable time

HOW TO FIND US

Direction: ¼ mile NE of Hugh Town

MAP   Page 256 (5B)
         OS Map 203 (ref SV 909109)

INNISIDGEN LOWER AND UPPER BURIAL CHAMBERS

ST MARY'S, ISLES OF SCILLY

Two Bronze Age cairns, about 30 metres (100 ft) apart, with stunning views towards St Martin's.

OPENING TIMES

Any reasonable time

HOW TO FIND US

Direction: 1¾ miles NE of Hugh Town

MAP   Page 256 (5B)
         OS Map 203 (ref SV 922127)

KING CHARLES'S CASTLE

TRESCO, ISLES OF SCILLY

At the end of a walk along the coast north of Tresco you will find the remains of this 16th-century castle, built for coastal defence.

KING CHARLES'S CASTLE

OPENING TIMES

Any reasonable time

HOW TO FIND US

Direction: Located ¾ mile NW of New Grimsby, coastal location approach with care

MAP   Page 256 (4A)
         OS Map 203 (ref SV 882161)

OLD BLOCKHOUSE

TRESCO, ISLES OF SCILLY

The remains of a small 16th-century gun tower, overlooking the white sandy bay at Old Grimsby.

OPENING TIMES

Any reasonable time

HOW TO FIND US

Direction: Located on Blockhouse Point, at the S end of Old Grimsby harbour

MAP   Page 256 (4A)
         OS Map 203 (ref SV 897155)

PORTH HELLICK DOWN BURIAL CHAMBER

ST MARY'S, ISLES OF SCILLY

Probably the best-preserved Bronze Age burial mound found on the Isles, featuring a passage and inner chamber.

OPENING TIMES

Any reasonable time

HOW TO FIND US

Direction: 1¾ miles E of Hugh Town

MAP   Page 256 (5B)
         OS Map 203 (ref SV 928108)

OTHER HISTORIC ATTRACTIONS

DISCOUNTED ENTRY TO OUR MEMBERS (DISCOUNTS MAY NOT APPLY ON EVENT DAYS)

THE ARTHURIAN CENTRE
CORNWALL – PL32 9TT

CROWNHILL FORT
DEVON – PL6 5BX

SHERBORNE CASTLE
DORSET – DT9 3PY

Walks past earthworks to ancient stones and battlefield site, with a nature trail and exhibition.

Victorian fortress built to defend the northern approaches to the Plymouth Naval Dockyard.

Accommodation is available at the fort. Please call for details.

Owned and managed by the Landmark Trust.

Late 16th-century castle originally built by Sir Walter Raleigh and set in 20 acres of glorious lakeside landscaped gardens.

ENTRY

20% discount for EH members

Discount does not extend to EH Corporate Partners

ENTRY

Half-price for EH members

Discount does not extend to accommodation

Discount does not extend to EH Corporate Partners

ENTRY

£2 entry to grounds for EH members, except on special event days.

Additional charge for interior.

Discount does not extend to EH Corporate Partners

OPENING TIMES

Easter-late Oct, daily   10am-5pm

OPENING TIMES

Apr-Oct, Sun-Fri   10am-5pm

OPENING TIMES

22 Mar-30 Oct, Sat-Sun & Tue-Thu & Bank Hols   11am-5pm

Last admission 4.30pm. Castle interior opens 2.30pm on Saturdays.

HOW TO FIND US

Directions: On B3314 at Slaughterbridge, Camelford

Tel: 01840 212450

HOW TO FIND US

Directions: N of Plymouth, off A386

Tel: 01752 793754

HOW TO FIND US

Directions: E of Sherborne, off A30

Tel: 01935 813182

MAP   Page 256 (5C)
       OS Map 200 (ref SX 109857)

MAP   Page 256 (6E)
       OS Map 201 (ref SX 487592)

MAP   Page 257 (4H)
       OS Map 183 (ref ST 649164)

Visit **www.english-heritage. org.uk** for up-to-date events information and the latest news.

Don't forget your membership card when you visit any of the properties listed in this handbook.

You can find out more about the work of English Heritage at **www.english-heritage.org.uk**

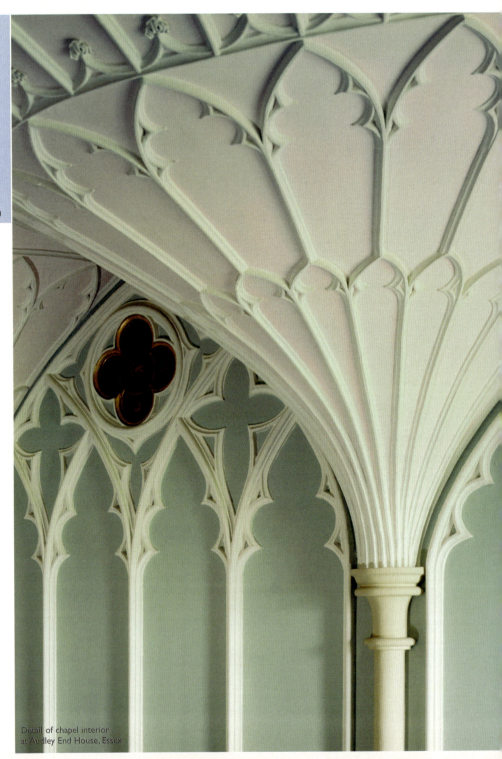

Detail of chapel interior
at Audley End House, Essex

EAST OF ENGLAND

East Anglia's long coastline has always been especially vulnerable to seaborne attack from Europe. Its beaches, backed only by dunes or low cliffs, are difficult to defend, providing a tempting landing ground for invaders. Much of this area's history is therefore enshrined in its coastal defences.

PROPERTIES

SEE INDIVIDUAL LISTINGS FOR DETAILS

BEDFORDSHIRE
Bushmead Priory, De Grey
Mausoleum, Houghton House,
Wrest Park

CAMBRIDGESHIRE
Denny Abbey and the
Farmland Museum, Duxford
Chapel, Isleham Priory Church,
Longthorpe Tower

ESSEX
Audley End House and
Gardens, Hadleigh Castle, Hill
Hall, Lexden Earthworks and
Bluebottle Grove, Mistley
Towers, Prior's Hall Barn, St
Botolph's Priory, St John's
Abbey Gate, Tilbury Fort,
Waltham Abbey Gatehouse
and Bridge

HERTFORDSHIRE
Berkhamsted Castle, Old
Gorhambury House, Roman
Wall of St Albans

NORFOLK
Baconsthorpe Castle, Berney
Arms Windmill, Binham Priory,
Binham Market Cross, Blakeney
Guildhall, Burgh Castle, Caister
Roman Site, Castle Acre: Bailey
Gate, Castle Acre Castle and
Castle Acre Priory, Castle
Rising Castle, Church of the
Holy Sepulchre, Cow Tower in
Norwich, Creake Abbey, Great
Yarmouth Row Houses &
Greyfriars' Cloisters, Grime's
Graves, North Elmham Chapel,
St Olave's Priory, Thetford
Priory, Thetford Warren Lodge,
Weeting Castle

SUFFOLK
Bury St Edmunds Abbey,
Framlingham Castle,
Landguard Fort, Leiston Abbey,
Lindsey/St James's Chapel,
Moulton Packhorse Bridge,
Orford Castle, Saxtead Green
Post Mill

Comprehensive
map of our sites
PAGE 260-261

Orford Castle

COASTAL DEFENCES SINCE HENRY VIII

The proximity of East Anglia to mainland Europe and the exposed nature of its beaches make this part of England easy to invade. As a result, a variety of strategically placed coastal defences have been built across the region.

Henry VIII commissioned a coastal defence system during the late 1530s, when invasion by France and other Roman Catholic powers seemed inevitable. Royal Commissioners identified King's Lynn, Weybourne, Lowestoft, Aldeburgh, Orford, the Orwell (Landguard and Harwich) and Tilbury as most in need of fortifications. These locations continued to influence the placement and construction of coastal defences for the next 400 years.

Today there are abundant remains of the defences which guarded our shores, from large forts to tiny pillboxes – they are fascinating monuments of our heritage and witnesses to the evolving demands of our national security. Key examples of coastal properties in the care of English Heritage include Burgh Castle, Framlingham and Orford Castles in Suffolk, Hadleigh Castle in Essex and Landguard and Tilbury Forts.

As well as caring for this priceless legacy, English Heritage also works with a number of partners in the area to enable the past and present to work together. By finding new uses for old buildings

and bringing past glories back to life, we can ensure that our invaluable heritage remains a positive asset.

Over the past year we have worked on a number of projects including the preservation of Greyfriars' Tower – a 400-year old lighthouse in King's Lynn which featured in the 2003 series of BBC's 'Restoration'.

We have also created a map-based database of the historic environment of the Thames Gateway. This identifies the hidden historic strengths of the area, as well as recognising broad environmental categories such as archaeology, patterns of human expansion and land management.

AUDLEY END HOUSE & GARDENS
ESSEX – CB11 4JF

Sir Thomas Audley was given the lands of Walden Abbey by Henry VIII, and adapted the abbey buildings as his mansion. His grandson Thomas, first Earl of Suffolk, rebuilt this mansion between 1610 and 1614. The new Audley End was truly palatial in scale, but Suffolk fell from power after 1618, and the family's resources dwindled.

The walled garden

The Great Hall

Charles II bought the house in 1668, and used it as a base when he attended the races at Newmarket. By the 1680s, Sir Christopher Wren was warning of the need for major repairs. The cost of these caused William III to cancel the mortgage and return Audley End to the Suffolk family.

The house declined in the 18th century and, when the Suffolk line died out in 1745, it was bought by the Countess of Portsmouth for her nephew and heir, Sir John Griffin Griffin. Following his inheritance, Griffin Griffin – also the fourth Baron Howard de Walden and first Baron Braybrooke – made changes to the house. By the time of his death in 1797, he had added a suite of neo-Classical rooms designed by Robert Adam and a Gothic chapel. Meanwhile, 'Capability' Brown had been employed to remodel the grounds.

Today, the house's interior is largely the result of ownership by the third Baron Braybrooke, who inherited it in 1825. He installed his extensive picture collection and filled the rooms with furnishings.

The fourth Baron Braybrooke's natural history collection also remains an appealing feature of the house. Audley End was requisitioned during World War II, after which the ninth

Lord Braybrooke resumed possession. In 1948, he sold it to English Heritage's predecessor, the Ministry of Works.

The Gardens

Much has been done recently to restore the park and the fine Victorian gardens – including the parterre – to their former glory. An artificial lake was created with water from the River Cam, and runs through delightful 18th-century parkland. The Classical Temple of Concorde, built in 1790 in honour of George III, and restored 19th-century formal parterre garden dominate the views from the back of the house.

Visitors can see Robert Adam's Tea House Bridge and ornamental garden buildings, and the Elysian Garden cascade. The thriving organic walled Victorian Kitchen Garden – with its box-edged paths, trained fruit and 52m (170ft) long vine house, still as it was in its Victorian heyday – is a memorable part of any visit.

Also worth visiting is the historic kitchen and dry laundry.

Audley End plays host to open-air concerts and craft and gardening shows during the summer months.

Please note

At certain times of the year access to the house is by guided tours only. Some rooms will not be open throughout the season. Please call to check.

In some rooms light levels are reduced to preserve vulnerable textiles and other collections.

www.english-heritage.org.uk/audleyend

⊤ Available for corporate and private hire.

NON-MEMBERS HOUSE & GARDENS	
Adult	£8.95
Concession	£6.70
Child	£4.50
Family	£22.40

NON-MEMBERS GARDENS ONLY	
Adult	£4.60
Concession	£3.50
Child	£2.30
Family	£11.50

OPENING TIMES

House:		
3-21 Mar, Thu-Mon (tours only)	10am-4pm
23 Mar-3 Oct, Wed-Mon (tours available)	12pm-5pm
6-31 Oct, Thu-Mon (tours only)	10am-4pm
Gardens:	
3-21 Mar, Thu-Mon	10am-5pm
23 Mar-3 Oct, Wed-Mon	10am-6pm
6-31 Oct, Thu-Mon	10am-5pm

HOW TO FIND US

Direction: 1 mile W of Saffron Walden on B1383 (M11 exits 8 and 10)

Train: Audley End 1¼ miles. Please note: Footpath runs alongside a busy main road.

Bus: Hedingham/Viceroy 59, Stansted Transit 301 from ⌷ Audley End

Call for special events information Tel: 01799 522399 (information line)

Local Tourist Information Saffron Walden: 01799 510444 Cambridge: 01223 464732

Disabled access (ground floor and gardens only).

Family learning resources available.

Information sheets in French, Dutch, German and Japanese.

No photography or stiletto heels allowed in house.

Plants and organic vegetables on sale.

MAP	Page 261 (5F) OS Map 154 (ref TL 525382)

BACONSTHORPE CASTLE
NORFOLK

The remains of a 15th-century castle, built by Sir John Heydon during the Wars of the Roses. The exact date when building first began is not known, since Sir John did not apply for the statutory royal licence necessary to construct a fortified house. In the 1560s, Sir John's grandson added the outer gatehouse, which was inhabited until the 1920s, when one of the turrets fell down. The ruins, of red brick and knapped flint, are reflected in the lake, enlarged from the original castle moat.

OPENING TIMES

Any reasonable time

HOW TO FIND US

Direction: 3/4 mile N of village of Baconsthorpe off unclassified road, 3 miles E of Holt

Train: Sheringham 4½ miles

MAP   Page 261 (1H)
       OS Map 133 (ref TG 121382)

Looking for a unique present?

Why not browse our online shop at **www.english-heritage. org.uk/shopping**

BERKHAMSTED CASTLE
HERTFORDSHIRE

The remains of a large 11th-century motte-and-bailey castle, with notable earthworks.

OPENING TIMES

All year, daily, Summer 10am 6pm
                  Winter 10am-4pm
Closed   25 Dec and 1 Jan

HOW TO FIND US

Direction: By 🚆 Berkhamsted

Bus: From surrounding areas

Train: Berkhamsted, adjacent

MAP   Page 260 (6D)
       OS Map 165 (ref SP 995082)

BERNEY ARMS WINDMILL
NORFOLK

One of Norfolk's best and largest extant marsh mills, built to grind a constituent of cement and in use until 1951, finally pumping water to drain surrounding marshland.

NON-MEMBERS

Adult	£2.30
Concession	£1.70
Child	£1.20

OPENING TIMES

24 Mar-30 Sep, pre-booked groups only

BERNEY ARMS WINDMILL

HOW TO FIND US

Direction: 3½ miles NE of Reedham on the N bank of River Yare. Accessible by hired boat, or by footpath from Halvergate (3½ miles). ¼ mile walk from train

Train: Berney Arms ¼ mile

Tel: 01493 857900

MAP   Page 261 (3K)
       OS Map 134 (ref TG 465049)

BINHAM PRIORY
NORFOLK

The extensive remains of a Benedictine priory. The original nave of the priory is still in use as the parish church.

Featured in Simon Schama's television series, 'A History of Britain'.

Managed by Binham Parochial Church Council.

OPENING TIMES

Any reasonable time

HOW TO FIND US

Direction: ¼ mile NW of village of Binham-on-Wells on road off B1388

Bus: Sanders 45/6 Norwich-Fakenham

Tel: 01328 830362

MAP   Page 261 (1H)
       OS Map 132 (ref TF 982399)

BINHAM MARKET CROSS

NORFOLK

Medieval cross on the site of an annual fair held from Henry I's reign until the 1950s.

Managed by Binham Parochial Church Council.

OPENING TIMES

Any reasonable time

HOW TO FIND US

Direction: Located on the Binham village green adjacent to the Priory

Bus: Sanders 45/6 Norwich-Fakenham

MAP	Page 261 (1H)
	OS Map 132 (ref TF 984396)

BLAKENEY GUILDHALL

NORFOLK

The vaulted basement of a 14th-century merchant's house.

Managed by Blakeney Parish Council.

OPENING TIMES

Any reasonable time

HOW TO FIND US

Direction: In Blakeney off A149

Train: Sheringham 9 miles

Bus: Norfolk Green 36 Sheringham – Hunstanton

Tel: 0845 300 6116

MAP	Page 261 (1H)
	OS Map 133 (ref TG 028441)

BURGH CASTLE

NORFOLK

Walls of a Roman 'Saxon Shore' fort, built in the late 3rd century.

Managed by Norfolk Archaeological Trust.

OPENING TIMES

Any reasonable time

HOW TO FIND US

Direction: At far W end of Breydon Water on unclassified road, 3 miles W of Great Yarmouth

Train: Great Yarmouth 5 miles

Bus: First 6/7 from Great Yarmouth

MAP	Page 261 (3K)
	OS Map 134 (ref TG 475047)

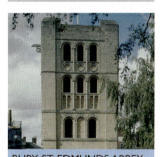

BURY ST EDMUNDS ABBEY

SUFFOLK

The Norman Tower and 14th-century Abbey Gate, with the extensive ruins of the Benedictine abbey church and precinct.

Managed by St Edmundsbury Borough Council.

OPENING TIMES

Any reasonable time

HOW TO FIND US

Direction: E end of town centre

Train: Bury St Edmunds 1 mile

Bus: From surrounding areas

Tel: 01284 764667

MAP	Page 261 (4G)
	OS Map 155 (ref TL 857642)

BUSHMEAD PRIORY

BEDFORDSHIRE – MK44 2LD

The medieval refectory of this Augustinian priory contains the original timber roof, wall paintings and stained glass.

NON-MEMBERS

Adult	£2.00
Concession	£1.50
Child	£1.00

OPENING TIMES

1 Jul-31 Aug. Pre-booked group access at weekends only

HOW TO FIND US

Direction: Located off B660, 2 miles S of Bolnhurst

Train: St Neots 6 miles

Tel: 01525 860152

MAP	Page 260 (4E)
	OS Map 153 (ref TL 115607)

CAISTER ROMAN SITE

NORFOLK

The remains of this Roman fort include a defensive wall, a gateway and buildings along a main street.

Managed by Great Yarmouth Borough Council.

OPENING TIMES

Any reasonable time

HOW TO FIND US

Direction: Near Caister-on-Sea, 3 miles N of Great Yarmouth

Train: Great Yarmouth 3 miles

Bus: First Bus 6-8, 602-4 from Great Yarmouth

MAP	Page 261 (2K)
	OS Map 134 (ref TG 517123)

CASTLE ACRE BAILEY GATE

NORFOLK

The north gate of this medieval fortified town, also protected by a bank and ditch.

OPENING TIMES

Any reasonable time

HOW TO FIND US

Direction: Located in Castle Acre, 5 miles N of Swaffham

MAP   Page 261 (2G)
       OS Map 132 (ref TF 817151)

CASTLE ACRE CASTLE

NORFOLK

The remains of a Norman manor house, which was later fortified to become a castle, with extensive earthworks. The castle formed part of William de Warenne's Norfolk estates.

OPENING TIMES

Any reasonable time

HOW TO FIND US

Direction: Located at the E end of Castle Acre, 5 miles N of Swaffham

MAP   Page 261 (2G)
       OS Map 132 (ref TF 819152)

CASTLE ACRE PRIORY

NORFOLK   SEE OPPOSITE PAGE

CASTLE RISING CASTLE

NORFOLK – PE31 6AH

A fine 12th-century keep, set amid huge defensive earthworks and once the palace and home of Isabella, the 'She Wolf' of France, dowager Queen of England. The keep walls stand to their original height.

Owned and managed by Mr Greville Howard.

NON-MEMBERS

Adult	£3.85
Concession	£3.10
Child	£2.20
Family ticket	£11.50

OPENING TIMES

19 Mar-1 Nov, daily	10am-6pm
2 Nov-31 Mar, Wed-Sun	10am-4pm
Closed	24-26 Dec

HOW TO FIND US

Direction: Located 4 miles NE of King's Lynn off A149

Train: King's Lynn 4½ miles

Bus: First 410/1 King's Lynn-Hunstanton

Tel: 01553 631330

Audio tours (charged).
Disabled access (exterior, only toilets).
Dogs on leads (restricted areas).

MAP   Page 261 (2G)
       OS Map 132 (ref TF 666246)

CHURCH OF THE HOLY SEPULCHRE, THETFORD

NORFOLK

The ruined nave of a priory church of the Canons of the Holy Sepulchre, the only surviving remains in England of a house of this order.

OPENING TIMES

Any reasonable time

HOW TO FIND US

Direction: Located on the W side of Thetford off B1107

Bus: From surrounding areas

Train: Thetford ¾ mile

MAP   Page 261 (3H)
       OS Map 144 (ref TL 865831)

COW TOWER, NORWICH

NORFOLK

A circular, detached brick tower standing on the riverside, which formed part of the city of Norwich's 14th-century defences.

Managed by Norwich City Council.

OPENING TIMES

Any reasonable time

HOW TO FIND US

Direction: In Norwich, near cathedral

Bus: From surrounding areas

Train: Norwich ½ mile

Tel: 01603 213434

MAP   Page 261 (2J)
       OS Map 134 (ref TG 240092)

CASTLE ACRE PRIORY

NORFOLK – PE31 6AH

The delightful village of Castle Acre boasts an extraordinary wealth of history, and is one of the best examples of Norman estate planning. Situated on the Peddars Way, Castle Acre was originally built as a fortified town, protected by its own banks, gateways and ditch.

While the town provided for the material needs of the occupants of the castle, the Cluniac priory was built to cater for their spiritual requirements. Castle Acre Priory was inspired by the monastery at Cluny in France and was home to a community of monks until 1537, when Henry VIII disbanded all monastic houses. The village stands on the Pilgrim routes to Thetford, Bromholm Priory and Walsingham.

The priory's ruins span seven centuries and include a beautiful 12th-century church with an elaborately decorated west front, still rising to its full height, a 15th-century gatehouse and a porch and prior's lodging still fit to live in.

The recreated herb garden situated next to the visitor centre grows herbs that the monks would have used for medicinal, culinary and decorative purposes.

At the other end of the village stand the ruins of the castle with its impressive earthworks. The Bailey Gate in the village centre is also worth a look (see opposite page).

www.english-heritage.org.uk/castleacre

NON-MEMBERS

Adult	£4.30
Concession	£3.20
Children	£2.20
Family ticket	£10.80

OPENING TIMES

24 Mar-30 Sep, daily	10am-6pm
1 Oct-31 Mar, Wed-Sun	10am-4pm
Closed	24-26 Dec and 1 Jan

HOW TO FIND US

Direction: ¼ mile W of village of Castle Acre, 5 miles N of Swaffham

Tel: 01760 755394

Disabled access (ground floor and grounds only).

Family learning resources available.

MAP	Page 261 (2G)
	OS Map 132 (ref TF 814148)

www.english-heritage.org.uk/eastofengland

CREAKE ABBEY
NORFOLK

The ruins of the church of an Augustinian abbey, later converted to an almshouse

OPENING TIMES

Any reasonable time

HOW TO FIND US

Direction: N of North Creake off B1355

MAP	Page 261 (1H)
	OS Map 132 (ref TF 856395)

DE GREY MAUSOLEUM, FLITTON
BEDFORDSHIRE

A remarkable treasure house of sculpted tombs and monuments from the 16th to 19th centuries, commemorating the de Grey family of Wrest Park.

OPENING TIMES

Weekends only. Contact the keykeeper in advance: Mrs Stimson, 3 Highfield Road, Flitton (01525 860094)

DE GREY MAUSOLEUM, FLITTON

HOW TO FIND US

Direction: Through Flitton, attached to the church, on an unclassified road 1½ miles W of A6 at Silsoe

Train: Flitwick 2 miles

MAP	Page 260 (5E)
	OS Map 153 (ref TL 059359)

DENNY ABBEY AND THE FARMLAND MUSEUM
CAMBRIDGESHIRE – CB5 9PQ

Founded in 1159 by Benedictine monks, with a unique history of successive occupation by Benedictines, Knights Templars and finally Franciscan nuns. Their patron, the Countess of Pembroke, converted most of the church into her house: after the Dissolution this survived as a farmhouse, with the refectory as its barn.

Managed by the Farmland Museum Trust.

ENTRY MUSEUM AND ABBEY NON-MEMBERS

Adult	£3.80
Concession	£3.00
Child	£1.60
Family ticket	£9.60

DENNY ABBEY AND THE FARMLAND MUSEUM

OPENING TIMES

24 Mar-31 Oct, daily   12pm-5pm

HOW TO FIND US

Direction: Located 6 miles N of Cambridge on A10

Train: Waterbeach 3 miles

Bus: Stagecoach in Cambridge 19 Cambridge-Ely

Tel: 01223 860489/860988

Disabled access (museum and abbey ground floor only).

Dogs on leads (restricted areas only).

Tearooms/restaurant (weekends only).

MAP	Page 261 (4F)
	OS Map 154 (ref TL 492685)

DUXFORD CHAPEL
CAMBRIDGESHIRE

This medieval chapel was once part of a hospital.

Managed by South Cambridgeshire District Council.

OPENING TIMES

Any reasonable time

HOW TO FIND US

Direction: Adjacent to Whittlesford station off A505

Train: Whittlesford, adjacent

MAP	Page 261 (4F)
	OS Map 154 (ref TL 485473)

FRAMLINGHAM CASTLE
SUFFOLK   GO TO PAGE 132

GREAT YARMOUTH ROW HOUSES & GREYFRIARS' CLOISTERS

NORFOLK - NR30 2RQ

Great Yarmouth's Row 111 and The Old Merchant's House are fine examples of traditional Row Houses, which were developed in the 17th century and are unique to the town. Features of both houses are the Dutch-style exteriors with patterned brick and flint walling, and square clay tiles on the floors and within passageways. Inside the houses, you can see a range of historical fittings, including wall anchors, door-knockers, hinges and brackets. To reflect the changing history of the rows, both houses include models of some of the tenants who inhabited them in the 1870s and 1930s.

Greyfriars' Cloisters are the remains of a 13th-century friary of Franciscan 'grey friars', with wall paintings dating from c.1300. Greyfriars' Cloisters unusually survived the dissolution of the friary in 1538; after 400 years of re-use, they were finally rediscovered after the bombing during World War II.

New for 2005
The new Middlegate garden now links Old Merchant's House, Row 111 and the Nelson Museum, and features a herb garden and a central sculpture reflecting the history of Great Yarmouth.

GREAT YARMOUTH ROW HOUSES

Insect, bird and bat boxes have been included to encourage wildlife. The garden site was previously an urban wasteland and the project was led by English Heritage and Great Yarmouth Borough Council.

NON-MEMBERS

Adult	£3.30
Concession	£2.50
Child	£1.70

OPENING TIMES

24 Mar-30 Sept, daily 12pm-5pm
Free guided tour of Greyfriars' Cloisters every Friday at 10.30am. Please call site for details.

HOW TO FIND US

Direction: Great Yarmouth, follow signs for Historic Quay

Train: Great Yarmouth ½ mile

Bus: From surrounding areas

Tel: 01493 857900

Family learning resources available.

MAP	Page 261 (2K) OS Map 134 (Houses ref TG 525072, Cloisters ref TG 524073)

GRIME'S GRAVES

NORFOLK – IP26 5DE

GRIME'S GRAVES

Grime's Graves is the only Neolithic flint mine open to visitors in Britain. First named Grim's Graves by the Anglo-Saxons, after the pagan god Grim, it was not until some of them were excavated in 1870 that they were found to be flint mines dug over 5,000 years ago.

The mines provided the flint to make tools. Today, visitors can descend 10 metres (30 feet) by ladder into one excavated shaft. This is also a site of Special Scientific Interest, as it is home to a wide variety of flora and fauna.

NON-MEMBERS

Adult	£2.60
Concession	£2.00
Child	£1.30
Family	£6.50

No entry to the mines for children under 5 years of age

OPENING TIMES

3-31 March, Thu-Mon 10am-5pm
1 Apr-30 Sep, daily 10am-6pm
6-31 Oct, Thu-Mon 10am-5pm

HOW TO FIND US

Direction: Located 7 miles NW of Thetford off A134

Train: Brandon 3½ miles

Bus: First 130 Bury St Edmunds – Mildenhall, alight Santon Downham; then 2 miles

Tel: 01842 810656

Disabled access (exhibition area only; access track rough).
Dogs on leads (restricted areas).
Family learning resources available.

MAP	Page 261 (3G) OS Map 144 (ref TL 817899)

FRAMLINGHAM CASTLE

SUFFOLK – IP8 9BT

Framlingham is a magnificent example of a late 12th-century castle. Built by Roger Bigod, Earl of Norfolk, the castle, together with Framlingham Mere, was designed both as a stronghold and as a symbol of power and status – as befitted one of the most influential people in the court of Henry II. Architecturally, the castle is notable for its curtain wall and mural towers, an early example of this design.

The castle fulfilled a number of roles. It was at the centre of the struggle between the Bigod barons and the Crown, and Mary Tudor mustered her supporters here in 1553, before being crowned Queen. At the end of the 16th century it was a prison; later still a poorhouse and school were built in the grounds. Today, the imposing stone walls and crenellated towers with their ornate Tudor chimneys dominate, while the grassy earthworks around the castle are subdued reminders of busier times. To the west, the Mere provides a stunning setting.

While visiting, why not take a walk around the magnificent Framlingham Mere and the castle's outer courts and moats? Or perhaps negotiate the impressive wall-walk and take in the beautiful views of the surrounding countryside, or enjoy one of Framlingham's many pubs or tearooms.

Please note
Entry also includes access to the Lanman Trust's Museum of local history.

www.english-heritage.org.uk/framlinghamcastle

Gate Tower

NON-MEMBERS,

Adult	£4.30
Concession	£3.20
Child	£2.20
Family ticket	£10.80

OPENING TIMES

24 Mar-30 Sep, daily	10am-6pm
1-31 Oct, daily	10am-5pm
1 Nov-31 Mar, daily	10am-4pm
Closed	24-26 Dec and 1 Jan

HOW TO FIND US

Direction: In Framlingham on B1116

Train: Wickham Market 6½ miles; Saxmundham 7 miles

Bus: First/Goldline 64A, 82A from Ipswich (passes ≥ Ipswich on Mon-Sat, ≥ Saxmundham Sundays, ≥ Woodbridge all days)

Tel: 01728 724189

Local Tourist Information Woodbridge: 01394 382240

Disabled access (grounds and ground floor only).

Family learning resources available.

MAP	Page 261 (4J)
	OS Map 156 (ref TM 287637)

HADLEIGH CASTLE
ESSEX

The impressive remains of a mighty fortress constructed over seven centuries ago, overlooking the Essex marshes. The barbican and two towers remain standing today.

New for 2005
Conservation work to stabilise the ruins and ground around the castle took place in 2004. So far, archaeologists have discovered that medieval workmen may also have experienced the same slippage problems. They have also uncovered evidence of activity during Roman times at the site.

OPENING TIMES
Any reasonable time

HOW TO FIND US
Direction: ¾ mile S of A13 at Hadleigh

Train: Leigh-on-Sea 1½ miles by footpath

Bus: First and Arriva Southend services from surrounding areas to within ½ mile

Tel: 01760 755161

Disabled access (hilly).

MAP   Page 261 (7G)
       OS Map 154 (ref TL 485473)

HILL HALL
ESSEX – CM6 7QQ

This fine Elizabethan mansion features some of the earliest external Renaissance architectural detail in the country, plus rare period wall paintings of mythical and biblical subjects. Hill Hall has now been divided into private houses, but parts remain open to the public by prior arrangement.

NON-MEMBERS
Adult	£3.00
Concession	£2.50
Child	£1.50

OPENING TIMES
Open 24 Mar-30 Sep. Accessible by pre-booked group tours on a Wednesday only. To book, please call 01223 582700

HOW TO FIND US
Direction: 3 miles SE of Epping. Entrance ½ mile N of Theydon Mount

Underground: Epping 2½ miles

MAP   Page 261 (6F)
       OS Map 167 (ref TQ 489995)

HOUGHTON HOUSE
BEDFORDSHIRE

This early 17th-century mansion was reputedly the inspiration for the House Beautiful in John Bunyan's *Pilgrim's Progress*. Today, its remains still contain elements that justify the description, including work attributed to Inigo Jones.

OPENING TIMES
Any reasonable time

HOW TO FIND US
Direction: 1 mile NE of Ampthill off A421, 8 miles S of Bedford

Train: Flitwick or Stewartby, both 3 miles

Bus: Stagecoach in Northants 142/3, Arriva 223 Bedford – Flitwick

MAP   Page 260 (5E)
       OS Map 153 (ref TL 039395)

ISLEHAM PRIORY CHURCH

CAMBRIDGESHIRE

134

An early Norman church, Isleham Priory has survived in a surprisingly unaltered state, despite being converted into a barn for use by a local farmer.

OPENING TIMES

Any reasonable time. Contact the key-keeper, Mrs R Burton, 18 Festival Road, Isleham – 5 mins walk

HOW TO FIND US

Direction: Located in centre of Isleham, 16 miles NE of Cambridge on B1104

Train: Newmarket 8½ miles, Ely 9 miles

MAP	Page 261 (4G)
	OS Map 143 (ref TL 642743)

LANDGUARD FORT

SUFFOLK – IP11 3TX

Originally built during the 16th century, the remains of the extant fort date back to the 18th century and feature alterations made during the past 100 years. Landguard overlooks the Orwell Estuary.

LANDGUARD FORT

Please call David Tolliday (01394 277767) or David Wood (01473 218245) for details and charges for special events and guided tours

The nearby Felixstowe Museum in the old submarine mining building contains collections relevant to the site and local area (see page 142 for full details).

Managed by Landguard Fort Trust.

NON-MEMBERS

Adult	£3.00
Concession	£2.50
Child	£1.00

Free entry for children under 5 and wheelchair users.

OPENING TIMES

27 Mar-30 Apr, daily	10am-5pm
1 May-30 Sep, daily	10am-6pm
1-31 Oct, daily	10am-5pm

Last admission 1 hour before closing

HOW TO FIND US

Direction: Located 1 mile S of Felixstowe town centre – follow brown-and-white tourist signs to Landguard Point and Nature Reserve from A14

Train: Felixstowe 2½ miles

Bus: First 75-7 Ipswich-Felixstowe Dock to within ¾ miles of site

MAP	Page 261 (5J)
	OS Map 169 (ref TM 284319)

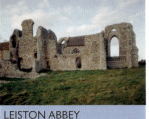

LEISTON ABBEY

SUFFOLK

LEISTON ABBEY

The remains of an abbey of the Premonstratensian order of 'white canons', with a 16th-century brick gatehouse.

Managed by Pro Corda College.

OPENING TIMES

Any reasonable time

HOW TO FIND US

Direction: N of Leiston off B1069

Bus: First/Goldline 64, 81A, 82A Ipswich-Aldeburgh (pass close Saxmundham)

Train: Saxmundham 5 miles

MAP	Page 261 (4K)
	OS Map 156 (ref TM 445642)

LEXDEN EARTHWORKS AND BLUEBOTTLE GROVE

ESSEX

This section of earthworks is part of a series which were designed to protect Iron Age Colchester and were later added to by the conquering Romans. At their peak, the earthworks at Lexden encompassed about 12 square miles.

Managed by Colchester Borough Council.

LEXDEN EARTHWORKS AND BLUEBOTTLE GROVE

OPENING TIMES
Any reasonable time

HOW TO FIND US
Direction: 2 miles W of Colchester off A604. Lexden Earthworks are on Lexden Straight Rd. To visit Bluebottle Grove from Lexden, turn left into Heath Rd, left into Church Lane, right into Beech Hill and follow the brown-and-white tourist signs to the site

Train: Colchester or Colchester Town, both 2½ miles

Bus: Network Colchester 5 from Colchester

Tel: 01206 282931

MAP   Page 261 (5H)
       OS Map 168 (Lexden Earthworks
       ref TL 965246, Bluebottle Grove
       ref TL 975245)

LINDSEY/ST JAMES'S CHAPEL

SUFFOLK

A beautiful thatched 13th-century chapel with lancet windows.

OPENING TIMES
All year: daily   10am-4pm

HOW TO FIND US
Direction: Located on an unclassified road ½ mile E of Rose Green and 8 miles E of Sudbury

Train: Sudbury 8 miles

Disabled access (single step).

MAP   Page 261 (5H)
       OS Map 156 (ref TM 445642)

LONGTHORPE TOWER
CAMBRIDGESHIRE – PE1 1HA

The tower displays the finest 14th-century domestic wall paintings in northern Europe of secular and spiritual subjects, including The Wheel of Life, The Nativity and King David.

NON-MEMBERS
Adult	£2.30
Concession	£1.70
Child	£1.20

OPENING TIMES
1 Jul-31 Aug, Sat	12pm-5pm
All other days, pre-booked tours only	

HOW TO FIND US
Direction: Located 2 miles W of Peterborough on A47

Train: Peterborough 1½ miles

Bus: Stagecoach in Peterborough Citi 2, Kime 9 from city centre (passing Peterborough)

Tel: 01223 582700

Parking (not at site).

MAP   Page 260 (3E)
       OS Map 142 (ref TL 162984)

MISTLEY TOWERS
ESSEX

The remains of a church designed by Robert Adam and built in 1776. It is unusual in having towers at both the east and west ends.

Managed by Mistley Thorn Residents' Association.

OPENING TIMES
Key available from Mistley Quay Workshops: 01206 393884

HOW TO FIND US
Direction: Located on B1352, 1½ miles E of A137 at Lawford, 9 miles E of Colchester

Train: Mistley ¼ mile

Bus: First 103/4 Colchester-Harwich

Disabled access (exterior only).
Dogs on leads (restricted areas).

MAP   Page 261 (5H)
       OS Map 169 (ref TM 116320)

MOULTON PACKHORSE BRIDGE

SUFFOLK

Four-arched bridge built during the 15th century and spanning the River Kennett.

OPENING TIMES

Any reasonable time

HOW TO FIND US

Direction: In Moulton off B1085, 4 miles E of Newmarket

Train: Kennett 2 miles

MAP	Page 261 (4G)
	OS Map 154 (ref TL 698645)

NORTH ELMHAM CHAPEL

NORFOLK

NORTH ELMHAM CHAPEL

This ruin of an 11th-century chapel, possibly built on the site of the cathedral of the Anglo-Saxon bishops of East Anglia, was converted into a fortified manor house and enclosed by earthworks in the 14th century by Hugh le Despencer, Bishop of Norwich.

Managed by North Elmham Parish Council.

OPENING TIMES

Any reasonable time

HOW TO FIND US

Direction: Located 6 miles N of East Dereham on B1110

MAP	Page 261 (2H)
	OS Map 132 (ref TF 988216)

OLD GORHAMBURY HOUSE

HERTFORDSHIRE

The decorated remains of an impressive Elizabethan mansion, demonstrating the extent to which the Renaissance influenced architecture in England.

OPENING TIMES

All year (except 1 Jun), any reasonable time

HOW TO FIND US

Direction: On foot by permissive 2-mile path: any reasonable time. By car (1 May-30 Sep, Thurs pm only), drive to Gorhambury Mansion and walk across the gardens

Train: St Albans Abbey 3 miles, St Albans 3½ miles

Bus: Arriva 300/1, 340 St Albans-Hemel Hempstead to start of drive

MAP	Page 260 (6E)
	OS Map 166 (ref TL 110076)

ORFORD CASTLE

SUFFOLK – IP12 2ND

This unique polygonal keep survives almost intact. It was built between 1165 and 1173 by Henry II to help control the barons of Norfolk and Suffolk. The castle was built to a highly innovative design, and the progress of its construction is detailed in royal documents. Recent archaeological work has provided a clearer understanding of how the castle worked, and a new painting by Frank Gardiner shows how the keep, together with the lost outer defences, would have looked.

New for 2005
New reconstruction painting and guidebook.

NON-MEMBERS

Adult	£4.30
Concession	£3.20
Child	£2.20
Family ticket	£10.80

OPENING TIMES

24 Mar-30 Sep, daily	10am-6pm
1 Oct-31 Mar, Thu-Mon	10am-4pm
Closed	24-26 Dec and 1 Jan

HOW TO FIND US

Direction: In Orford on B1084, 20 miles NE of Ipswich

Train: Wickham Market 8 miles

ORFORD CASTLE

Bus: Country Travel 160, 182 Woodbridge-Orford (passes 🚆 Melton)

Tel: 01394 450472

🅿️ 🏛️ 📷 🎧 🎭 ⚠️

Family learning resources available.

MAP Page 261 (4J)
     OS Map 166 (ref TL 110076)

PRIOR'S HALL BARN, WIDDINGTON

ESSEX

One of the finest surviving medieval barns in south east England, and representative of the aisled barns found in north west Essex.

OPENING TIMES

1 Apr-30 Sep, Sat-Sun   10am-6pm

HOW TO FIND US

Direction: In Widdington, on unclassified road 2 miles SE of Newport, off B1383

Train: Newport 2 miles

Bus: Stansted Transit 301 Bishops Stortford-Saffron Walden (passing 🚆 Audley End)

✕ ♿

MAP Page 261 (5F)
     OS Map 167 (ref TL 537318)

ROMAN WALL, ST ALBANS

HERTFORDSHIRE

Several hundred yards of the wall built c.AD 200 to defend the Roman city of Verulamium. The remains of towers and foundations of a gateway can still be seen.

OPENING TIMES

Any reasonable time

HOW TO FIND US

Direction: Located on the S side of St Albans, ½ mile from the centre, off the A4147

Train: St Albans Abbey ½ mile, St Albans 1¼ miles

Bus: From surrounding areas

MAP Page 260 (6E)
     OS Map 166 (ref TL 137066)

SAXTEAD GREEN POST MILL

SUFFOLK – IP13 9QQ

This corn mill, the whole body of which revolves on its base, was one of many that were built in Suffolk from the late 13th century. It is still in working order, even though milling ceased in 1947. Climb the wooden stairs to the various floors, which are full of fascinating mill machinery.

SAXTEAD GREEN POST MILL

NON-MEMBERS

Adult	£2.60
Concession	£2.00
Child	£1.30

OPENING TIMES

25 Mar-30 Sep, Fri-Sat   12pm-5pm

HOW TO FIND US

Direction: 2½ miles NW of Framlingham on A1120

Train: Wickham Market 9 miles

Bus: Country Travel 160, 182 Woodbridge – Orford (passes close to 🚆 Woodbridge)

Tel: 01728 685789

📷 🎧 📷 ✕ ⚠️

MAP Page 261 (4J)
     OS Map 156 (ref TM 253644)

ST BOTOLPH'S PRIORY

ESSEX

The nave of the first Augustinian priory in England, with impressive arcading across its west end.

Managed by Colchester Borough Council.

OPENING TIMES

Any reasonable time

HOW TO FIND US

Direction: Nr Colchester Town station.

Train: Colchester Town, adjacent

Bus: From surrounding areas

Tel: 01206 282931

MAP Page 261 (5H)
     OS Map 168 (ref TL 999249)

ST JOHN'S ABBEY GATE
ESSEX

THETFORD PRIORY
NORFOLK

THETFORD WARREN LODGE
NORFOLK

This fine abbey gatehouse, in East Anglian flushwork, is all that now survives of the Benedictine abbey of St John.

Managed by Colchester Borough Council.

OPENING TIMES

Any reasonable time

HOW TO FIND US

Direction: S side of central Colchester

Train: Colchester Town ¼ mile

Bus: From surrounding areas

Tel: 01206 282931

MAP   Page 261 (5H)
      OS Map 168 (ref TL 998248)

ST OLAVE'S PRIORY
NORFOLK

Remains of an Augustinian priory founded nearly 200 years after the death of St Olave the patron saint of Norway, in 1030.

OPENING TIMES

Any reasonable time

HOW TO FIND US

Direction: Located 5½ miles SW of the town of Great Yarmouth on A143

Train: Haddiscoe 1¼ miles

Dogs on leads (restricted areas only).

MAP   Page 261 (3K)
      OS Map 134 (ref TM 459996)

The Priory of Our Lady of Thetford was founded in 1103 by Roger Bigod. The ruins, including the remains of the impressive gatehouse and priors lodging, still stand. In the 13th century, a Lady Chapel was added to the church. According to legend, the Virgin Mary appeared in a vision to locals, requesting that this chapel be built in her honour. During the subsequent construction, the old statue of Our Lady was found to have a hollow in the head containing relics of saints. In 1536, the 'King's visitors' descended on the priory and, despite Henry VIII's son Henry Fitzroy being buried here, it was dissolved.

OPENING TIMES

Any reasonable time

HOW TO FIND US

Direction: Located on the W side of Thetford, near the station

Train: Thetford ¼ mile

Bus: From surrounding areas

MAP   Page 261 (3G)
      OS Map 144 (ref TL 866834)

Medieval gamekeeper's or hunting lodge within the forest.

OPENING TIMES

Any reasonable time

HOW TO FIND US

Direction: Located 2 miles W of Thetford off B1107

Train: Thetford 2½ miles

Bus: First 130 Bury St Edmunds-Mildenhall (pass close ⊞ Thetford)

MAP   Page 261 (3G)
      OS Map 144 (ref TL 839841)

TILBURY FORT
ESSEX – RM18 7NR

The artillery fort at Tilbury on the Thames estuary protected London from the 16th century through to World War II.

TILBURY FORT

Henry VIII built the first fort, and nearby Elizabeth I rallied her army waiting for the Armada. The present fort – the most complete example of its type in England – was begun in 1672 under Charles II. It housed powerful artillery to stop warships, a garrison to repel a land attack, and two magazines that stored vast quantities of gunpowder.

Visitors can now enter one of Tilbury's later magazines through dark and atmospheric passages. A new exhibition examines the history of the fort, including the evolution of its design and its important role in the defence of London's river. For those with an interest in military history there are new displays of guns and gunpowder barrels and information on advances in military engineering.

New for 2005
There will be a new audio tour which will include Elizabeth I's Armada speech and a description of life at the fort by Nathan Makepiece, the Fort's Master Gunner.

'Sharpe', the historical TV drama set during the Napoleonic Wars, was filmed here.

NON-MEMBERS

Adult	£3.30
Concession	£2.50
Children	£1.70
Family ticket	£8.30
£1.30 to fire anti-aircraft gun	

OPENING TIMES

24 Mar-30 Sep, daily	10am-6pm
1-31 Oct, daily	10am-5pm
1 Nov-31 Mar, Thu-Mon	10am-4pm

HOW TO FIND US
Direction: Located ½ mile E of Tilbury off A126

Train: Tilbury Town 1½ miles

Bus: Rail shuttle 🚆 Tilbury – Tilbury Ferry, then ¼ mile

Ferry: Gravesend-Tilbury Ferry, then ¼ mile

Tel: 01375 858489

🏃 ♿ E 📷 🍴 ♿ 🎧 🐕 📷 🛡

⚠

Disabled access (exterior, magazines and fort square).

Dogs on leads (restricted areas).

Family learning resources available.

MAP	Page 261 (7G)
	OS Map 177 (ref TQ 651753)

WALTHAM ABBEY GATEHOUSE AND BRIDGE
ESSEX

At this site you can see a late 14th-century abbey gatehouse, part of the cloister and Harold's Bridge, named after the last Saxon King of England.

Managed by Lee Valley Park.

OPENING TIMES
Any reasonable time

HOW TO FIND US
Direction: In Waltham Abbey off A112

Train: Waltham Cross 1¼ miles

Bus: Frequent services by different operators from 🚆 Waltham Cross

Tel: 01992 702200

🎧 ♿ Sensory trail guide

MAP	Page 261 (6F)
	OS Map 166 (Gatehouse ref TL 381007, Harold's Bridge ref TL 382009)

WEETING CASTLE
NORFOLK

The ruins of a substantial early medieval manor house, surrounded by a shallow rectangular moat.

OPENING TIMES
Any reasonable time

HOW TO FIND US
Direction: Located 2 miles N of Brandon off B1106

Train: Brandon 1¼ miles

🐕

MAP	Page 261 (3G)
	OS Map 144 (ref TL 778891)

Check *Heritage Today* for news and information on forthcoming events and exclusive members' offers.

WREST PARK BEDFORDSHIRE – MK45 4HS

This is one of the most magnificent gardens in England, but one of the least well known. Unlike 'Capability' Brown's natural landscape styling, favoured during the late 18th century, Wrest Park's formal gardens provide a fascinating history of gardening styles, laid out over 150 years and inspired by the great gardens of Versailles in France.

The Pavilion from the Long Water

Wrest Park was the home of the de Grey family from the 13th century until 1917. The gardens are celebrated for their rare survival of a formal layout of wooded walks and canals from the early 18th century, centred on the architectural highlight of the pavilion designed by Thomas Archer in 1710. Subsequent generations added garden buildings such as the Bath House and the Chinese Pavilion, valuing the special atmosphere of the established garden even when more fashionable landscapers would have swept it away.

The old manor house was demolished when the present house was completed by 1834. The new house was designed by Thomas, Earl de Grey, an enthusiast for 18th-century French architecture. It is set further north from the site of the old house, and new formal gardens were laid out between the

house and the woodland garden. The Orangery, Italian garden and Parterre with magnificent lead sculptures date from the 19th century.

Please note
There is no public access to the house. Entry to gardens only.

www.english-heritage.org.uk/ wrestpark

NON-MEMBERS

Adult	£4.30
Concession	£3.20
Child	£2.20
Family ticket	£10.80

OPENING TIMES

26 Mar-30 Sep,
Sat-Sun & Bank Hols   10am-6pm
1-31 Oct, Sat-Sun   10am-5pm

HOW TO FIND US

Direction: ¾ mile E of Silsoe off A6, 10 miles S of Bedford

Train: Flitwick 4 miles

Bus: Stagecoach in Northants X1, X52 Bedford – Luton

Tel: 01525 860152

Buggies available for disabled visitors. Family learning resources available.

MAP	Page 260 (5E)
	OS Map 153 (ref TL 091355)

www.english-heritage.org.uk/eastofengland

OTHER ATTRACTIONS

DISCOUNTED ENTRY TO OUR MEMBERS (DISCOUNTS MAY NOT APPLY ON EVENT DAYS)

FELIXSTOWE MUSEUM

SUFFOLK

ENTRY

Half-price for EH members.

Discount does not extend to EH Corporate Partners

OPENING TIMES

Easter Sunday - 31 Oct, Sundays and Bank Holiday Mondays,

1 Jun-28 Sep, Wednesdays only, 1pm-5.30pm (last admission 5pm)

Direction: Located 1 mile S of Felixstowe, near the docks

Train: Felixstowe 2½ miles

Bus: First Eastern Counties service 75/7 Ipswich – Felixstowe Dock to within ½ mile of the site

Tel: 01394 674355 for admission prices and further details

MAP   Page 261 (5J)
          OS Map 169 (ref TM 283320)

FLAG FEN EXCAVATIONS

CAMBRIDGESHIRE

ENTRY

Reduced entry for EH members, please call site for details.

Discount does not extend to EH Corporate Partners

OPENING TIMES

Please call the site for full details of opening hours

Direction: 2 miles S of Wittlesey Rail Station to the East of Peterborough; 3 miles from Peterborough city centre

Tel: 01733 313414

MAP   Page 260 (3E)
          OS Map 142 (ref TL 225989)

TIME AND TIDE MUSEUM

NORFOLK

Come and find out about Great Yarmouth's fascinating history, its rich maritime and fishing heritage. Wander down a typical 1913 'Row', experience the heady atmosphere of a 1950's fishwharf, take the wheel of a coastal Drifter and hear gripping tales of wreck and rescue. Located in a Victorian herring curing works, there is something for all the family, with lively hands on displays and free audio guides.

ENTRY

25% discount on all ticket categories for English Heritage Members

OPENING TIMES

21 Mar-31 Oct		
Mon-Sun		10am-5pm
1 Nov-30 Mar		
Mon and Fri		10am-4pm
Sat-Sun		12pm-4pm
Closed	23-26 Dec and 1 Jan	

Tel: 01493 745526 for admission prices and further details

www.museums.norfolk.gov.uk

MAP   Page 261 (2K)
          OS Map 142 (ref TL 225989)

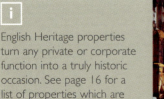

ℹ️

English Heritage properties turn any private or corporate function into a truly historic occasion. See page 16 for a list of properties which are available for hire.

ENGLISH HERITAGE

TOURS THROUGH TIME

A RANGE OF FULLY GUIDED HISTORICAL TOURS
IN ASSOCIATION WITH BROOKLAND TRAVEL

ENGLISH HERITAGE'S UNIQUE HISTORICAL TOURS

YOUR TOUR INCLUDES:

- Free entry to English Heritage sites
- Expert commentary throughout the day
- Specialist talks and guided tours on location
- Free guidebooks
- Discounts in English Heritage gift shops
- Comfortable coach travel
- Dinner, bed and breakfast on overnight tours, many of which stay in historic hotels

Tours Through Time provide a window to the past and enable you to explore some of the most intriguing and beautiful historic sites of England.

Places are limited. Book early to avoid disappointment by contacting Brookland Travel. **BOOK NOW** on **0845 121 2863**

INDULGE YOURSELF WITH A ONE DAY OR OVERNIGHT TOUR

Take the chance to walk amongst the stones at Stonehenge, explore the secret tunnels of Dover Castle, roam Cornwall's spectacular coastline, follow in the footsteps of the Duke of Wellington or enjoy a special tour of HMS Victory and historic Portsmouth.

HOW TO BOOK

For bookings or further information please contact Brookland Travel:

Monday to Friday 9am – 5pm

BY PHONE

0845 121 2863 (local rate)

BY EMAIL

mail@brookland-travelbreaks.co.uk

VISIT OUR WEBSITE

www.english-heritage.org.uk/ toursthroughtime

OR WRITE TO US

ENGLISH HERITAGE TOURS THROUGH TIME
Brookland Travel, 1st Floor, 22 High East Street,
Dorchester, Dorset DT1 1EZ

Kirby Hall

EAST MIDLANDS

The East Midlands provides a rich and diverse backdrop steeped in history and legend, from the rugged landscape of the Peak District National Park to Sherwood Forest, home of the legendary hero Robin Hood.

www.english-heritage.org.uk/eastmidlands

PROPERTIES

SEE INDIVIDUAL LISTINGS FOR DETAILS

DERBYSHIRE
Arbor Low Stone Circle and Gib Hill Barrow, Bolsover Castle, Bolsover Cundy House, Hardwick Old Hall, Hob Hurst's House, Nine Ladies Stone Circle, Peveril Castle, Sutton Scarsdale Hall, Wingfield Manor

LEICESTERSHIRE
Ashby de la Zouch Castle, Jewry Wall, Kirby Muxloe Castle

LINCOLNSHIRE
Bolingbroke Castle, Gainsborough Old Hall, Lincoln Medieval Bishops' Palace, Sibsey Trader Windmill, Tattershall College

NORTHAMPTONSHIRE
Chichele College, 78 Derngate, Eleanor Cross Geddington, Kirby Hall, Rushton Triangular Lodge

NOTTINGHAMSHIRE
Mattersey Priory, Rufford Abbey

RUTLAND
Lyddington Bede House

Comprehensive map of our sites
PAGE 262-263

Peveril Castle

CASTLES, POETS AND ROBIN HOOD

With beautiful countryside, picturesque villages and famous historic characters, the East Midlands has something for everyone. And from the Norman Peveril Castle perched high in the Peak District to the caves at Creswell Crags where Ice Age cave art was recently discovered, English Heritage is working to protect it all.

Rutland, the smallest county in England, is home to Lyddington Bede House, which was originally one wing of a medieval palace belonging to the Bishops of Lincoln. The neighbouring county of Lincolnshire offers some of the finest stretches of waterways in Britain, while Northamptonshire gives a sense of serenity from its rolling hills

and tranquil villages. If you visit between May and September, you may see evidence of the mysterious art of well dressing, which is still practised in Derbyshire. Thought to have originated in pagan times, this ancient art involves decorating springs and wells with pictures made from local plants and flowers.

Other historical figures add to the rich heritage of this area. Bess of Hardwick, who became the second most powerful and wealthy woman of the Elizabethan era, has links with many properties in the region including Hardwick Old Hall, Hardwick New Hall, Wingfield Manor and Bolsover Castle. Lord Byron also lived in the area, at Newstead Abbey in

Nottinghamshire, which narrowly missed out on a place in the final of the 2004 series of the BBC's 'Restoration'.

English Heritage works with partners in the area to bring the past and present together.

One of the projects we have contributed to over the past year is the Castleton Centre. This new focal point for visitors to Castleton and Peveril Castle is being developed by the Peak District National Park, English Heritage and other partners in the area. We are also working closely with the East Midlands Development Agency to place the historic environment at the forefront of future tourism developments in the region.

www.english-heritage.org.uk/eastmidlands

ARBOR LOW STONE CIRCLE AND GIB HILL BARROW

DERBYSHIRE

The region's most important prehistoric site, Arbor Low is a Neolithic henge monument atmospherically set amid high moorland. Within an earthen bank and ditch, a circle of some 50 white limestone slabs, all now fallen, surrounds a central stone 'cove' – a feature found only in major sacred sites. Nearby is enigmatic Gib Hill, a large burial mound.

Entry: The farmer who owns right of way to property may levy a charge.

Managed by Peak District National Park Authority.

OPENING TIMES

Daily, in summer	10am-6pm
Daily, rest of year	10am-4pm
Closed	24-26 Dec and 1 Jan

HOW TO FIND US

Direction: ½ mile W of A515, 2 miles S of Monyash

Train: Buxton 10 miles

Bus: First 181 from Sheffield, TM Travel 202 from Derby, Hulleys 171 from Bakewell, all to Parsley Hay, then 1 mile

Tel: 01629 816200

MAP Page 262 (2E) OS Map 119 (ref SK 160636)

ASHBY DE LA ZOUCH CASTLE

LEICESTERSHIRE   SEE OPPOSITE PAGE

BOLINGBROKE CASTLE

LINCOLNSHIRE

The remains of a 13th-century hexagonal castle, birthplace in 1367 of the future King Henry IV, with adjacent earthworks. Besieged and taken by Cromwell's Parliamentarians in 1643.

Managed by Heritage Lincolnshire.

OPENING TIMES

Any reasonable time

HOW TO FIND US

Direction: In Old Bolingbroke, 16 miles N of Boston off A16

Train: Thorpe Culvert 10 miles

Tel: 01529 461499

MAP Page 263 (2J) OS Map 122 (ref TF 349650)

BOLSOVER CASTLE

DERBYSHIRE   GO TO PAGE 150

BOLSOVER CUNDY HOUSE

DERBYSHIRE

This 17th-century conduit house used to supply water to Bolsover Castle. It has recently been restored, with a solid stone-vaulted roof.

Managed by Bolsover Civic Society.

BOLSOVER CUNDY HOUSE

OPENING TIMES

Any reasonable time

HOW TO FIND US

Direction: Off M1 at junctions 29 or 30, follow signs for Bolsover Castle. In Craggs Road, Bolsover, 6 miles E of Chesterfield on A362

Train: Chesterfield 6 miles

Bus: Stagecoach in Chesterfield service 81-3, Chesterfield - Bolsover

Tel: 01246 822844 (Bolsover Castle)

MAP Page 263 (2F) OS Map 141 (ref SK 470707)

CHICHELE COLLEGE

NORTHAMPTONSHIRE

Remains of a college (communal residence) for clergy serving the parish church, founded by Archbishop Chichele in 1431. The site is used regularly to display works of art.

For full details, visit www.eastnorthamptonshire.gov.uk

Managed by Cultural Community Partnerships.

OPENING TIMES

Quadrangle – any reasonable time. For the chapel, contact the keykeeper, Mrs D Holyoak, 12 Lancaster St, Higham Ferrers. Or telephone 01933 314157

HOW TO FIND US

Direction: In Higham Ferrers

Train: Wellingborough 5 miles

Bus: Stagecoach in Northants 46 from Wellingborough

Tel 01933 655401

Dogs on leads (restricted areas only).

MAP Page 263 (6G) OS Map 153 (ref SP 960687)

ASHBY DE LA ZOUCH CASTLE

LEICESTERSHIRE – LE65 1BR

Ashby Castle forms the backdrop to the famous jousting scenes in Sir Walter Scott's classic novel of 1819, *Ivanhoe*. Now a ruin, the castle began as a manor house in the 12th century. It only achieved castle status in the 15th century, by which time the hall and buttery had been enlarged, with a solar to the east and a large integral kitchen added to the west.

Between 1474 and his execution by Richard III in 1483, Edward IV's Chamberlain Lord Hastings added the chapel and the impressive keep-like Hastings Tower – a castle within a castle. Visitors can now climb the 24-metre (78ft) tower, which offers fine views. Later the castle hosted many royal visitors, including Henry VII, Mary Queen of Scots, James I and Charles I.

A Royalist stronghold during the Civil War, the castle finally fell to Parliament in 1646, and was then made unusable. An underground passage from the kitchen to the tower, probably created during this war, can still be explored today.

www.english-heritage.org.uk/ashby

New for 2005

A three year conservation programme has just been completed, offering visitors improved facilities and an attractive picnic area.

NON-MEMBERS

Adult	£3.30
Concession	£2.50
Child	£1.70
Family ticket	£8.30

OPENING TIMES

24 Mar-30 Jun, Thu-Mon	10am-5pm
1 Jul-31 Aug, daily	10am-6pm
1 Sep-31 Oct, Thu-Mon	10am-5pm
1 Nov-31 Mar, Thu-Mon	10am-4pm
Closed	24-26 Dec and 1 Jan

HOW TO FIND US

Direction: In Ashby de la Zouch, 12 miles S of Derby on A511. Restricted parking on site, please park in town car park

Train: Burton on Trent 9 miles

Bus: Arriva 9, 25/7 Burton on Trent-Ashby de la Zouch; Arriva 118, 218 Leicester-Swadlincote

Local Tourist Information 01530 411767

Tel: 01530 413343

Disabled access (grounds only).
Parking (restricted on site, please park in town car park - charge applies).

MAP	Page 262 (4E)
	OS Map 128 (ref SK 361166)

BOLSOVER CASTLE DERBYSHIRE

'By an unlikely miracle,' wrote the historian and champion of the castle, Mark Girouard, 'the keep at Bolsover has survived into this century as an almost untouched expression in stone of the lost world of Elizabethan chivalry and romance.'

The house you see today stands on the site of a medieval castle built by the Peverel family shortly after the Norman Conquest. Sir Charles Cavendish bought the old castle and began work on his 'Little Castle' project in 1612. His creation – despite its embattled appearance – was not designed for defence, but for elegant living.

Sir Charles intended the house as a retreat from the world to an imaginary golden age of chivalry and pleasure. His son, William, later Duke of Newcastle, inherited the Little Castle in 1616 and set about its completion, assisted by the designer John Smythson. William then added the stately rooms of the Terrace Range and, in 1634, invited the Stuart court to a masque specially written for the occasion. Finally, William constructed the Riding School, in which he indulged his passion for training horses.

The symbolic and erotic wall paintings in the Little Castle were recently conserved, as was the original unique painted decoration to the panelling. The castle battlements and the Venus Garden have been restored and

the fountain, with 23 new statues, plays again for the first time in centuries. Part of the Riding School has been developed into a Discovery Centre.

Last year, a series of paintings depicting Roman emperors and empresses were returned to the building. Known as the Caesar paintings, they were commissioned by William Cavendish in the 17th century and copied from an original set created by the great Venetian artist Titian. The paintings are now of great importance, as the original set by Titian were destroyed by fire in Spain in 1734.

Bolsover Castle regularly hosts living history events, open-air concerts and Shakespeare plays. It also has an interactive audio tour and a Discovery Centre with audio-visual displays. There is reasonable disabled access to the main castle and good access to the grounds: however, the Little Castle is not accessible to wheelchairs.

Travel to Bolsover Castle, Hardwick Old Hall and other local attractions on a 1948 vintage coach (thereby gaining half-price entry). Services run 29-30 May and then every Sunday until 11 Sept, plus every Thursday from 7 July to 8 Sept.

For a full timetable, visit www.cosycoach.co.uk or call Cosy Coach Tours on 0114 248 9139.

www.english-heritage.org.uk/ bolsovercastle

⊤ Available for corporate and private hire.

▮ Licensed for civil wedding ceremonies.

New visitor centre

151

NON-MEMBERS

Adult	£6.60
Concession	£5.00
Child	£3.30
Family ticket	£16.50

OPENING TIMES

24 Mar-30 Apr, Thu-Mon	10am-5pm
1 May-31 Aug, daily	10am-6pm
1 Sep-31 Oct, Thu-Mon	10am-5pm
1 Nov-31 Mar, Thu-Mon	10am-4pm
Closes Saturdays	4pm

Closed 24-26 Dec and 1 Jan (and may close early for evening events)

HOW TO FIND US

Direction: In Bolsover, 6 miles E of Chesterfield on A632. Off M1 at junctions 29 or 30.

Train: Chesterfield 6 miles

Bus: Stagecoach in Chesterfield 81-3 Chesterfield-Bolsover

Tel: 01246 822844

Local Tourist Information (Chesterfield): 01246 345777

Family learning resources available.

Parking (in Castle car park off main gate, also coach drop-off point).

MAP   Page 263 (2F)
OS Map 120 (ref SK 470707)

Lion mask on the Venus Fountain

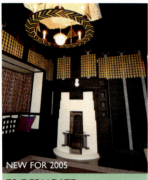

NEW FOR 2005

78 DERNGATE

NORTHAMPTONSHIRE

152

The house re-designed by Charles Rennie Mackintosh for model-manufacturer W.J. Bassett-Lowke. Carefully restored to its 1917 appearance in 2003, it is amongst Mackintosh's last architectural works and is the only Mackintosh house open in England. Supporting exhibitions explore the Mackintosh designs and celebrate the life and work of Bassett-Lowke.

Managed by the 78 Derngate Northampton Trust.

NON-MEMBERS

Adult	£5.50
Concession, inc. child	£4.00
Family ticket	£13.50
School parties (per head)	£2.50

Discount does not extend to EH Corporate partners

OPENING TIMES

23 Mar-27 Nov, Wed-Sun & Bank Hol Mon   10.30am-5pm

Last admission   3.45pm

Visits must be booked, please call 01604 603407

HOW TO FIND US

Direction: In Northampton, close to Derngate theatre

MAP	Page 263 (6G)
	OS Map 152 (ref SP 759603)

ELEANOR CROSS, GEDDINGTON

NORTHAMPTONSHIRE

In 1290, Eleanor of Castile, the wife of Edward I, died at Harby, Nottinghamshire. The beautiful tomb that Edward erected to her memory can still be seen today in Westminster Abbey. The places where her funeral cortège rested on the journey south to Westminster were marked by stone crosses. Only three of these crosses now remain intact: in the centre of Waltham Cross, Herts; at Hardingstone, on the edge of Northampton, and also here in Geddington.

OPENING TIMES

Any reasonable time

HOW TO FIND US

Direction: Located in the village of Geddington, off A43 between Kettering and Corby

Train: Kettering 4 miles

Bus: Stagecoach in Northants 8 Kettering-Corby

MAP	Page 263 (5G)
	OS Map 141 (ref SP 894830)

GAINSBOROUGH OLD HALL

LINCOLNSHIRE – DN21 2NB

A little-known gem, Gainsborough Old Hall is among the best-preserved medieval manor houses in England. Partly brick and partly timber-framed, and mainly later 15th century with Elizabethan additions, it has a kitchen with an enormous fireplace, a noble great hall, and an imposing lodgings tower.

Managed by Lincolnshire County Council.

NON-MEMBERS

Adult	£3.25
Concession	£2.50
Child	£2.50
Family ticket	£9.00

Small charge to special events for EH members. Discount for groups of 30 or more.

OPENING TIMES

24-26 Mar, Mon-Sat	10am-5pm
27 Mar-31 Oct, Mon-Sat	10am-5pm
Sun	1pm-4.30pm
1 Nov-31 Mar, Mon-Sat	10am-5pm
Closed	24-26, 31 Dec and 1 Jan

HOW TO FIND US

Direction: In Gainsborough, opposite the library

Train: Gainsborough Central ½ mile, Gainsborough Lea Road 1mile

Bus: From surrounding areas

Tel: 01427 612669

Disabled access (most of ground floor).

MAP	Page 263 (1G)
	OS Map 112 (ref SK 813900)

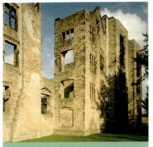

HARDWICK OLD HALL

DERBYSHIRE – S44 5QJ

This large, ruined house, finished in 1591, was the birthplace and family home of Bess of Hardwick, one of the most remarkable women of the Elizabethan Age. Next to it is the New Hall she built in the 1590s. An audio tour is available at Hardwick Old Hall telling the wonderful story of Bess of Hardwick.

Managed by EH and owned by the National Trust.

NON-MEMBERS

Adult	£3.30
Concession	£2.50
Child	£1.70
Family ticket	£8.30

National Trust members admitted free, but small charge at EH events. Tickets for the New Hall (National Trust) and joint tickets for both properties available at extra cost.

OPENING TIMES

24 Mar-30 Sep, Wed, Thu, Sat, Sun
10am-6pm

1-31 Oct, Wed, Thu, Sat, Sun
10am-5pm

HOW TO FIND US

Direction: 9½ miles SE of Chesterfield, off A6175, from J29 of M1

Train: Chesterfield 8 miles

Bus: Cosy Coaches C1 from Chesterfield (Sun, Jun-Aug only); otherwise Stagecoach in Chesterfield 737, 747 Sheffield/Chesterfield-Nottingham, alight Glapwell 'Young Vanish', 1½ miles

HARDWICK OLD HALL

Tel: 01246 850431

Toilets (in National Trust car park).

MAP	Page 263 (2F)
	OS Map 120 (ref SK 462637)

HOB HURST'S HOUSE

DERBYSHIRE

A square prehistoric burial mound with an earthwork ditch and outer bank. Named after a local goblin.

Managed by the Peak District National Park Authority.

OPENING TIMES

Any reasonable time

HOW TO FIND US

Direction: From unclassified road off B5057, 9 miles W of Chesterfield

Train: Chesterfield 9 miles

Bus: Hulleys 170, TM Travel X67 from Chesterfield to within 2 miles

Tel: 01629 816200

MAP	Page 262 (2E)
	OS Map 119 (ref SK 287692)

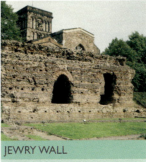

JEWRY WALL

LEICESTERSHIRE

A length of Roman wall over 9 metres (30 ft) high, with a museum displaying the archaeology of Leicester and its region.

JEWRY WALL

OPENING TIMES

Daily, summer	10am-6pm
Daily, rest of year	10am-4pm
Museum:	
Open Sat only	11am-4.30pm
Closed	24-26 Dec and 1 Jan

HOW TO FIND US

Direction: In St Nicholas St, W of Church of St Nicholas

Train: Leicester ¾ mile

Bus: From surrounding areas

Tel: 01162 254971
(Jewry Wall Museum)

Parking (by museum, within St Nicholas Circle).

MAP	Page 263 (4F)
	OS Map 140 (ref SK 582045)

KIRBY HALL

NORTHAMPTONSHIRE   GO TO PAGE 155

KIRBY MUXLOE CASTLE

LEICESTERSHIRE – LE9 9MD

Begun in the 1480s by Lord Hastings, but never completed, Kirby Muxloe Castle is currently closed while English Heritage undertakes extensive conservation work to the brickwork and moat bridge. Visitors are welcome to view the work from outside the castle area, around the perimeter of the moat. The conservation work is due to be completed in 2006.

KIRBY MUXLOE CASTLE

OPENING TIMES

Currently closed

HOW TO FIND US

Direction: 4 miles W of Leicester off B5380; close to M1 junction 21A, northbound exit only

Train: Leicester 5 miles

Bus: Arriva 63, 152-4 from Leicester

Tel: 01162 386886

154

MAP   Page 263 (4F)
        OS Map 140 (ref SK 524046)

LYDDINGTON BEDE HOUSE

RUTLAND – LE15 9LZ

Lyddington Bede House was originally one wing of a medieval rural palace belonging to the Bishops of Lincoln. Although it is not known when it was first built, the land was certainly owned by the church in the time of William the Conqueror. The property was seized by the Crown in 1547 and was then passed on to Lord Burghley who turned it into an almshouse for the poor in the 1600s. Visitors can wander through the bedesmen's rooms, with their tiny windows and fireplaces, as well as the Great Chamber which features a beautiful ceiling cornice. An on-site audio tour reconstructs some of the major changes during the past 700 years, and outside there is a small herb garden.

LYDDINGTON BEDE HOUSE

NON-MEMBERS

Adult	£3.30
Concession	£2.50
Child	£1.70
Family ticket	£8.30

OPENING TIMES

24 Mar-31 Oct, Thu-Mon 10am-5pm

HOW TO FIND US

Direction: In Lyddington, 6 miles N of Corby; 1 mile E of A6003, next to the church

Bus: Rutland Flyer 1 Corby-Melton Mowbray (passes close ≠ Oakham)

Tel: 01572 822438

Disabled access (ground floor only).

MAP   Page 263 (5G)
        OS Map 141 (ref SP 876970)

MATTERSEY PRIORY

NOTTINGHAMSHIRE

The remains of a small Gilbertine monastery, which was founded for six canons in 1185.

OPENING TIMES

Any reasonable time

HOW TO FIND US

Direction: ¾ mile down rough drive, 1 mile E of Mattersey off B6045

Train: Retford 7 miles

MAP   Page 263 (1G)
        OS Map 112 (ref SK 703896)

NINE LADIES STONE CIRCLE

DERBYSHIRE

This Early Bronze Age circle, 10 metres (33ft) across, is adjacent to other prehistoric religious sites on Stanton Moor.

Managed by Peak District National Park Authority.

NINE LADIES STONE CIRCLE

OPENING TIMES

Any reasonable time

HOW TO FIND US

Direction: From an unclassified road off A6, 5 miles SE of Bakewell

Train: Matlock 4½ miles

Bus: Hulleys 170 Matlock-Bakewell to within 1 mile

Tel: 01629 816200

MAP   Page 262 (2E)
        OS Map 119 (ref SK 249635)

PEVERIL CASTLE

DERBYSHIRE   GO TO PAGE 157

RUFFORD ABBEY

NOTTINGHAMSHIRE

Remains of a 17th-century country house, incorporating parts of a 12th-century Cistercian abbey and set in the Rufford Country Park.

OPENING TIMES

1 Apr-31 Oct, daily	10am-5pm
1 Nov-31 Mar, daily	10am-4pm
Closed	24-26 Dec and 1 Jan

HOW TO FIND US

Direction: 2 miles S of Ollerton off A614

Train: Mansfield 8 miles

Bus: Stagecoach in Bassetlaw 33 Nottingham-Worksop; F1/2 Heanor/Nottingham-Clumber

Tel: 01623 822944

Occasional charge for members on event days.

Parking (charge applies – not managed by EH).

Shop – craft centre.

MAP   Page 263 (2F)
        OS Map 120 (ref SK 646648)

Kirby Hall

KIRBY HALL

NORTHAMPTONSHIRE – NN17 5EN

Kirby Hall is one of the great Elizabethan houses, built in the hope of receiving the Queen on her annual 'progresses' around the country. The exceptional, richly carved decoration heralds the arrival in England of new ideas about architecture and design.

Although the house is partly ruined, the Great Hall and state rooms remain intact, and have been refitted and redecorated to authentic 17th- and 18th-century designs. Historical paint analysis and archaeological investigations have been undertaken to find out the significance of colour schemes in the history of this house.

The best rooms in the house were built by Sir Christopher Hatton and reserved for royal visitors. James I paid several visits to Hatton's nephew, another Christopher Hatton, and Sir Christopher Hatton the fourth added the great

gardens (described as 'ye finest garden in England') in the late 17th century. They are now partly restored and laid out in an elaborate 'cutwork' design.

The gardens and ground floor of the building are both easily accessible by wheelchair.

The 1999 film of Jane Austen's *Mansfield Park* was filmed here.

www.english-heritage.org.uk/ kirbyhall

Owned by the Earl of Winchilsea and managed by EH.

NON-MEMBERS

Adult	£4.30
Concession	£3.20
Child	£2.20
Family ticket	£10.80

OPENING TIMES

24 Mar-30 Jun, Thu-Mon	10am-5pm
1 Jul-31 Aug, daily	10am-6pm
1 Sep-31 Oct, Thu-Mon	10am-5pm
1 Nov-31 Mar, Thu-Mon	10am-4pm
Closed	24-26 Dec and 1 Jan

HOW TO FIND US

Direction: On an unclassified road off A43, 4 miles NE of Corby

Train: Kettering 9 miles

Tel: 01536 203230

Disabled access (grounds, gardens and ground floor only).

Dogs on leads (restricted areas).

MAP	Page 263 (5G)
	OS Map 141 (ref SP 926927)

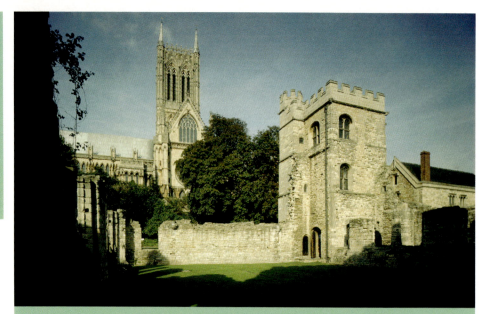

LINCOLN MEDIEVAL BISHOPS' PALACE

LINCOLNSHIRE – LN2 1PU

Constructed in the late 12th century, the medieval bishops' palace was once one of the most important buildings in England. As the administrative centre of the largest diocese in the country, its architecture reflected the enormous power and wealth of the bishops as princes of the church.

Built by St Hugh before 1200, the East Hall range is the earliest example of a roofed domestic hall in the country. The chapel range and entrance tower were built by Bishop William Alnwick, who modernised the palace in the 1430s. Having hosted visits from Henry VIII and James I, the palace was sacked by royalist troops during the Civil War in 1648. Built on hillside terraces, it has views of the cathedral and the Roman, medieval and modern city. The palace also contains a heritage garden and vineyard. To make your visit even more enjoyable, there is an award-winning audio tour.

www.english-heritage.org.uk/lincolnbishops

NON-MEMBERS

Adult	£3.60
Concession	£2.70
Child	£1.80
Family ticket	£9.00

OPENING TIMES

24 Mar-30 Jun, daily	10am-5pm
1 Jul-31 Aug, daily	10am-6pm
1 Sep-31 Oct, daily	10am-5pm
1 Nov-31 Mar, Thu-Mon	10am-4pm
Closed	24-26 Dec and 1 Jan

HOW TO FIND US

Direction: Located on the S side of Lincoln Cathedral

Train: Lincoln 1 mile

Bus: From surrounding areas

Tel: 01522 527468

Family learning resources available.
Parking (limited disabled parking on site).

MAP	Page 263 (2H)
	OS Map 121 (ref SK 978717)

PEVERIL CASTLE

DERBYSHIRE – S33 8WQ

This castle, perched high above the pretty village of Castleton, offers breathtaking views of the Peak District. Founded soon after the Norman Conquest of 1066 by one of King William's most trusted knights, William Peverel, the castle played an important role in guarding the Peak Forest area.

When 'Castle Peak', as it was known in the Middle Ages, passed into the hands of Henry II in 1155, he made a number of additions. Most notable was the great square keep, with its round-headed windows, built in 1176.

Improvements were made to the castle during the 13th century. It was also at this time that the Earl of Derby forcibly seized Peveril. By 1400, the castle ceased to be of strategic importance, but due to its impregnability was often used as a prison.

After extensive conservation work on the keep, English Heritage has erected a walkway at first-floor level, enabling visitors to enter two chambers previously inaccessible: a medieval garderobe and a small room with beautiful views of the surrounding countryside. The spiral stairway to the base of the keep has been illuminated using solar power.

New displays for 2005.

www.english-heritage.org.uk/peveril

NON-MEMBERS

Adult	£3.00
Concession	£2.30
Children	£1.50
Family ticket	£7.50

OPENING TIMES

24 Mar-30 Apr, daily	10am-5pm
1 May-31 Aug, daily	10am-6pm
1 Sep-31 Oct, daily	10am-5pm
1 Nov-31 Mar, Thu-Mon	10am-4pm
Closed	24-26 Dec and 1 Jan

HOW TO FIND US

Direction: Via the market place in Castleton; 15 miles W of Sheffield on A6187

Train: Sheffield-Hope 2½ miles

Bus: First/Stagecoach in Chesterfield 272-4 ⊠ Sheffield-Castleton, then 1 mile

Tel: 01433 620613

Family learning resources available.
Parking (in town).
Toilets (in town).

MAP	Page 262 (2E)
	OS Map 110 (ref SK 149826)

www.english-heritage.org.uk/eastmidlands

RUSHTON TRIANGULAR LODGE

NORTHAMPTONSHIRE – NN14 1RP

This triangular building was designed and built by Sir Thomas Tresham between 1593 and 1597. The Lodge is a testament to Tresham's Roman Catholicism: the number three, symbolising the Holy Trinity, is apparent everywhere. There are three floors, trefoil windows and three triangular gables on each side. On the entrance front is the inscription 'Tres Testimonium Dant' ('there are three that give witness'), a quote from the Gospel of St John in the Bible referring to the Holy Trinity. It is also a pun on Tresham's name; his wife called him 'Good Tres' in her letters.

NON-MEMBERS

Adult	£2.30
Concession	£1.70
Child	£1.20

OPENING TIMES

24 Mar-31 Oct, Thu-Mon 10am-5pm

HOW TO FIND US

Direction: 1 mile W of Rushton, on unclassified road; 3 miles from Desborough on A6

Train: Kettering 5 miles

RUSHTON TRIANGULAR LODGE

Bus: Stagecoach in Northants 19 Kettering-Market Harborough, alight Desborough, then 2 miles

Tel: 01536 710761

Dogs on leads (restricted areas only). Parking (nearby lay-by).

MAP	Page 263 (5G)
	OS Map 141 (ref SP 830831)

SIBSEY TRADER WINDMILL

LINCOLNSHIRE – PE22 0SY

This six-storey mill, built in 1877, still works today. The tearoom, which was nominated one of Lincolnshire's top ten tearooms in 2003 by *Lincolnshire Life* magazine, sells produce made from the mill's organic, stone-ground flour.

Managed by Ian Ansell. T: 07718 320449.

NON-MEMBERS

Adult	£2.00
Concession	£1.50
Child	£1.00

SIBSEY TRADER WINDMILL

OPENING TIMES

24 Mar-27 Sep,	
Sat, Tue & Bank Hols	10am-6pm
Sun	11am-6pm
28 Sep-13 Nov, Sat	10am-6pm
Sun	11am-6pm
Mill only:	
14 Nov-17 Mar, Sat	11am-5pm
Closed	24-26 Dec and 1 Jan

HOW TO FIND US

Direction: ½ mile W of Sibsey off A16, 5 miles N of Boston

Train: Boston 5 miles

Bus: Various services and operators from Boston to Sibsey, then ½ mile

Tel: 01205 750036

Disabled access (exterior only).

MAP	Page 263 (3J)
	OS Map 122 (ref TF 345510)

SUTTON SCARSDALE HALL

DERBYSHIRE

This 18th-century remodelling of an earlier house is now in ruins, but visitors can see the fragments of its former rich plaster decoration. Furniture, fittings and roof lead were all sold off after World War I, and panelled rooms from the hall are housed in museums in Philadelphia and Los Angeles.

SUTTON SCARSDALE HALL

OPENING TIMES

Summer, daily	10am-6pm
Rest of year, daily	10am-4pm
Closed	24-26 Dec and 1 Jan

HOW TO FIND US

Direction: Between Chesterfield and Bolsover, 1½ miles S of Arkwright Town

Train: Chesterfield 5 miles

Bus: Aston 48 from Chesterfield

MAP	Page 263 (2F) OS Map 120 (ref SK 442689)

TATTERSHALL COLLEGE

LINCOLNSHIRE

Remains of a grammar school for church choristers, built in the mid-15th century by Ralph, Lord Cromwell, the builder of nearby Tattershall Castle, now in the care of the National Trust.

Tattershall College is managed by Heritage Lincolnshire.

OPENING TIMES

Any reasonable time

HOW TO FIND US

Direction: In Tattershall, 14 miles NE of Sleaford on A153

Train: Ruskington (U) 10 miles

Bus: Brylaine 5 Lincoln-Boston (passing close ⮕ Lincoln and Boston)

Tel: 01529 461499

MAP	Page 263 (2H) OS Map 122 (ref TF 213578)

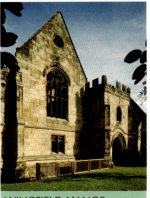

WINGFIELD MANOR

DERBYSHIRE – DE55 7NH

A huge, ruined country mansion, Wingfield Manor was built in the 1440s by Ralph, Lord Cromwell, Treasurer of England. Mary Queen of Scots was imprisoned here in 1569, 1584 and 1585. Unoccupied since the 1770s, the manor's late-Gothic Great Hall and the High Tower are testaments to its heyday.

TV's *Peak Practice* and Zeffirelli's film *Jane Eyre* have been filmed at the manor.

Wingfield Manor is contained within a private working farm and partly surrounds the farmhouse. Visitors are asked to respect the privacy of the owners and keep to the official routes. No visits outside listed opening hours.

NON-MEMBERS

Adult	£3.30
Concession	£2.50
Children	£1.70

OPENING TIMES

24 Mar-30 Oct, Thu-Mon	10am-5pm
1 Nov-31 Mar, Sat-Sun	10am-4pm
Closed	24-26 Dec and 1 Jan

Opening hours may change from those shown above. Please check with the site before you visit

WINGFIELD MANOR

HOW TO FIND US

Direction: 17 miles N of Derby; 11 miles S of Chesterfield on B5035; ½ mile S of South Wingfield. From M1 junction 28, W on A38, A615 (Matlock Road) at Alfreton, 1½ miles and turn onto B5035

Train: Alfreton 4 miles

Bus: Stagecoach in Chesterfield 140 Matlock-Alfreton

Tel: 01773 832060

Parking (none on site).
Orientation guide available.

MAP	Page 262 (3E) OS Map 119 (Ref SK 374548)

i

Sign-up on-line for our email Members' Newsletter at **www.english-heritage.org.uk**

i

English Heritage membership makes a lovely gift.

Call 0870 333 1181 or visit **www.english-heritage.org.uk/gift** for more details.

i

Don't forget to check opening dates and times before you visit.

OTHER HISTORIC ATTRACTIONS

DISCOUNTED ENTRY TO OUR MEMBERS (DISCOUNTS MAY NOT APPLY ON EVENT DAYS)

ALTHORP

NORTHAMPTONSHIRE

ENTRY

Adult	£10.50
Senior Citizen	£8.50
Child 5-17	£5.50
under-5s	free
Family Ticket	£26.50

Please book tickets in advance.

Discount does not extend to EH Corporate Partners, EH members receive free admission to the upstairs rooms of the house, including the Picture Gallery and State Bedrooms.

OPENING TIMES

Call site or visit www.althorp.com for details

Tel 01604 770107

MAP   Page 263 (6F)
         OS Map 152 (ref SP 682651)

ASHBY MUSEUM

LEICESTERSHIRE

ENTRY

Free for EH members and visitors to Ashby de la Zouch Castle on production of entry ticket.

Discount does not extend to EH Corporate Partners.

OPENING TIMES

Call site or visit www.leics.gov.uk for details

Tel 01530 560090

MAP   Page 262 (4E)
         OS Map 128 (ref SK 358169)

BELVOIR CASTLE

LINCOLNSHIRE

ENTRY

Reduction for EH members, please call site for details.

Discount does not extend to EH Corporate Partners.

OPENING TIMES

Call site or visit www.belvoircastle.com for details

Tel 01476 870262

MAP   Page 263 (3G)
         OS Map 130 (ref SK 820337)

BOSWORTH BATTLEFIELD

LEICESTERSHIRE

ENTRY

One EH member free with each paying member; not valid on special event days.

Discount does not extend to EH Corporate Partners.

OPENING TIMES

Call site or visit www.leics.gov.uk for details

Tel 01455 290429

MAP   Page 262 (4E)
         OS Map 140 (ref SK 403001)

MOIRA FURNACE

LEICESTERSHIRE

ENTRY

One EH member free with each paying member; not valid on special event days.

Discount does not extend to EH Corporate Partners

OPENING TIMES

Call site or visit www.leics.gov.uk for details

Tel: 01283 224667

MAP   Page 262 (4E)
         OS Map 128 (ref SK 314151)

PAPPLEWICK PUMPING STATION

NOTTINGHAMSHIRE

ENTRY

Free for EH members on static days and half price on steaming days.

Discount does not extend to EH Corporate Partners

OPENING TIMES

Call site or visit www.papplewick pumpingstation.co.uk for details

Tel: 01159 632938

MAP   Page 263 (3F)
         OS Map 120 (ref SK 583521)

FESTIVAL OF HISTORY

13–14 August 2005 Kelmarsh Hall, Northamptonshire

Don't miss the greatest weekend in history

- Unique historic setting
- Historic market
- Medieval jousting
- Dramatic battles
- Childrens' activites
- Celebrity lectures
- Music & dance
- Crafts & pastimes
- Members' discount and fast track access

Meet Britain's best historical performers. Experience the past from the Roman Empire to the Swinging Sixties. Barter at the historic market, enjoy music, dance and an unrivalled celebrity lecture programme.

EARLY BOOKING PRICES APPLY. Book now on **0870 333 1183**

THE KNIGHTS' TOURNAMENT

NEW FOR 2005

Follow your favourite knight as they battle it out in a national contest of jousting, archery, sword fighting, mounted skill at arms and falconry. Then see the grand final at the Festival of History.

Portchester Castle, Hampshire	May	14 & 15
Audley End House & Gardens, Essex	June	11 & 12
Kirby Hall, Corby, Northamptonshire	June	25 & 26
Belsay Hall, Northumberland	July	16 & 17
Pendennis Castle, Falmouth, Cornwall	August	2 & 3
Festival of History, Kelmarsh Hall, Northamptonshire	August	13 & 14

To book call **0870 333 1183** or visit
www.english-heritage.org.uk/events

Witley Court –
balustrade

WEST MIDLANDS

Set at the heart of the country, the rich and varied history of the West Midlands is reflected by the diversity of its historical attractions.

PROPERTIES

SEE INDIVIDUAL LISTINGS FOR DETAILS

HEREFORDSHIRE
Arthur's Stone, Edvin Loach Old Church, Goodrich Castle, Longtown Castle, Mortimer's Cross Water Mill, Rotherwas Chapel, Wigmore Castle

SHROPSHIRE
Acton Burnell Castle, Boscobel House and the Royal Oak, Buildwas Abbey, Cantlop Bridge, Clun Castle, Haughmond Abbey, Iron Bridge, Langley Chapel, Lilleshall Abbey, Mitchell's Fold Stone Circle, Moreton Corbet Castle, Old Oswestry Hill Fort, Stokesay Castle, Wenlock Priory, White Ladies Priory, Wroxeter Roman City

STAFFORDSHIRE
Croxden Abbey, Wall Roman Site

WEST MIDLANDS
Halesowen Abbey

WARWICKSHIRE
Kenilworth Castle

WORCESTERSHIRE
Leigh Court Barn, Witley Court

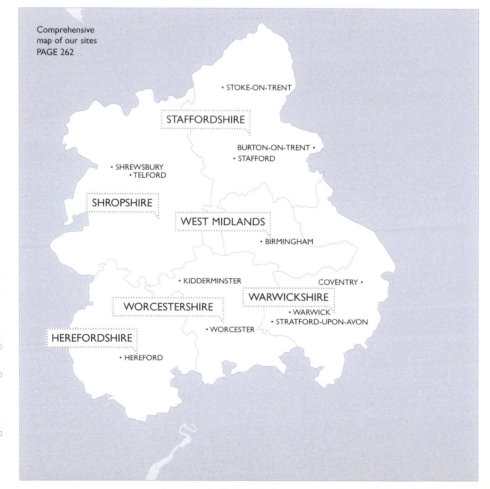

Comprehensive map of our sites
PAGE 262

• STOKE-ON-TRENT

STAFFORDSHIRE

BURTON-ON-TRENT •
• STAFFORD

• SHREWSBURY
• TELFORD

SHROPSHIRE

WEST MIDLANDS

• BIRMINGHAM

• KIDDERMINSTER

COVENTRY •

WARWICKSHIRE
• WARWICK
• STRATFORD-UPON-AVON

WORCESTERSHIRE
• WORCESTER

HEREFORDSHIRE
• HEREFORD

Stokesay Castle

THE HISTORIC WEST MIDLANDS

The Midlands is a region both rich and diverse in its heritage. Each of the counties that make up the region boasts an often unexpected wealth of historic association and a large number of beautiful and significant historic properties. Quiet and picturesque Shropshire, for example, has Stokesay Castle, one of the most perfectly preserved medieval fortified manor houses in England. It is also home to the World Heritage Site of Ironbridge, where the Industrial Revolution began and the modern world was forged.

The Midlands are likewise blessed with magnificent countryside, from the Staffordshire Peak District to the Malvern Hills and the beautiful Wye Valley in Herefordshire, where stands Goodrich Castle, a majestic medieval fortress. Witley Court, amid the rolling hills of Worcestershire, was once among England's finest country mansions: now a spectacular ruin, it offers a striking glimpse into a world of Victorian splendour and extravagance.

The region also has associations with many famous historical figures. It is the birthplace both of the poet and playwright William Shakespeare and the naturalist Charles Darwin; Charles II fled from Cromwell's troops to the safe hideaways of Boscobel House and the Royal Oak; while romantic Kenilworth Castle has links with Simon de Montfort, the tragic King Edward II, and Queen Elizabeth I and her favourite Robert Dudley, Earl of Leicester.

As well as caring for and managing many properties and ruins in the region – including the highly unusual Wigmore Castle – English Heritage undertakes projects to repair and restore these nationally important sites.

Recently, conservation work has begun on Leicester's Gatehouse, built by Sir Robert Dudley, in the 16th century to recieve and entertain Elizabeth I. Despite regular care and maintenance, the building has deteriorated in recent years, and has been closed to the public.

The first phase of restoration work is due for completion in 2005, involving extensive repairs to the exterior and interior of the gatehouse. A second phase of interior development is planned for the next year. This will secure the gatehouse's future as an exciting historical venue for public visits, educational use and corporate events.

www.english-heritage.org.uk/westmidlands

ACTON BURNELL CASTLE

SHROPSHIRE

The warm red sandstone shell of a fortified 13th-century manor house. It was the site of the first parliament at which the commons were formally represented.

OPENING TIMES

Any reasonable time

HOW TO FIND US

Direction: Located in Acton Burnell, signposted from A49, 8 miles S of Shrewsbury

Train: Shrewsbury or Church Stretton, both 8 miles

MAP	Page 262 (4B)
	OS Map 126 (ref SJ 534019)

ARTHUR'S STONE

HEREFORDSHIRE

ARTHUR'S STONE

Situated near the Welsh border, Arthur's Stone is an impressive prehistoric burial chamber formed of large blocks of stone.

OPENING TIMES

Any reasonable time

HOW TO FIND US

Direction: 7 miles E of Hay-on-Wye off B4348 near Dorstone

Bus: Stagecoach in South Wales 39, Yeomans Canyon 40 Hereford – Brecon to within ¾ mile

MAP	Page 262 (7B)
	OS Map 148 (ref SO 319431)

BOSCOBEL HOUSE AND THE ROYAL OAK

SHROPSHIRE   SEE OPPOSITE PAGE

BUILDWAS ABBEY

SHROPSHIRE – TF8 7BW

The extensive ruins of a Cistercian abbey, including much of its fine 12th-century church. In a woodland setting beside the River Severn, not far from the Iron Bridge.

NON-MEMBERS

Adult	£2.60
Concession	£2.00
Child	£1.30

BUILDWAS ABBEY

OPENING TIMES

24 Mar-31 May, Thu-Mon	10am-5pm
1 Jun-31 Aug, daily	10am-6pm
1-30 Sep, Thu-Mon	10am-5pm

HOW TO FIND US

Direction: On S bank of River Severn on A4169, 2 miles W of Ironbridge

Train: Telford Central 6 miles

Bus: Arriva 96 Telford-Shrewsbury (passes close to ≥ Telford Central)

Tel: 01952 433274

Disabled access is limited.

MAP	Page 262 (4C)
	OS Map 127 (ref SJ 643043)

CANTLOP BRIDGE

SHROPSHIRE

This single-span, cast-iron road bridge over the Cound Brook was designed by the great engineer Thomas Telford, who was instrumental in shaping industrial Shropshire and the West Midlands.

OPENING TIMES

Any reasonable time

HOW TO FIND US

Direction: ¾ mile SW of Berrington on an unclassified road off A458

Train: Shrewsbury 5 miles

MAP	Page 262 (4B)
	OS Map 126 (ref SJ 517062)

BOSCOBEL HOUSE AND THE ROYAL OAK

SHROPSHIRE – ST19 9AR

Boscobel House was built around 1632, when John Gifford of Whiteladies converted a timber-framed farmhouse into a hunting lodge.

The Gifford family were Catholic, at a time when the religion was outlawed. Tradition holds that the true purpose of Boscobel was to serve as a secret place for the shelter of Catholics in time of need.

The house was, however, destined for greater importance. Following the execution of King Charles I in 1649, his eldest son made a brave attempt to regain the throne, but in 1651 his hopes were crushed at Worcester in the final conflict of the Civil War. Young Charles was forced to flee for his life.

Initially, the future King Charles II set out to cross the River Severn into Wales, but found his way blocked by Cromwell's patrols.

He sought refuge at Boscobel and hid first in what is now known as the Royal Oak and then spent the night in a priest-hole in the attic. He was escorted to other safe houses before escaping to France.

Boscobel later became a much visited place, although it remained a working farm. Sold to Walter Evans in 1812, it stayed in his family during the 19th century. In 1918, it was bought by the Earl of Bradford.

www.english-heritage.org.uk/boscobel

NON-MEMBERS

Adult	£4.60
Concession	£3.50
Child	£2.30
Family ticket	£11.50

NON-MEMBERS GROUNDS ONLY

Adult	£1.50
Concession	£1.10
Child	£0.80

The White Room

OPENING TIMES

24 Mar-31 May, Thu-Mon 10am-5pm
1 Jun-31 Aug, daily 10am-6pm
1 Sep-31 Oct, Thu-Mon 10am-5pm
Last entry one hour before closing.

HOW TO FIND US

Direction: On minor road from A41 to A5, 8 miles NW of Wolverhampton. 5 mins drive from M54 J3

Train: Cosford 3 miles

Tel: 01902 850244

Parking (coaches welcome).

MAP	Page 262 (4C)
	OS Map 127 (ref SJ 838082)

CLUN CASTLE

SHROPSHIRE

The spectacular riverside ruins of a Welsh Border Norman castle, its keep unusually set on the side of its mound.

OPENING TIMES

Any reasonable time

HOW TO FIND US

Direction: In Clun, off A488, 18 miles W of Ludlow

Train: Hopton Heath 6½ miles; Knighton 6½ miles

Guidebooks available from Stokesay Castle.

MAP — Page 262 (5B)
OS Map 137 (ref SO 299809)

CROXDEN ABBEY

STAFFORDSHIRE

CROXDEN ABBEY

The impressive remains of an abbey of Cistercian 'white monks', including towering fragments of its 13th-century church, infirmary and 14th-century abbot's lodging.

OPENING TIMES

All year round — 10am-5pm

HOW TO FIND US

Direction: 5 miles NW of Uttoxeter off A522

Train: Uttoxeter 6 miles

MAP — Page 262 (3D)
OS Map 128 (ref SK 066397)

EDVIN LOACH OLD CHURCH

HEREFORDSHIRE

A traditional English churchyard, Edvin Loach contains both a 19th-century church and the remains of an 11th-century church.

OPENING TIMES

Any reasonable time

HOW TO FIND US

Direction: Located 4 miles N of Bromyard on an unclassified road off B4203

MAP — Page 262 (6C)
OS Map 149 (ref SO 663584)

GOODRICH CASTLE

HEREFORDSHIRE   GO TO PAGE 170

HALESOWEN ABBEY

WEST MIDLANDS – B62 8RJ

Contact Regional Office on 0121 625 6820 for details.

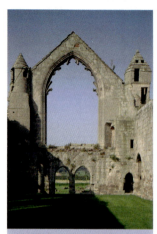

HAUGHMOND ABBEY

SHROPSHIRE

Extensive remains of a 12th-century Augustinian abbey. An exhibition commemorates 600 years since the nearby Battle of Shrewsbury. Picnic area and light refreshments available.

Introductory display and exhibition in the Museum explains the history of the Abbey and provides information about objects found on site and their relation to monastic life.

NON-MEMBERS

Adult	£2.60
Concession	£2.00
Children	£1.30

OPENING TIMES

24 Mar-31 May, Thu-Mon	10am-5pm
1 Jun-31 Aug, daily	10am-6pm
1-30 Sep, Thu-Mon	10am-5pm

HAUGHMOND ABBEY

HOW TO FIND US

Direction: Located 3 miles NE of Shrewsbury off B5062

Train: Shrewsbury 3½ miles

Bus: Arriva 519 Shrewsbury – Newport

Tel: 01743 709661

🅿️ ♿ 🏛️ 📷 🍴 🖼️ ⚠️
Disabled access (not easy).

MAP   Page 262 (4B)
        OS Map 126 (ref SJ 542152)

IRON BRIDGE

SHROPSHIRE   GO TO PAGE 171

KENILWORTH CASTLE

WARWICKSHIRE GO TO PAGE 172

LANGLEY CHAPEL

SHROPSHIRE

A small chapel tranquilly set all alone in charming countryside. Its atmospheric interior contains a perfect set of 17th-century timber furnishings, including a musicians' pew.

OPENING TIMES

Any reasonable time

HOW TO FIND US

Direction: 1½ miles S of Acton Burnell, on an unclassified road off A49; 9½ miles S of Shrewsbury

Train: Shrewsbury 7½ miles

MAP   Page 262 (5B)
        OS Map 149 (ref SO 663584)

LEIGH COURT BARN

WORCESTERSHIRE

This striking example of medieval architecture is the largest cruck structure in the UK. Once part of Leigh Court Manor, the barn has ten bays and two porches.

OPENING TIMES

24 Mar-30 Sep, Thu-Sun and Bank Hol Mons   10am-6pm

HOW TO FIND US

Direction: 5 miles W of Worcester on an unclassified road off A4103

Train: Worcester Foregate Street 5 miles

Bus: Bromyard Omnibus 417 from Worcester to within 1 mile

MAP   Page 262 (6C)
        OS Map 150 (ref SO 783535)

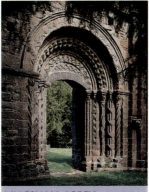

LILLESHALL ABBEY

SHROPSHIRE

LILLESHALL ABBEY

The extensive, evocative ruins of an abbey of Augustinian canons, dissolved in 1538, feature the remains of the 12th- and 13th-century church and cloister buildings, surrounded by lawns and ancient yew trees.

OPENING TIMES

24 Mar-30 Sep	10am-5pm
Closed	1 Oct-31 Mar

HOW TO FIND US

Direction: On an unclassified road off A518, 4 miles N of Oakengates

Train: Oakengates 4½ miles

Bus: Arriva 83, 481 Telford – Stafford (passes close to ≷ Telford Central and Stafford) to within 1 mile

Tel: 0121 625 6820 (Regional office)

Guidebooks from Haughmond Abbey, or upon order.

MAP   Page 262 (4C)
        OS Map 127 (ref SJ 738142)

ℹ️

Sign-up on-line for our email Members' Newsletter at **www.english-heritage.org.uk**

ℹ️ Visit **www.english-heritage. org.uk** for up-to-date events information and the latest news.

GOODRICH CASTLE

HEREFORDSHIRE – HR9 6HY

This fortress stands majestically on its old red sandstone crag commanding the passage of the River Wye into the picturesque wooded valley at Symonds Yat. A fortification may have been established here in the mists of prehistory, as aerial photography has traced ditches surrounding the site that appear to represent an Iron Age fort.

Within the courtyard of the castle proper stands a beautifully proportioned square keep, built in the 12th century. By 1102 the site was known as 'Godric's Castle', after its first lord, the English thegn Godric. Today we know it as Goodrich Castle.

The fortress played its part in the wars between Stephen and Matilda in the 12th century, and in 1216 witnessed a crushing defeat of the besieging barons beneath its walls by William Marshal, Earl of Pembroke.

William's five sons were all successively lords of the castle: but all had died in tragic circumstances without heirs by 1245.

In 1247, Goodrich passed to Henry III's half-brother, William de Valence, who renovated the defences and living quarters in the most up-to-date style. It is his great red sandstone castle which graces this beautiful part of Herefordshire today.

During the Civil War, Goodrich was held successively by both sides. Sir Henry Lingen's Royalists eventually surrendered in 1646 under threats of undermining, and a deadly Parliamentarian mortar – the famous 'Roaring Meg' – has now returned to the castle after over 350 years.

www.english-heritage.org.uk/ goodrichcastle

NON-MEMBERS

Adult	£4.30
Concession	£3.20
Child	£2.20
Family ticket	£10.80

OPENING TIMES

24 Mar-31 May	10am-5pm
1 Jun-31 Aug	10am-6pm
1 Sep-31 Oct	10am-5pm
1 Nov-28 Feb, Thu-Mon	10am-4pm
1-31 Mar	10am-5pm
Closed	24-26 Dec and 1 Jan

HOW TO FIND US

Direction: 5 miles S of Ross-on-Wye off A40

Bus: Stagecoach in Wye & Dean 34 Monmouth – Ross-on-Wye (with connection from Gloucester) to within ½ mile

Tel: 01600 890538

Family learning resources available. Parking (400 yards from castle).

MAP Page 262 (7C)
OS Map 162 (ref SO 577200)

IRON BRIDGE

SHROPSHIRE

The world's first iron bridge was cast by local ironmaster Abraham Darby and erected over the River Severn in 1779. Set in a spectacular wooded gorge, Iron Bridge is now Britain's best known industrial monument and a World Heritage Site.

Iron Bridge is the perfect place to begin a tour of the many industrial, ceramic, decorative arts and living history museums in the area, and of the many other English Heritage sites nearby.

These include Buildwas Abbey, Wenlock Priory, Wroxeter Roman City and Stokesay Castle.

Latest research into how the bridge was constructed shows that 70% of the parts were 'made to fit'. A half-sized replica built for a TV programme is on view at Blist's Hill Museum. The toll house display was opened in 2003 by Her Majesty the Queen.

OPENING TIMES

Any reasonable time

HOW TO FIND US

Direction: Adjacent to A4169

Bus: From Telford (all services pass close to ≋ Telford Central and Wellington Telford West)

MAP   Page 262 (4C)
       OS Map 127 (ref SJ 672034)

KENILWORTH CASTLE
WARWICKSHIRE – CV8 1NE

Kenilworth Castle has been intimately linked with some of the most important names in English history. Today, with its impressive Norman keep, John of Gaunt's great hall, and the magnificent buildings built for Queen Elizabeth I, it is amongst the largest castle ruins in England.

The castle in its landscape is a remarkable time-capsule of medieval and Tudor history. The Norman keep remains at the centre of King John's expansion of the defences from 1210, including the curtain walls and defensive towers of the outer court. A moat led to an enormous mere or shallow lake, effectively putting the castle on an island.

Kenilworth was granted to Simon de Montfort by Henry III in 1253. Simon was the leader of a reforming campaign, which resulted in civil war and his death in 1265 at the Battle of Evesham. His supporters were besieged here for nine months, until overcome by disease. As crown property, the castle thereafter passed to the Duchy of Lancaster. In 1327, Edward II was imprisoned here and forced to renounce the throne, before his transfer to Berkeley Castle and alleged murder by red hot poker.

By 1394, John of Gaunt created the splendid great hall and private apartments of the inner court, turning the fortress into a palace. Back in royal ownership, it became a place of leisure for Henry VIII. Edward VI granted it to the Dudleys, and Elizabeth I's favourite, Robert Dudley, Earl of Leicester, added more

fine buildings to receive the queen and her court. Kenilworth became the focus of extravagant hospitality and festivities: the elaborate gatehouse, stables and recreated Tudor garden still bear witness to this high point in its history.

Tales woven by Sir Walter Scott in his book *Kenilworth* (1821) – concerning Dudley, his wife who died in strange circumstances, and the Virgin Queen – still lend extra glamour to the castle, but it never saw such glories again. After the Civil War, Kenilworth was partially demolished by Parliamentary troops; it fell into ruin and its great lake was drained away.

The castle was saved for the nation in 1938. It remains a powerful reminder of great leaders, their glories, pleasures and rebellions. It also offers stunning countryside views – with the Millennium trail from the castle to the Pleasaunce one of the best ways to enjoy them.

During the summer months you can make the most of the tea room at the castle. An interactive model and gift shop can also be found at the site.

www.english-heritage.org.uk/
kenilworthcastle

The Barn

173

NON-MEMBERS

Adult	£4.95
Concession	£3.70
Child	£2.50
Family ticket	£12.40

OPENING TIMES

24 Mar-31 May	10am-5pm
1 Jun-31 Aug	10am-6pm
1 Sep-31 Oct	10am-5pm
1 Nov-28 Feb	10am-4pm
1-31 Mar	10am-5pm
Closed	24-26 Dec and 1 Jan

HOW TO FIND US

Direction: In Kenilworth off A46. Clearly signposted from the town centre, off B4103

Train: Warwick and Coventry 5 miles

Bus: 12 Coventry – Leamington Spa, X16 Stratford-upon-Avon – Leamington Spa, X17 Coventry – Warwick, 539 Warwick – Kenilworth to within a few minutes walk. Travel line: 0870 608 2608

Local Tourist Information Kenilworth: 01926 748900

Audio tours (also in French and German).

Disabled visitors are advised to use the north entrance, opposite the Queen and Castle public house; phone in advance for access.

Family learning resources available.

Tearoom (Open Easter-Oct daily, Tel: 01926 864376).

MAP	Page 262 (5E)
	OS Map 140 (ref SP 278723)

174

MITCHELL'S FOLD STONE CIRCLE

SHROPSHIRE

Bronze Age stone circle set in dramatic moorland on Stapeley Hill. It once consisted of some 30 stones, 15 of which are still visible.

Managed by Shropshire County Council.

OPENING TIMES

Any reasonable time

HOW TO FIND US

Direction: 16 miles SW of Shrewsbury

Train: Welshpool 10 miles

Bus: Minsterley/Arriva 553 Shrewsbury – Bishop's Castle (passes close to ⇌ Shrewsbury) to within 1 mile

Tel: 01939 232771

MAP	Page 262 (5B)
	OS Map 137 (ref SO 304984)

MORETON CORBET CASTLE

SHROPSHIRE

The Corbet family replaced their fortified house with a stone castle in about 1239. This was extended in 1538, and again in the 1580s with a great Elizabethan wing, now itself a spectacular ruin.

OPENING TIMES

Any reasonable time

HOW TO FIND US

Direction: In Moreton Corbet off B5063; 7 miles NE of Shrewsbury

Train: Yorton 4 miles

Bus: Arriva/First X64 Shrewsbury – Hanley (passes close to ⇌ Shrewsbury and Stoke-on-Trent) to within 1 mile

Guidebooks from Buildwas and Haughmond Abbeys.

LONGTOWN CASTLE

HEREFORDSHIRE

This striking cylindrical keep, perched atop a large earthen motte, was built c.1200 and offers magnificent views of the Black Mountains. The walls are about 4.5 metres (15 feet) thick.

OPENING TIMES

Any reasonable time

HOW TO FIND US

Direction: Located 4 miles WSW of Abbey Dore, off B4347

MAP	Page 262 (7B)
	OS Map 161 (ref SO 321291)

MAP	Page 262 (4C)
	OS Map 126 (ref SJ 561231)

MORTIMER'S CROSS WATER MILL

HEREFORDSHIRE – HR6 9PE

A rare one-man-operated 18th-century water mill in part working order. There are attractive gardens and woodland walks. Nearby there is a stone weir and the significant Aymestrey Limestone Quarry.

There are special day and evening guided tours for groups, and every Bank Holiday Monday is a demonstration grinding day. Please call for details.

NON-MEMBERS

Adult	£4.00
Concession	£3.50
Child	£2.50
Under 5	Free

OPENING TIMES

Easter-30 Sep, Sat-Sun 10am-4pm
Other times by arrangement

HOW TO FIND US

Direction: Located 7 miles NW of Leominster on B4362

Train: Leominster 7½ miles

Tel: 01568 708820

Disabled access (exterior and ground floor only).

Warning (there are steep river banks and sluice channels which are hazardous at all times).

MAP   Page 262 (6B)
        OS Map 148 (ref SO 426637)

OLD OSWESTRY HILL FORT

SHROPSHIRE

A large Iron Age fort with a series of five ramparts, an elaborate western entrance and unusual earthwork cisterns.

OPENING TIMES

Any reasonable time

HOW TO FIND US

Direction: 1 mile N of Oswestry, off an unclassified road off A483

Train: Gobowen 2 miles

Bus: Arriva 2, 53, 63 from 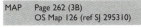 Gobowen

MAP   Page 262 (3B)
        OS Map 126 (ref SJ 295310)

ROTHERWAS CHAPEL

HEREFORDSHIRE

The family chapel of the Roman Catholic Bodenham family. The originally simple medieval building has 16th-century features, a rebuilt 18th-century tower, and a mid-Victorian side chapel and high altar.

OPENING TIMES

Any reasonable time. Key keeper located at nearby filling station

HOW TO FIND US

Direction: 1½ miles SE of Hereford on B4399, left into Chapel Road

Train: Hereford 3½ miles

Bus: First 78 from Hereford

Disabled access (kissing gate).

MAP   Page 262 (7B)
        OS Map 149 (ref SO 536383)

i

English Heritage members can take up to 6 children, as part of a family group, into our properties at no extra cost (see page 6).

STOKESAY CASTLE SHROPSHIRE – SY7 9AH

Stokesay Castle is the finest and best preserved 13th-century fortified manor house in England. It offers visitors a unique glimpse into a distant age, when strength and elegance were combined.

Interior of the hall

Detail of carved overmantel in the Solar

The castle stands amid peaceful countryside near the Welsh border, sited in a picturesque group with its timber-framed 17th-century gatehouse and the parish church.

Stokesay's magnificent great hall, with its gabled windows, almost untouched since medieval times, also retains its original staircase. There is, too, an open octagonal hearth and an innovative and fine cruck-built timber roof.

It was Lawrence of Ludlow, one of the most renowned wool merchants of his era, who began building this fortified manor house soon after 1281. The completion of his work is perhaps indicated by the licence to crenellate, which he obtained from Edward I for the three-storied south tower.

The house's impressive solar chamber boasts a breathtaking Jacobean fireplace. The chief feature of this is an elaborately carved overmantel, which was originally painted in gold, pink, red, green and white.

Across the courtyard stands the truly delightful 17th-century gatehouse, built in about 1640. This is an elaborate example of the regional style of timber framing, with a highly decorated exterior and two brick chimney stacks, one of which is original.

The audio tour at Stokesay will help you to imagine the castle as the centre of medieval life in the district. A successful combination of impressive fortification and comfortable residence, its grounds include cottage-style gardens. The site includes an extensive gift shop.

www.english-heritage.org.uk/ stokesay

NON-MEMBERS

Adult	£4.60
Concession	£3.50
Children	£2.30
Family ticket	£11.50

OPENING TIMES

24 Mar-31 May, Thu-Mon	10am-5pm
1 Jun-31 Aug, daily	10am-6pm
1 Sep-31 Oct, Thu-Mon	10am-5pm
1 Nov-28 Feb, Fri-Sun	10am-4pm
1-31 Mar, Thu-Mon	10am-5pm
Closed	24-26 Dec and 1 Jan

HOW TO FIND US

Direction: 7 miles NW of Ludlow off A49

Train: Craven Arms 1 mile

Bus: Arriva/Whittlebus 435 Shrewsbury – Ludlow

Tel: 01588 672544

Local Tourist Information Ludlow: 01584 875053

Disabled access (call custodian for details).

Family learning resources available.

Parking (300m from the main entrance across rough grass but disabled visitors may be set down closer to the entrance). Please call in advance.

Tearoom (Seasonal: 1 Apr-31 Oct).

MAP   Page 262 (5B)
       OS Map 148 (ref SO 436817)

WALL ROMAN SITE (LETOCETUM)

STAFFORDSHIRE – WS14 0AW

178

Wall was an important staging post on Watling Street, the Roman military road to North Wales. It provided overnight accommodation for travelling Roman officials and imperial messengers. The foundations of an inn and bathhouse can be seen, and many of the excavated finds are displayed in the on-site museum.

Managed by EH and owned by the National Trust.

NON-MEMBERS

Adult	£2.90
Concession	£2.20
Child	£1.50

National Trust members admitted free, but small charge on EH special events days

OPENING TIMES

24 Mar-31 May	10am-5pm
1 Jun-31 Aug	10am-6pm
1 Sep-31 Oct	10am-5pm

HOW TO FIND US

Direction: Off A5 at Wall, near Lichfield

Train: Shenstone 1½ miles

Tel: 01543 480768

Audio tours (£1.50 for National Trust members).

MAP   Page 262 (4D)
       OS Map 139 (ref SK 098066)

WENLOCK PRIORY

SHROPSHIRE – TF13 6HS

The ruins of a large Cluniac priory, Wenlock was once part of the Europe-wide network of the immense French Abbey of Cluny. The remains include a rare monk's washbasin and a finely decorated chapter house.

NON-MEMBERS

Adult	£3.30
Concession	£2.50
Child	£1.70

OPENING TIMES

24 Mar-31 May, Thu-Mon	10am-5pm
1 Jun-31 Aug	10am-6pm
1 Sep-31 Oct, Thu-Mon	10am-5pm
1 Nov-28 Feb, Fri-Sun	10am-4pm
1-31 Mar, Thu-Mon	10am-5pm
Closed	24-26 Dec and 1 Jan

HOW TO FIND US

Direction: In Much Wenlock

Train: Telford Central 9 miles

Bus: Shropshire Bus 436/7 Shrewsbury – Bridgnorth (passes close to Shrewsbury)

Tel: 01952 727466

MAP   Page 262 (5C)
       OS Map 127 (ref SJ 625001)

WHITE LADIES PRIORY

SHROPSHIRE

The remains of the late 12th-century church of a small nunnery of 'white ladies' or Augustinian canonesses, surrounded by picturesque woodland.

OPENING TIMES

1 Apr-31 Oct	Any reasonable time
Closed	1 Nov-31 Mar

HOW TO FIND US

Direction: Located 1 mile SW of Boscobel House off an unclassified road between A41 and A5; 8 miles NW of Wolverhampton

Train: Cosford 2½ miles

MAP   Page 262 (4C)
       OS Map 127 (ref SJ 826076)

Check *Heritage Today* for news and information on forthcoming events and exclusive members' offers.

WIGMORE CASTLE
HEREFORDSHIRE

Once the stronghold of the turbulent Mortimer family, Wigmore Castle was abandoned by the 17th century. Now it is among the most remarkable ruins in England, largely buried up to first floor level by earth and fallen masonry. Yet many of its fortifications survive to full height, including parts of the keep on its towering mound.

OPENING TIMES

Any reasonable time

HOW TO FIND US

Direction: Located 8 miles W of Ludlow on A4110. Accessible via footpath ¾ mile from the village on Mortimer Way

Train: Bucknell 6 miles, Ludlow 10 miles

Bus: R & B 735 from Ludlow, Mon only

P ♀ ♂ ♛ ⚠

Toilets (including disabled) at the Village Hall and also the Compasses Hotel by arrangement, Tel: 01568 770705.

There are steep steps to the summit, which are hazardous in icy conditions. Children must stay under close control and should not climb the walls or banks. Strong footwear is recommended. There is no custodial presence.

MAP   Page 262 (6B)
       OS Map 148 (ref SO 408693)

Kenilworth Castle

WITLEY COURT AND GARDENS

WORCESTERSHIRE – WR6 6JT

A hundred years ago, Witley Court was one of England's great country houses, holding many extravagant parties. Today it is a spectacular ruin, remaining from a disastrous fire in 1937.

View across the front pool

The spectacular ruins of this once great house are surrounded by magnificent landscaped gardens – the 'Monster Work' of William Nesfield – which still contain huge stone fountains. The largest, representing Perseus and Andromeda, which has now been restored, was described as making the 'noise of an express train' when it was fired.

Before 1846, when William Humble Ward (later first Earl of Dudley) inherited Witley Court, the land surrounding the house was laid out in the English landscape style originated by Lord Foley. As part of Ward's transformation of the estate, he called in the leading landscape designer of the time, William Andrews Nesfield, whose skills in designing intricate and elegant parterres were complemented by his great ability as an artist and engineer.

Nesfield started work in 1854, creating the south parterre with its great Perseus and Andromeda fountain. His scheme involved elegantly designed plantings of clipped evergreens and shrubs, with parterres that were enclosed by more clipped evergreens.

The central avenue of planting from the house led through the fountains to the Golden Gates, terminating the south parterre. The east parterre garden with its Flora Fountain was designed in the *Parterre de Broderie* style, meaning that it was intended to have the appearance of embroidery, with its box-edged shapes filled with coloured gravel and flowers.

Following a disastrous fire in 1937, the Witley Estate, including its gardens, fell into long decline. English Heritage has now restored the south garden.

The Woodland Walks in the North Park pass many different species of tree and shrub, acquired from all over the world to create a showpiece. A new garden in 'The Wilderness' is part of the Contemporary Heritage Garden project, designed by Colvin and Moggridge. This provides yet more opportunities for walking within Witley Court's grounds.

Attached to Witley Court is Great Witley Church, which has a superb baroque interior (not managed by English Heritage). The church also has a tea room close by, and

Witley Court has a superb gift shop. The Perseus and Andromeda fountain is back in working order, even the original high cascades are operating. Please call the site (01299 896636) for details of the fountain firing.

www.english-heritage.org.uk/ witleycourt

NON-MEMBERS

Adult	£4.95
Concession	£3.70
Child	£2.50
Family ticket	£12.40

OPENING TIMES

24 Mar-31 May	10am-5pm
1 Jun-31 Aug	10am-6pm
1 Sep-31 Oct	10am-5pm
1 Nov-28 Feb, Thu-Mon	10am-4pm
1-31 Mar	10am-5pm
Closed	24-26 Dec and 1 Jan

HOW TO FIND US

Direction: 10 miles NW of Worcester on A443

Train: Droitwich Spa 8½ miles

Bus: Yarranton 758 Worcester – Tenbury Wells (passes close to ⇌ Worcester Foregate Street)

Tel: 01299 896636

Local Tourist Information Droitwich Spa: 01905 774312

Disabled access (exterior and grounds only).

Family learning resources available.

Tearooms open daily, Apr-Sep and Sat and Sun, Oct (not managed by EH).

Perseus and Andromeda fountain

Waterfall in the park

MAP	Page 262 (6C)
	OS Map 150 (ref SO 769649)

North wall of the frigidarium

WROXETER ROMAN CITY

SHROPSHIRE – SY5 6PH

Wroxeter was the fourth largest city in Roman Britain. Much of the site where it stood has escaped subsequent development, and so it can provide extensive information about what the city was like. Originally a legionary fortress, it later developed into a thriving civilian city populated by retired soldiers and traders.

Today, the most impressive features are the second-century municipal baths and the remains of the huge wall dividing them from the exercise hall, right in the city's heart. All around were the roads, houses and trading stalls of the settlement. The site museum explains how the city worked and gives an insight into the lives of those who lived there. It includes artefacts from the site.

www.english-heritage.org.uk/wroxeter

NON-MEMBERS

Adult	£4.00
Concession	£3.00
Child	£2.00
Family ticket	£10.00

OPENING TIMES

24 Mar-31 May	10am-5pm
1 Jun-31 Aug	10am-6pm
1 Sep-31 Oct	10am-5pm
1 Nov-28 Feb	10am-4pm
1-31 Mar	10am-5pm
Closed	24-26 Dec and 1 Jan

HOW TO FIND US

Direction: Located at Wroxeter, 5 miles E of Shrewsbury on B4380

Train: Shrewsbury 5½ miles; Wellington Telford West 6 miles

Bus: Arriva 96 Telford – Shrewsbury (passes close to ⬛ Telford Central)

Tel: 01743 761330

Family learning resources available.

MAP	Page 262 (4B)
	OS Map 126 (ref SJ 565087)

The Royal Oak at Boscobel House (see page 167)

OTHER HISTORIC ATTRACTIONS

DISCOUNTED ENTRY TO OUR MEMBERS (DISCOUNTS MAY NOT APPLY ON EVENT DAYS)

STONELEIGH ABBEY

WARWICKSHIRE – CV8 2LF

Originally founded for Cistercian Monks, Stoneleigh Abbey reflects a rich mix of history. Charles I was entertained here, Jane Austen uses descriptions of it in two of her novels and Queen Victoria visited it in 1858. The estate comprises a medieval gatehouse – one of the few in Britain still standing and complete, the Great West Wing with State Rooms decorated in fine, free-hand plasterwork and a Gothic Revival riding school and stables. Tearoom facilities available.

ENTRY (WEST WING & STABLES)

Adult	£6.00
Senior Citizens	£4.00
Child	£2.50

One child free with each Adult ticket

ENTRY (GROUNDS ONLY)

Per Person	£2.50

10% discount to EH members
All prices are subject to change and are correct at time of going to print.

OPENING TIMES

Good Friday-31 Oct
Tue, Wed, Thu, Sun and Bank Hols
Guided Tours   11am, 1pm, 3pm
Grounds open   10am-5pm

HOW TO FIND US

Direction: B4115 off the A452/A46, just a short journey from Kenilworth Castle

Tel: 01926 858535

www.stoneleighabbey.org

MAP   Page 262 (5E)
OS Map 140 (ref SP 318712)

Flowers at Brodsworth Hall Gardens

YORKSHIRE

The people of Yorkshire have an ancient and abiding pride in this northern land of majestic landscapes and ancient kingdoms. And there is a fierce sense of independence, which has often revealed itself in rebellion and the struggle for power.

PROPERTIES

SEE INDIVIDUAL LISTINGS FOR DETAILS

EAST YORKSHIRE
Burton Agnes Manor House, Howden Minster, Skipsea Castle

NORTH LINCOLNSHIRE
Gainsthorpe Medieval Village, St Peter's Church, Thornton Abbey and Gatehouse

NORTH YORKSHIRE
Aldborough Roman Site, Byland Abbey, Clifford's Tower, Easby Abbey, Fountains Abbey, Helmsley Castle, Kirkham Priory, Marmion Tower, Middleham Castle, Mount Grace Priory, Pickering Castle, Piercebridge Roman Bridge, Richmond Castle, Rievaulx Abbey, St Mary's Church, Scarborough Castle, Spofforth Castle, Stanwick Iron Age Fortifications, Steeton Hall Gateway, Wharram Percy Deserted Medieval Village, Wheeldale Roman Road, Whitby Abbey

SOUTH YORKSHIRE
Brodsworth Hall and Gardens, Conisbrough Castle, Monk Bretton Priory, Roche Abbey

Comprehensive map of our sites
PAGE 265

• RICHMOND

WHITBY •

• NORTHALLERTON

SCARBOROUGH •

HELMSLEY •

NORTH YORKSHIRE

BRIDLINGTON •

• HARROGATE

YORK •

EAST YORKSHIRE

• BRADFORD

• LEEDS

KINGSTON-UPON-HULL •

WEST YORKSHIRE

• WAKEFIELD

NORTH LINCOLNSHIRE

NORTH EAST LINCOLNSHIRE

• DONCASTER

SOUTH YORKSHIRE

• SHEFFIELD

Wharram Percy Deserted Medieval Village

DIVERSITY AND DELIGHT OF YORKSHIRE

From medieval villages and ancient abbeys to castle strongholds and country houses, the region's role in shaping national events is clearly displayed in the vast diversity of Yorkshire's English Heritage sites.

Over the past year, English Heritage has used archaeology and new scientific techniques to reveal even more about many of its sites.

At Brodsworth Hall and Gardens, Head Gardener Dave Avery has used a Heritage Lottery Fund grant to spend the last five years painstakingly and lovingly restoring the gardens to their 1860s heyday. It has been an incredible journey, which has

involved identifying a completely new cultivar of fern, reviving long neglected plants such as Cyclamen repandum, and planting over 100,000 snowdrop bulbs by hand.

Recent archaeological finds at Helmsley Castle have revealed that, far from being a minor castle, Helmsley is a 'Cradle of English Chivalry'. These discoveries are displayed in exhibitions in the award-winning contemporary visitor centre, and used in a new audio-tour. Access at the castle has also been improved.

At Scarborough Castle, three thousand years of Yorkshire's turbulent coastal history are

explored in new exhibitions and displays of artefacts excavated from the site, and at Byland Abbey, new interpretation in the museum explores the importance of the impressive ruins.

At Wharram Percy Deserted Medieval Village, new research by English Heritage has changed our understanding of why so many medieval villages were deserted by their residents. It has also revealed that life at Wharram could be both violent and short. Yet skeletal examinations have shown that Anglo-Saxon medical skills were anything but primitive, with cranial surgery being performed on even the poorest of society's classes.

www.english-heritage.org.uk/yorkshire

BRODSWORTH HALL AND GARDENS
SOUTH YORKSHIRE – DN5 7XJ

Built in the 1860s, Brodsworth Hall is designed in the Italianate style and was furnished in the opulent fashion of the time. Much of its original scheme survives to the present day, making it one of England's most complete surviving Victorian country houses. English Heritage has chosen to conserve rather than restore the interiors, recounting the tale of how a once opulent Victorian house has grown comfortably old and inviting to all.

The flower garden

Charles Sabine Augustus Thell-usson inherited the Brodsworth Estate in 1859. He commissioned a new mansion – Brodsworth Hall – to replace the original house, and this was lived in by successive members of the family until 1988.

The history of the house is brought alive through the 'Maids and Mistresses' exhibition. Displays, photographs and audio material show what life was like for women at Brodsworth over the last 150 years. Other exhibitions offering an insight into life at Brodsworth include 'Serving the House', 'Discovering Chintz', 'Family Life' and 'The Gardens'.

Garden Statue

For Garden Lovers

The gardens have been subst-antially restored since English Heritage took over management of the property in 1990, and are now a copybook example of 1860s design. Many years of pruning and tree removal have opened up vistas last enjoyed before World War 1.

The flower garden displays a fine selection of authentic period bedding plants, and the romantic views from the restored summer-house take in the quarry garden, paths, bridges and garden buildings. Of special interest are the restored woodland garden, the statue walks and the fern dell, which is planted with unusual plant specimens.

The gardens at Brodsworth Hall are a delight in any season, but here are our suggested dates for viewing specific collections. Please bear in mind that the exact display times are subject to seasonal variation.

Feb /Mar
130,000 snowdrops and 36 varieties of daffodil.

Apr
14,000 bulbs and 5,000 tulips form the spring bedding.

May
Laburnum Arch in flower.

May/June
Rose display and over 100 historic varieties of geranium at peak.

July
Summer bedding around the fountain; 250 varieties of ferns at their best.

Oct
Ornamental trees display their autumn colours.

Nov-Jan
Over 400 yew trees and many laurels provide shelter for a bracing winter walk.

BRODSWORTH HALL & GARDENS

The kitchen

For Families:

The garden has picnic tables and large areas of grass for expending energy! The hall has two rooms on the first floor with activities for children and activity sheets to keep youngsters interested throughout the furnished interiors. A dedicated baby changing room is available in the toilets. Visitors please note that prams and back carriers for babies are not allowed in the fragile interiors of the hall. However, staff can provide small padded pushchairs and slings for visitors' use.

For visitors with mobility needs, a complimentary return buggy service is available to transport visitors from the car park to the hall or tea room. There are over 2 miles of smooth paths and benches throughout the gardens to enable visitors to rest and enjoy the atmosphere, although some steps and steep slopes limit access to certain parts of the garden.

The hall is accessed by ramps and although extensive, has seats along the route for visitors to use, many handrails and a lift to enable visitors to enjoy the first floor.

New for 2005

Garden Explorer packs to help children and families to investigate the gardens.

www.english-heritage.org.uk/brodsworthhall

The dining room

NON-MEMBERS HOUSE & GARDENS:	
Adult	£6.60
Concession	£5.00
Child	£3.30

NON-MEMBERS GARDENS ONLY:	
Adult	£4.60
Concession	£3.50
Child	£2.30

OPENING TIMES

House:
19 Mar-2 Oct, Tue-Sun and Bank Hols 1pm-5pm
3-31 Oct, Sat-Sun 12pm-4pm
Gardens and Tearoom:
19 Mar-30 Oct, daily 10am-5.30pm
Gardens, Tearoom, Shop & Servants' Wing:
1 Nov-31 Mar, Sat-Sun 10am-4pm
Last admission ½ hour before closing

HOW TO FIND US

Direction: In Brodsworth, 5 miles NW of Doncaster off A635 Barnsley Road; from junction 37 of A1(M)

Train: South Elmsall 4 miles; Moorthorpe 4½ miles; Doncaster 5½ miles

Bus: Yorkshire Traction 211 Doncaster-Barnsley (passing close ⊠ Doncaster and passing ⊠ South Elmsall & Moorthorpe). Alight at Pickburn, Five Lanes End, thence ½ mile walk

Local Tourist Information Doncaster: 01302 734309

Tel: 01302 724969 (info-line)

Family learning resources available.
No cameras (house).

MAP	Page 265 (5G)
	OS Map 111 (ref SE 506070)

ALDBOROUGH ROMAN SITE

N. YORKSHIRE – YO51 9EP

This was the principal town of the Brigantes, whose earlier tribal stronghold can be seen at Stanwick. The remains include parts of the Roman defences and two spectacular mosaic pavements. Further clues to the Roman town can be found in the village, from its layout to the Roman masonry reused in the 14th-century church. The on-site museum displays local Roman finds.

NON-MEMBERS

Adult	£2.60
Concession	£2.00
Child	£1.30

OPENING TIMES

19 Mar-31 Jul, Thu-Mon	10am-5pm
1-31 Aug, daily	10am-5pm
1-30 Sep, Thu-Mon	10am-5pm

HOW TO FIND US

Direction: Located in Aldborough, ¾ mile SE of Boroughbridge on a minor road off B6265; within 1 mile of junction of A1 and A6055

Bus: Arriva/Harrogate Coach Travel 142 ⇌ York-Ripon

Tel: 01423 322768

Family learning resources available. Dogs on leads (restricted areas only).

MAP	Page 265 (3G)
	OS Map 99 (ref SE 405662)

English Heritage membership makes a lovely gift.

Call 0870 333 1181 or visit **www.english-heritage.org.uk/ gift** for more details.

BRODSWORTH HALL AND GARDENS

S. YORKSHIRE   GO TO PAGE 188

BURTON AGNES MANOR HOUSE

E. YORKSHIRE

A rare and well-preserved example of a Norman house, encased in brick during the 17th and 18th centuries.

OPENING TIMES

1 Apr-31 Oct, daily	11am-5pm

The nearby Burton Agnes Hall and Gardens are privately owned and are not managed by English Heritage

HOW TO FIND US

Direction: In Burton Agnes village, 5 miles SW of Bridlington on A166

Train: Nafferton 5 miles

Bus: E Yorkshire 744 ⇌ York-Bridlington

MAP	Page 265 (3J)
	OS Map 101 (ref TA 102632)

BYLAND ABBEY

N. YORKSHIRE – YO61 4BD

This ruin, set on the edge of the beautiful North York Moors National Park, was once one of the great northern Cistercian monasteries. It is a truly outstanding example of early Gothic architecture, and its splendid decorated tiles are a testament to its earlier magnificence.

Both Rievaulx Abbey and Helmsley Castle are within reasonable travelling distance.

New for 2005

The updated museum combines examples of the intricate stonework that once adorned the abbey with new displays and family-friendly books and activities.

NON-MEMBERS

Adult	£2.90
Concession	£2.20
Child	£1.50

OPENING TIMES

19 Mar-31 Jul, Thu-Mon	10am-5pm
1-31 Aug, daily	10am-5pm
1-30 Sep, Thu-Mon	10am-5pm

HOW TO FIND US

Direction: 2 miles S of A170, between Thirsk and Helmsley; near Coxwold village

Train: Thirsk 10 miles

Bus: Stephensons 31/X, Moorsbus M15 York-Helmsley

Tel: 01347 868614

Family learning resources available. Parking (opposite the Abbey). Toilets (Abbey Inn opposite the Abbey).

MAP	Page 265 (2G)
	OS Map 100 (ref SE 549789)

CLIFFORD'S TOWER

N. YORKSHIRE – YO1 9SA

In 1068-9, William the Conqueror built two motte and bailey castles in York, to strengthen his military hold on the north. Clifford's Tower, an unusual four-lobed keep built in the 13th century atop the mound of William's larger fortress, is now the principal surviving stonework remnant of York's medieval castle. The sweeping views of the city from the tower still show why it played such an important part in controlling northern England.

NON-MEMBERS

Adult	£2.80
Concession	£2.10
Child	£1.40
Family ticket	£7.00

OPENING TIMES

19 Mar-30 Sep, daily	10am-6pm
1-31 Oct, daily	10am-5pm
1 Nov-31 Mar, daily:	10am-4pm
Closed	24-26 Dec and 1 Jan

HOW TO FIND US

Direction: In Tower St, York

Train: York 1 mile

Bus: From surrounding areas

Tel: 01904 646940

Local Tourist Information York: 01904 621756

🅿 🏠 🚻 ⊠ 🍴 🛡 ⚠

Family learning resources available. Parking (local charge).

MAP	Page 265 (3G)
	OS Map 105 (ref SE 605515)

CONISBROUGH CASTLE

S. YORKSHIRE – DN12 3BU

The white, cylindrical keep of this 12th-century castle is a spectacular structure. Built of magnesian limestone , it is the only example of its kind in England. Recently restored, with two new floors and a roof, it is a fine example of medieval architecture, and was one of the inspirations for Sir Walter Scott's classic novel, *Ivanhoe*.

Managed by The Ivanhoe Trust.

OPENING TIMES

1 Apr-30 Sep, daily	10am-5pm
(last admission 4.20pm)	
1 Oct-31 Mar, daily	10am-4pm
(last admission 3.20pm)	

EH members admitted free or with a discount during special events.

Guided, evening and school party tours offered. Available for private hire and special events. Please call before Sat visits during summer, as the castle may close early for private functions.

HOW TO FIND US

Direction: Located NE of Conisbrough town centre off A630; 4½ miles SW of Doncaster

Train: Conisbrough ½ mile

Bus: From surrounding areas

Tel: 01709 863329

❄ 🅿 ♿ 🚻 🏠 ⊠ ⚠

Dogs on leads (restricted areas only).

Parking (visitors with disabilities, please call the site to reserve a space).

MAP	Page 265 (5G)
	OS Map 111 (ref SK 515989)

EASBY ABBEY

N. YORKSHIRE

The substantial remains of the medieval abbey buildings stand in a beautiful setting by the River Swale near Richmond. The ruins can be reached via a pleasant walk from Richmond Castle.

OPENING TIMES

1 Apr-30 Sep, daily	10am-6pm
1-31 Oct, daily	10am-5pm
1 Nov-31 Mar, daily	10am-4pm
Closed	24-26 Dec and 1 Jan

HOW TO FIND US

Direction: 1 mile SE of Richmond, off B6271

Bus: Arriva X26/7, 27/8 Darlington-Richmond (pass close ≋ Darlington) then 1½ miles

🅿 🏠 🍴 📷 ⚠

Guidebooks (from Richmond Castle).

MAP	Page 265 (2F)
	OS Map 92 (ref NZ 185003)

GAINSTHORPE MEDIEVAL VILLAGE

N. LINCOLNSHIRE

GAINSTHORPE MEDIEVAL VILLAGE

A deserted medieval village, one of the best-preserved examples in England, revealed in a labyrinth of grassy humps and bumps.

OPENING TIMES
Any reasonable time

HOW TO FIND US
Direction: Located on minor road W of A15; S of Hibaldstow; 5 miles SW of Brigg

Train: Kirton Lindsey 3 miles

MAP Page 265 (5J)
OS Map 112 (ref SE 954011)

HELMSLEY CASTLE
N.YORKSHIRE   GO TO PAGE 194

HOWDEN MINSTER
E.YORKSHIRE

The elaborate ruins of a medieval chancel and chapter house (viewable only from the outside), attached to the large cathedral-like minster, now the parish church.

OPENING TIMES
Any reasonable time
Closed   24-26 Dec and 1 Jan

HOW TO FIND US
Direction: In Howden; 23 miles W of Kingston Upon Hull, 25 miles SE of York, near the junction of A63 and A614

Train: Howden 1½ miles

Bus: East Yorkshire 155/6 Goole-Hull

Parking (street parking nearby).

MAP Page 265 (4H)
OS Map 106 (ref SE 748283)

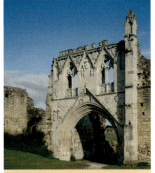

KIRKHAM PRIORY
N.YORKSHIRE – YO60 7JS

These intriguing ruins of an Augustinian priory include an elaborate gatehouse and monks' 'washroom', all set in the peaceful Derwent valley, an area of outstanding natural beauty in the Yorkshire Wolds. Explore the on-site interpretation, including the story of the secret visit of Winston Churchill and the role of the site in preparation for D-Day during World War II.

NON-MEMBERS
Adult	£2.90
Concession	£2.20
Child	£1.50

OPENING TIMES
19 Mar-30 Sep, daily   10am-6pm
1-31 Oct, Thur-Mon   10am-4pm

HOW TO FIND US
Direction: 5 miles SW of Malton, on a minor road off A64

Train: Malton 6 miles

Bus: Yorkshire Coastliner 840/2/3 Leeds-Scarborough (pass York and Malton) to within ¾ mile

Tel: 01653 618768

Family learning resources available.

MAP Page 265 (3H)
OS Map 100 (ref SE 736658)

MARMION TOWER
N.YORKSHIRE

A medieval gatehouse boasting a beautiful oriel window. There are fine medieval monuments, historically associated with the tower, in the adjacent church.

OPENING TIMES
1 Apr-30 Sep, daily   10am-6pm
1-31 Oct, daily   10am-5pm
1 Nov-31 Mar, daily   10am-4pm
Closed   24-26 Dec and 1 Jan

HOW TO FIND US
Direction: On A6108 in West Tanfield

Train: Thirsk 10 miles

MAP Page 265 (3F)
OS Map 99 (ref SE 268787)

You can find out more about the work of English Heritage at **www.english-heritage.org.uk**

193

HELMSLEY CASTLE

NORTH YORKSHIRE – YO62 5AB

The spectacular ruins of this 12th-century castle are situated on the edge of the medieval market town of Helmsley. Set amid massive earthworks and overlooking the Rye Valley, this impressive castle makes a dramatic sight.

The South Barbican and the outer ditch

This ancient castle now boasts two new features: an award-winning visitor centre which graces the grounds, and a striking exhibition within the castle buildings which tells the story of the fortress through interactive displays, an audio tour and an array of archaeological finds. These include some unique armour-piercing arrowheads, once at the forefront of military technology.

The castle was originally built by Walter Espec, one of the most powerful barons of his day, to mark the centre of his estate. It was consolidated by Robert de Roos in the late 12th and early 13th century, and remained in the de Roos family until 1478, when it was granted to George, Duke of Clarence. On his death, the castle passed to his brother Richard, Duke of Gloucester, who later became King Richard III.

When the monarch perished at the Battle of Bosworth in 1485, the castle was returned to the de Roos line. The Earls of Rutland subsequently inherited lordship of the castle

through marriage, and updated the west range of buildings into a fashionable Elizabethan residence.

Despite its medieval origins, the castle only saw action in the Civil War. Parliamentarian forces laid siege to Helmsley in 1644 and the occupants were eventually forced to surrender due to lack of food. Sir Thomas Fairfax was ordered to destroy the castle's many defences, including the symbolic keep, but took care to preserve the Elizabethan west range, which later became the home of his daughter in 1657.

Helmsley Castle regularly hosts living history events.

Access to all areas of the Castle has recently been improved, and there are plenty of places for picnics. Rievaulx and Byland Abbeys are both within reasonable travelling distance, including on foot via the Cleveland Way National Trail.

www.english-heritage.org.uk/ helmsleycastle

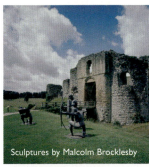
Sculptures by Malcolm Brocklesby

Visitor Centre

NON-MEMBERS

Adult	£4.00
Concession	£3.00
Child	£2.00
Family ticket	£10.00

OPENING TIMES

19 Mar-30 Sep, daily	10am-6pm
1 Oct-31 Mar, Thu-Mon	10am-4pm
Closed	24-26 Dec and 1 Jan

HOW TO FIND US

Direction: Near the town centre

Bus: Scarborough & District 128 from ⌦ Scarborough; Stephensons 31/X from York

Tel: 01439 770442

Family learning resources available.

Parking (large car park adjacent to castle; charge payable).

Toilets (in car park and town centre).

View of the North Barbican from the West

MAP	Page 265 (2G)
	OS Map 100 (ref SE 611836)

MIDDLEHAM CASTLE

N. YORKSHIRE – DL8 4QR

Middleham Castle was the childhood and favourite home of Richard III. This connection is still remembered in the town, and a requiem mass is held in the local church on the anniversary of Richard's death.

A Norman motte-and-bailey fortification existed at Middleham before the present castle was built between the 12th and 15th centuries. The earthworks are now dwarfed by the magnificent keep and masonry of what was once the 'Windsor of the North'.

An exhibition on some of the impressive personalities of the castle's past includes a replica of the beautiful Middleham Jewel, a 15th-century pendant decorated with a large sapphire which was found near the castle.

NON-MEMBERS

Adult	£3.30
Concession	£2.50
Child	£1.70

OPENING TIMES

19 Mar-30 Sep, daily	10am-6pm
1 Oct-31 Mar, Thu-Mon	10am-4pm
Closed	24-26 Dec and 1 Jan

HOW TO FIND US

Direction: Located at Middleham; 2 miles S of Leyburn on A6108

Bus: Dales & District 159 Ripon-Richmond

Tel: 01969 623899

Local Tourist Information Leyburn: 01969 623069

Disabled access (except keep).
Family learning resources available.
Toilets (in town centre).

MAP   Page 265 (2F)
       OS Map 99 (ref SE 127876)

MONK BRETTON PRIORY

S. YORKSHIRE

The sandstone ruins of a Cluniac monastery founded in 1153, including the remains of the 14th-century gatehouse.

OPENING TIMES

1 Apr-30 Sep, daily	10am-6pm
1-31 Oct, daily	10am-5pm
1 Nov-31 Mar, daily	10am-4pm
(managed by a key-keeper)	
Closed	24-26 Dec and 1 Jan

Charge may apply on event days

HOW TO FIND US

Direction: Located 1 mile E of Barnsley town centre, off A633

Train: Barnsley 2½ miles

Bus: From surrounding areas

MAP   Page 265 (5G)
       OS Map 111 (ref SE 373065)

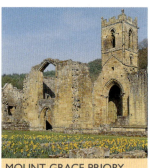

MOUNT GRACE PRIORY

N. YORKSHIRE – DL6 3JG

MOUNT GRACE PRIORY

Set amid woodland below the escarpment of the North York Moors and the Cleveland Way National Trail, the ruins of this 14th-century priory represent the best preserved 'charterhouse' of the 10 Carthusian monasteries in Britain. A reconstructed monk's cell and herb garden offer visitors a glimpse into the daily lives of the medieval residents. The gardens – remodelled in the early 20th century – are now a haven for wildlife, including the famous 'Priory Stoats'.

Owned by National Trust, maintained and managed by EH.

NON-MEMBERS

Adult	£3.60
Concession	£2.70
Child	£1.80
Family ticket	£9.00

NT members admitted free, except on special event days.

OPENING TIMES

19 Mar-30 Sep, daily	10am-6pm
1 Oct-31 Mar, Thu-Mon	10am-4pm
Closed	24-26 Dec and 1 Jan

Direction: 12 miles N of Thirsk; 6 miles NE of Northallerton, on A19

Train: Northallerton 6 miles

Bus: Arriva North East 80, 89 from Northallerton – Stokesley, alight Priory Road End, then ½ mile

Tel: 01609 883494

Local Tourist Information Northallerton: 01609 776864

Family learning resources available.

MAP   Page 265 (2G)
       OS Map 99 (ref SE 449985)

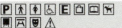

PICKERING CASTLE

N. YORKSHIRE – YO18 7AX

This splendid motte-and-bailey castle is well-preserved, with much of the original keep, towers and walls remaining. The castle was used by a succession of medieval kings as a royal hunting lodge.

There is an exhibition in the chapel.

NON-MEMBERS

Adult	£3.00
Concession	£2.30
Child	£1.50
Family ticket	£7.50

OPENING TIMES

19 Mar-30 Sep, daily	10am-6pm
1-31 Oct, Thu-Mon	10am-4pm

HOW TO FIND US

Direction: In Pickering; 15 miles SW of Scarborough

Train: Malton 9 miles; Pickering (N York Moors Rly) ¼ mile

Bus: Yorkshire Coastliner 840/2 from ≷ Malton; Scarborough & District 128 from ≷ Scarborough

Tel: 01751 474989

Disabled access (except motte).
Family learning resources available.

MAP	Page 265 (2H)
	OS Map 100 (ref SE 799845)

PIERCEBRIDGE ROMAN BRIDGE

N. YORKSHIRE

Remains of a Roman bridge, which once led to Piercebridge Roman Fort.

OPENING TIMES

Any reasonable time

HOW TO FIND US

Direction: At Piercebridge; 4 miles W of Darlington, on B6275

Train: Darlington 5 miles

Bus: Arriva 75/6 Darlington – Barnard Castle (passes close to ≷ Darlington)

MAP	Page 265 (1F)
	OS Map 93 (ref NZ 214155)

RICHMOND CASTLE

N. YORKSHIRE – DL10 4QW

Dramatically situated high on a rocky promontory, the castle's formidable keep overlooks the River Swale and the rooftops of the market town of Richmond. Originally built by the Normans to control the north, the castle's past as a fortress, barracks and prison is explored in an exciting exhibition, 'Castle, Commerce and Conscience'.

RICHMOND CASTLE

The Contemporary Heritage Garden is a place of contemplation, and offers commanding views of the surrounding area. According to legend, King Arthur lies sleeping in the cavern beneath the castle's keep.

NON-MEMBERS

Adult	£3.60
Concession	£2.70
Child	£1.80
Family ticket	£9.00

OPENING TIMES

19 Mar-30 Sep, daily	10am-6pm
1 Oct-31 Mar, Thu-Mon	10am-4pm
Closed	24-26 Dec and 1 Jan

HOW TO FIND US

Direction: In Richmond

Bus: Arriva X26/7, 27/8 Darlington – Richmond (passes close to ≷ Darlington)

Tel: 01748 822493

Family learning resources available.

MAP	Page 265 (2F)
	OS Map 92 (ref NZ 172007)

RIEVAULX ABBEY

N. YORKSHIRE   GO TO PAGE 200

Sign-up on-line for our email Members' Newsletter at **www.english-heritage.org.uk**

If you would like more information on properties, events and membership please call 0870 333 1181 or email **customers@ english-heritage.org.uk**

ROCHE ABBEY

S. YORKSHIRE – S66 8NW

198

Founded in 1147, the fine early Gothic transepts of this Cistercian monastery in South Yorkshire still survive to their original height. After the Dissolution of the Monasteries in the 16th century, a mob of locals descended on the abbey to pillage many of its treasures. This vividly recorded event is the most complete account in England of what occurred during this period. In the 18th century, Lancelot 'Capability' Brown transformed an already beautiful valley into a truly enchanting landscape, incorporating the ruins. Excavation has since revealed the complete layout of the original abbey.

NON-MEMBERS

Adult	£2.90
Concession	£2.20
Child	£1.50

OPENING TIMES

19 Mar-31 Jul, Thu-Mon	10am-5pm
1-31 Aug, daily	10am-5pm
1-30 Sep, Thu-Mon	10am-5pm

HOW TO FIND US

Direction: 1½ miles S of Maltby, off A634

Train: Conisbrough 7 miles

Bus: First 1, 2, 10, Powell 122 Rotherham-Maltby, then 1½ miles

Tel: 01709 812739

Family learning resources available.

MAP Page 265 (6G)
OS Map 111 (ref SK 544898)

ST MARY'S CHURCH, STUDLEY ROYAL

N. YORKSHIRE

This magnificent Anglican church was designed in the 1870s by William Burges and has been described as his "ecclesiastical masterpiece". It has a highly decorated interior including coloured marble, stained glass, a splendid organ and painted and gilded figures in all their original glory.

EH property managed by the National Trust as part of the Studley Royal Estate.

OPENING TIMES

| 1 Apr-30 Sep, daily | 1pm-5pm |

HOW TO FIND US

Direction: Located 2½ miles W of Ripon, off B6265; in the grounds of the Studley Royal Estate

Bus: Arriva 802 Wakefield-Leyburn, Sun, May-Sep only; otherwise Hutchinson 145 from Ripon (with connections from Harrogate), Thurs & Sat only

Tel: 01765 608888

Parking (at visitor centre).

MAP Page 265 (3F)
OS Map 99 (ref SE 275693)

ST PETER'S CHURCH, BARTON-UPON-HUMBER

N. LINCOLNSHIRE – DN18 5EX

With a history spanning over a millennium, this church features a remarkable Anglo-Saxon tower and baptistry and a large later medieval nave and chancel encompassing a range of architectural styles. One of the most studied churches in England, the results of excavations and research are displayed inside.

ST PETER'S CHURCH, BARTON-UPON-HUMBER

OPENING TIMES

| Daily | 1pm-3pm |
| Closed | 24-26 Dec and 1 Jan |
| Charge may apply on event days |

HOW TO FIND US

Direction: In Barton-upon-Humber

Train: Barton-upon-Humber ½ mile

Bus: Road Car/E Yorks 350 Hull-Cleethorpes Barton-upon-Humber

Tel: 01652 632516

MAP Page 265 (5J)
OS Map 112 (ref TA 035219)

SCARBOROUGH CASTLE

N. YORKSHIRE SEE OPPOSITE PAGE

SKIPSEA CASTLE

E. YORKSHIRE

The extensive earthworks of an abandoned fortified medieval borough, attached to an impressive motte and bailey castle dating from the Norman era.

OPENING TIMES

Any reasonable time

HOW TO FIND US

Direction: Located 8 miles S of Bridlington; W of Skipsea village

Train: Bridlington 9 miles

Dogs on leads (restricted areas only). Waterproof footwear recommended.

MAP Page 265 (3J)
OS Map 107 (ref TA 162551)

View of castle across bay

SCARBOROUGH CASTLE

NORTH YORKSHIRE – YO11 1HY

There is no better way to acquaint yourself with the popular seaside town of Scarborough than from the walls of the castle. Specially constructed viewing platforms now offer visitors wonderful views of the coastline and the town itself.

Built on the site of a prehistoric settlement and a fortified Roman signal station, Scarborough Castle defends a prominent headland between two bays, with sheer drops to the sea and only a narrow landward approach. Commanding this approach is Henry II's towering 12th-century keep, the centre-piece of fortifications developed over the centuries in response to repeated sieges – notably by rebel barons in 1312, and twice during the Civil War.

Though again strengthened with barracks and gun-batteries against Jacobite threats in 1746, the castle failed to defend the harbour against the American sea-raider John Paul Jones in 1779, and was itself damaged by German naval bombardment in 1914. During World War II it played the more covert role of hosting a secret listening post.

Scarborough itself is the oldest holiday resort in the country and first drew visitors to its mineral waters in the early 17th century.

New For 2005

This turbulent 3,000-year history is explored in new interactive displays this year, accompanied by free activity sheets, an audio tour, an investigative story box, and a new tearoom.

www.english-heritage.org.uk/ scarboroughcastle

NON-MEMBERS

Adult	£3.30
Concession	£2.50
Child	£1.70
Family ticket	£8.30

OPENING TIMES

19 Mar-30 Sep, daily	10am-6pm
1 Oct-31 Mar, Thu-Mon	10am-4pm
Closed	24-26 Dec and 1 Jan

HOW TO FIND US

Direction: Castle Road, E of the town centre

Train: Scarborough 1 mile

Bus: From surrounding areas

Tel: 01723 372451

Family learning resources available.

Parking (pre-booked parking only for disabled visitors, otherwise located in town centre).

MAP	Page 265 (2J)
	OS Map 101 (ref TA 050892)

RIEVAULX ABBEY NORTH YORKSHIRE – YO62 5LB

'Everywhere peace, everywhere serenity, and a marvellous freedom from the tumult of the world.' Those words, written over eight centuries ago by the monastery's third abbot, St Aelred, could describe Rievaulx today, for it is one of the most atmospheric of all the ruined abbeys of the north.

Words are not the only link to Rievaulx's distant medieval monks. Over the past few years, the site has become something of an archaeological treasure, with unexpected discoveries shedding new light on the lives of the abbey's former residents. Analysis of a flagon found by chance has revealed that the monks ate wild strawberries. A remote-controlled CCTV camera explored the hidden depths of a 16th-century drain that plunges deep underground, providing an insight into monastic hygiene. Further experimental archaeology has investigated the abbey's flourishing iron industry. And the rare find of a piece of 13th-century stained glass, with a depiction of a cockerel, has illustrated the extensive renewal and rebuilding of the abbey church in the Early English Gothic style. Meanwhile, archaeologists continue to study the wider landscape around Rievaulx, revealing the remarkable extent of the abbey's influence and industry.

Although much of what was built by the monks is in ruins, most of the presbytery (the eastern part of the abbey church) stands virtually to its full height. Built in the 13th century, its soaring height is a reminder of Rievaulx's original splendour. The abbey was founded by St Bernard of Clairvaux, as part of the missionary effort to reform Christianity in western Europe. Just 12 Clairvaux monks came to Rievaulx in 1131. From these modest beginnings, however, grew one of the wealthiest monasteries of medieval England and the first northern Cistercian monastery.

In the Middle Ages, wealthy families vied with each other to found churches. Rievaulx enjoyed the protection of Walter Espec, who provided much of the abbey's land. The monks of nearby Byland Abbey disputed land ownership with Rievaulx, which led to engineering works to divert the course of the River Rye which formed the boundary between their properties. You can still see traces of the old river and the channels dug by the monks.

A steady stream of monks came to Rievaulx Abbey, attracted by the prestige of Abbot Aelred, author and preacher, who was regarded then and after as a wise and saintly man. Following his death in 1167, the monks of Rievaulx sought canonisation for their former leader and, in the 1220s, they rebuilt the east part of their church in a much more elaborate style for his tomb.

Rievaulx was still a vibrant community when Henry VIII dissolved it in 1538. Its new owner, Thomas Manners, first Earl of Rutland, swiftly instigated the systematic destruction of the buildings. However, what was left behind still constitutes one of the most eloquent of all monastic sites, free 'from the tumult of the world'.

Don't miss the exciting exhibition, 'The Works of God and Man', which explores Rievaulx's history, employing a variety of lively and interactive displays.

Both Helmsley Castle and Byland Abbey are within reasonable travelling distance, including on foot via the Cleveland Way National Trail.

www.english-heritage.org.uk/ rievaulxabbey

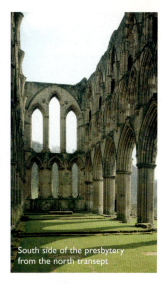

South side of the presbytery from the north transept

201

NON-MEMBERS

Adult	£4.00
Concession	£3.00
Child	£2.00

OPENING TIMES

19 Mar-30 Sep, daily	10am-6pm
1 Oct-31 Mar, Thu-Mon	10am-4pm
Closed	24-26 Dec and 1 Jan

HOW TO FIND US

Direction: In Rievaulx; 2¼ miles N of Helmsley, on minor road off B1257

Bus: Moorsbus from Helmsley (from ⬛ Scarborough) Sun, Apr-Oct, daily in Aug; from ⬛ York, Sun, Apr-Oct only; Scarborough & District 128 from Scarborough; Stephensons 31/X from York, alighting Helmsley, then 2½ miles

Tel: 01439 798228

Local Tourist Information Helmsley: 01439 770173

Audio tours (also available for the visually impaired, those with learning difficulties and in French and German).

Family learning resources available.

MAP	Page 265 (2G) OS Map 100 (ref SE 577850)

SPOFFORTH CASTLE

N. YORKSHIRE

202

This fortified medieval manor house was a home of the aristocratic Percy family. It has some fascinating features, including an undercroft built into the rock.

Managed by Spofforth-with-Stockeld Parish Council.

OPENING TIMES

1 Apr-30 Sep, daily	10am-6pm
1 Oct-31 Mar, daily	10am-4pm
(managed by a key-keeper)	
Closed	24-26 Dec and 1 Jan

HOW TO FIND US

Direction: 3½ miles SE of Harrogate; off A661 at Spofforth

Train: Pannal 4 miles

Bus: Harrogate & District 770/1 Harrogate-Leeds

Dogs on leads (restricted areas only).

MAP   Page 265 (4G)
       OS Map 104 (ref SE 360511)

Looking for a unique present? Why not browse our online shop at **www.english-heritage. org.uk/shopping**

STANWICK IRON AGE FORTIFICATIONS

N. YORKSHIRE

The tribal stronghold of the mighty Iron Age Brigantes, and possibly even the first capital of northern England, Stanwick features earthworks enclosing almost 3½ square kilometres (850 acres).

Today, visitors can still see the ramparts and an excavated section of the ditch, which has been cut into the rock.

OPENING TIMES

Any reasonable time

HOW TO FIND US

Direction: Located on a minor road off A6274, at Forcett Village

Train: Darlington 10 miles

Dogs on leads (restricted areas only).

MAP   Page 265 (1F)
       OS Map 92 (ref NZ 179124)

STEETON HALL GATEWAY

N. YORKSHIRE

A fine example of a small, well-preserved manorial gateway dating from the 14th century.

OPENING TIMES

Daily (exterior only)   10am-5pm

HOW TO FIND US

Direction: Located 4 miles NE of Castleford, on a minor road off A162 at South Milford

Train: South Milford 1 mile

Dogs on leads (restricted areas only).

MAP   Page 265 (4G)
       OS Map 105 (ref SE 484314)

THORNTON ABBEY AND GATEHOUSE

N. LINCOLNSHIRE

This abbey was founded in 1139 for a community of Augustinian canons from Kirkham Priory. It was reconstructed from the 1260s onwards as its prestige and riches grew. The remains of the church and cloisters survive within an extensive area of earthworks, and the ruins of a beautiful octagonal chapter house are notably fine. Most impressive, though, is the 14th-century gatehouse, recognised as one of the grandest in Europe.

OPENING TIMES

Abbey grounds:	
Daily	10am-6pm
Gatehouse:	
1 Apr-30 Sep, 1st and 3rd Sun of the month	12pm-6pm
1 Oct-31 Mar, 3rd Sun of the month	12pm-4pm
Charge may apply on event days	

HOW TO FIND US

Direction: 18 miles NE of Scunthorpe, on a road N of A160; 7 miles SE of the Humber Bridge, on a road E of A1077

Train: Thornton Abbey ¼ mile

Disabled access (except gatehouse interior and part of chapter ruins).
Dogs on leads (restricted areas only).

MAP   Page 265 (5J)
       OS Map 113 (ref TA 118189)

WHARRAM PERCY DESERTED MEDIEVAL VILLAGE

N. YORKSHIRE

This is one of about 3,000 ancient villages abandoned between the 11th and 18th centuries, and the foundations of more than 30 medieval peasant houses are still visible at the site, together with the ruined church. Excavation has revealed evidence of prehistoric occupation and also of a settlement dating back to the Bronze Age, with Roman farms and an Anglo-Saxon estate coming after. This is all revealed in new interpretation panels in 2005.

OPENING TIMES

Any reasonable time

HOW TO FIND US

Direction: 6 miles SE of Malton, on minor road from B1248; ½ mile S of Wharram-le-Street

Train: Malton 8 miles

P ⛨ ▦ ▣ ⚠

Guidebooks (available from Kirkham Priory or Pickering Castle).

Parking (¾ mile from site).

MAP   Page 265 (3H)
        OS Map 100 (ref SE 859644)

WHEELDALE ROMAN ROAD

N. YORKSHIRE

Mile-long stretch of Roman road across the moors, still with its hard core and drainage ditches.

The nearby railway station at Goathland was used in the Harry Potter films.

Managed by North York Moors National Park.

OPENING TIMES

Any reasonable time

HOW TO FIND US

Direction: S of Goathland; W of A169; 7 miles S of Whitby

Train: Goathland (N York Moors Rly) 4 miles

⚠ ⛨

MAP   Page 265 (2H)
        OS Map 94 (ref SE 806977)

Check *Heritage Today* for news and information on forthcoming events and exclusive members' offers.

Don't forget to check opening dates and times before you visit.

Mosaic pavement –
Aldborough Roman Town

www.english-heritage.org.uk/yorkshire

WHITBY ABBEY NORTH YORKSHIRE – YO22 4JT

Perched high on a cliff, the gaunt remains of this magnificent abbey stand tall above the picturesque seaside town of Whitby.

Arcading

The Abbey was founded in AD657 by St Hilda (known as Hild during her lifetime). Recent archaeological research – undertaken by English Heritage – suggests that the abbey was once a bustling settlement, a modern sophisticated town of its day, worthy of royal patronage and home to saints such as Caedmon.

The Abbey was destroyed during a Viking invasion in AD867, but one of William the Conqueror's knights revived it in the late 1070s. By 1220, his Norman church proved inadequate for the many pilgrims so rebuilding began. After its dissolution by Henry VIII in 1538, Whitby Abbey passed to the Cholmley family, who built a mansion largely out of materials plundered from the monastery.

Whitby Abbey did not suffer as much destruction as many other former abbeys following the dissolution as it was (and still is) used by shipping as a navigation point.

A new visitor centre now nestles within the walls of the Cholmley family mansion, as part of a major interpretation and access project encompassing the whole of the headland. This area has been hailed as one of the most important archaeological sites in the country. The visitor centre houses archaeological material excavated at Whitby, as well as computer-generated images revealing how the headland has changed over time. Rich finds from the Anglo-Saxon and medieval abbeys are also exhibited, together with objects relating to the Cholmley family.

One of the aims of the project has been to enhance and protect the natural beauty and historic character of the headland. As work at the headland progressed, English Heritage carried out research excavations which have added to our understanding of Whitby's complex past, including the discovery of a rare 17th-century 'hard garden' – inspired by Cholmley's visits to France and Spain – now restored. Continuing research may yield further insights into the past of this historically important abbey.

Spectacular audio-visual displays recreate the medieval abbey and the 17th-century house, its interiors and gardens. Visitors can also gain an insight into the people who have lived in Whitby, from St Hilda to Bram Stoker, author of *Dracula*.

Please note
From the Whitby harbour area, the abbey can only be directly reached on foot via the 199 'abbey steps' (or Caedmon's Trod) : alternatively a well-signposted road leads from the town outskirts to the clifftop abbey.

www.english-heritage.org.uk/whitbyabbey

NON-MEMBERS

Adult	£4.00
Concession	£3.00
Child	£2.00
Family ticket	£10.00

OPENING TIMES

19 Mar-30 Sep, daily	10am-6pm
1-31 Oct, daily	10am-5pm
1 Nov-31 Mar, Thu-Mon	10am-4pm
Closed	24-26 Dec and 1 Jan

HOW TO FIND US

Direction: On cliff top, E of Whitby

Train: Whitby ½ mile

Bus: From surrounding areas

Tel: 01947 603568

Local Tourist Information Whitby: 01947 602674

Disabled access (south entrance parking, charged).
Dogs on leads (restricted areas only).
Family learning resources available.
Parking (charge payable).
Tearoom (managed by Youth Hostel Association).

MAP	Page 265 (1J)
	OS Map 94 (ref NZ 903112)

Visitor centre

OTHER HISTORIC ATTRACTIONS

DISCOUNTED ENTRY TO OUR MEMBERS (DISCOUNTS MAY NOT APPLY ON EVENT DAYS)

THE ARCHAEOLOGICAL RESOURCE CENTRE (ARC), YORK

N. YORKSHIRE – YO1 8NN

Become an archaeologist and handle real ancient artefacts, piecing together the past and finding out what life was like centuries ago.

ENTRY

Adult	£4.50
Concession	£4.00
Child	£4.00

15% reduction for English Heritage members (owned by York Archaeological Trust).

OPENING TIMES

School term, Mon-Fri	10am-3.30pm
School holidays, Mon-Sat	11am-3pm

Tel: 01904 543402/543403

www.vikingjorvik.com

MAP	Page 265 (3H)
	OS Map 105 (ref SE 606519)

CASTLE HOWARD

N. YORKSHIRE – YO60 7DA

Magnificent 18th-century house with extensive collections and breathtaking grounds. Gift shops, plant centre, childrens' adventure playground, boat trips, farm shop and cafés.

Managed by The Castle Howard Estate.

ENTRY

Adult	£9.50
Concession	£8.50
Child	£6.50

EH DISCOUNT

Adult	£2.00 off
Others	£1.50 off

Discount available only with house and garden ticket.

OPENING TIMES

1 Mar-6 Nov, daily,	from 10am

Please call for times or visit www.castlehoward.co.uk

Tel: 01653 648333

MAP	Page 265 (3H)
	OS Map 100 (ref SE 716701)

DUNCOMBE PARK, HELMSLEY

N. YORKSHIRE – YO62 5EB

The recently restored family home of Lord and Lady Feversham is surrounded by over 300 acres of stunning grounds and parkland.

Managed by Duncombe Park Estate Ltd.

ENTRY

Adult	£6.50
Concession	£5.00

Entry to house and gardens for EH members £2.50. Discount not available during special events

DUNCOMBE PARK, HELMSLEY

OPENING TIMES

1 May-30 Oct	

Please call for times or visit www.duncombepark.com

Tel: 01439 770213

MAP	Page 265 (2G)
	OS Map 100 (ref SE 604830)

JORVIK, YORK

N. YORKSHIRE – YO1 9WT

Explore York's past on the very site where archaeologists uncovered remains of the Viking Age city of 'Jorvik', and journey through a reconstruction of actual Viking Age streets.

ENTRY

Adult	£7.45
Concession	£6.30
Child	£5.25

15% reduction for English Heritage members.

OPENING TIMES

Apr-Oct, daily	10am-5pm
Nov-Mar, daily	10am-4pm

Tel: 01904 543402/543403

www.vikingjorvik.com

MAP	Page 265 (4H)
	OS Map 105 (ref SE 604516)

MERCHANT ADVENTURERS' HALL, YORK

N. YORKSHIRE – YO1 9XD

Europe's finest medieval guildhall, built 1357-1361 and largely unaltered. It now operates as a registered museum.

Managed by The Company of Merchant Adventurers of the City of York.

ENTRY

Adult	£2.50
Concession	£2.00
Child	£1.00

Half price admission for English Heritage members.

OPENING TIMES

Oct-Mar, Mon-Sat	9am-3.30pm
Apr-Sep, Mon-Thu	9am-5pm
Apr-Sep, Fri & Sat	9am-3.30pm
Apr-Sep, Sun	12pm-4pm
Closed Christmas and New Year	
Tel: 01904 654818	

MAP	Page 265 (3H)
	OS Map 105 (ref SE 605517)

Don't forget your membership card when you visit any of the properties listed in this handbook.

FOUNTAINS ABBEY

RIPON, N. YORKSHIRE – HG4 3DY

Fountains Abbey has been described as the 'crown and glory of all that monasticism has left us in England'. There are 800 years of history to be explored in the 320-hectare (790-acre) estate, a World Heritage Site combining architecture and landscape of outstanding historical and aesthetic importance. The ruins of the Cistercian abbey, which was founded in 1132, are the largest such remains in Europe and provide a dramatic focal point for the landscape garden, which was laid out during the first half of the 18th century by William and John Aislabie.

Fountains Mill, one of Europe's oldest surviving mills, once supplied the monks of Fountains Abbey with flour for baking. It has now been in continuous use for more than 800 years. Today, visitors can see the magnificent water wheel turning as it has for centuries, and explore the life and times of the mill through displays and ancient artefacts.

Other features within the estate include St Mary's Church, a masterpiece of Victorian Gothic design (see page 198), and the Elizabethan mansion, Fountains Hall, built partly with stone from the abbey. St Mary's Church also provides a focus for the medieval deer park.

FOUNTAINS ABBEY

Managed by the National Trust. English Heritage works in partnership with the National Trust to protect this site.

NON-MEMBERS FOUNTAINS ABBEY & WATER GARDEN

Adult	£5.50
Concession	£3.00
Family ticket	£15.00

EH members admitted free to this NT site. Reduction for groups if booked in advance. Guided tours available. Deer Park: free of charge. Parking £2.50, free to members.

OPENING TIMES

Abbey and Water Garden:	
Mar-Oct 10am-5pm daily	
Nov-Feb 10am-4pm daily	
Closed Fridays Nov-Jan	
Deer Park: open daily during daylight hours	
Closed	24-25 Dec

HOW TO FIND US

Direction: 4 miles W of Ripon, off B6265

Bus: Hutchinson 812 from 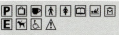 York, with connections from Harrogate on Harrogate & District 36, Suns, May-Sep only; Arriva 802 from Wakefield and Leeds, Suns, May-Sep only; otherwise Hutchinson 145 from Ripon (with connections from Harrogate), Thurs & Sat only; Minibus hopper service from Ripon-Fountain's Abbey: Tel: 01423 526555

Tel: 01765 608888

Box office: 01765 643199

Disabled access (not suitable for three-wheel battery cars).

MAP	Page 265 (3F)
	OS Map 99 (ref SE 275683)

NORTH WEST

A land of steep-sided mountains falling into deep, black lakes, of sweeping moors and dales, the North West is a poet's paradise and a paragon of natural beauty.

www.english-heritage.org.uk/northwest

PROPERTIES

SEE INDIVIDUAL LISTINGS FOR DETAILS

CHESHIRE
Beeston Castle, Chester Castle: Agricola Tower and Castle Walls, Chester Roman Amphitheatre, Sandbach Crosses

CUMBRIA
Ambleside Roman Fort, Bow Bridge, Brough Castle, Brougham Castle, Castlerigg Stone Circle, Carlisle Castle, Clifton Hall, Countess Pillar, Furness Abbey, Hadrian's Wall (see p222), Hardknott Roman Fort, King Arthur's Round Table, Lanercost Priory, Mayburgh Henge, Penrith Castle, Piel Castle, Ravenglass Roman Bath House,

Shap Abbey, Stott Park Bobbin Mill, Wetheral Priory Gatehouse

LANCASHIRE
Goodshaw Chapel, Sawley Abbey, Warton Old Rectory, Whalley Abbey Gatehouse

MERSEYSIDE
St George's Hall

Comprehensive map of our sites
PAGE 264 & 266

HADRIAN'S WALL

• CARLISLE

• PENRITH

• WHITEHAVEN

CUMBRIA

• ULVERSTON

LANCASHIRE

• BLACKPOOL
• PRESTON

GREATER MANCHESTER

MERSEYSIDE
• MANCHESTER

• LIVERPOOL

CHESHIRE
• CHESTER

Stott Park Bobbin Mill

INDUSTRY AND ROMANCE

From the industrial heritage in the south of the region to the romantic ruins in the north, this area offers visitors an impressive range of history.

For a stunning overview of this awesome landscape, you could do no better than climbing to the top of the impressive keep at Carlisle Castle. From here, the magnificent panorama stretches from the Lakes to the Pennines, the Solway Firth to the Grampians.

Another castle with fantastic views is Beeston Castle in the south of the region. It perches on a sheer rocky crag, defending some delightful countryside. Much further north, Brougham Castle stands on the spectacularly beautiful banks of the Cumbrian River Eamont.

The Industrial Revolution is brought to life at Stott Park Bobbin Mill, near Lake Windermere. At this working mill and museum you can learn the fascinating story of the cotton industry, wooden bobbin manufacturing and the people who worked there.

If you have a literary interest, Furness Abbey – a site much loved by William Wordsworth – is definitely worth a visit. The church, set in the 'vale of deadly nightshade', has long been perceived as a very romantic building.

English Heritage often works with local organisations to ensure the preservation of the region's important buildings and monuments.

Recently, we have been involved in a bid to achieve World Heritage Status for the city of Liverpool. In partnership with Liverpool City Council, the Liverpool Culture Company and a range of other bodies, the Historic Environment of Liverpool Project (HELP) is helping to tackle the city's historic buildings at risk. Surveys will also be carried out across Merseyside and within Liverpool itself to ensure that the history of the city is better understood.

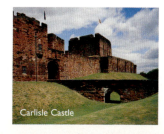
Carlisle Castle

AMBLESIDE ROMAN FORT
CUMBRIA

These remains of a 1st and 2nd-century fort, built to guard the Roman road from Brougham to Ravenglass, give a clear idea of what such forts were like.

Managed by the National Trust.

OPENING TIMES
Any reasonable time

HOW TO FIND US
Direction: 182 metres W of Waterhead car park, Ambleside

Train: Windermere 5 miles

Bus: Stagecoach in Cumbria 555/6, 599 from Windermere

MAP	Page 266 (6D)
	OS Map 90 (ref NY 372034)

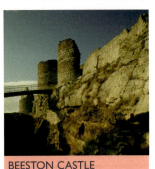

BEESTON CASTLE
CHESHIRE – CW6 9TX

Standing majestically on a sheer rocky crag, Beeston has perhaps the most stunning views of any castle in England. Its history stretches back more than 4,000 years to when it was a Bronze Age hillfort. The huge castle was built in 1226 and soon became a royal stronghold, only falling centuries later during the Civil War.

The *Castle of the Rock* exhibition outlines the history of this strategic site from prehistoric

BEESTON CASTLE

times, through the Middle Ages to the Civil War.

Please note
Steep climb (no disabled access to the top of the hill)

NON-MEMBERS
Adult	£3.60
Concession	£2.70
Child	£1.80
Family ticket	£9.00

OPENING TIMES
24 Mar-30 Sep, daily	10am-6pm
1 Oct-31 Mar, daily	10am-4pm
Closed	24-26 Dec and 1 Jan

HOW TO FIND US
Direction: Located 11 miles SE of Chester, on minor road off A49

Train: Chester 10 miles

Bus: Arriva 83 from Chester

Tel: 01829 260464

Local Tourist Information Chester 01244 402111

Family learning resources available.

MAP	Page 264 (7D)
	OS Map 117 (ref SJ 537593)

BOW BRIDGE
CUMBRIA

This late-medieval stone bridge across Mill Beck carries an old route to nearby Furness Abbey (see page 216), which was founded in 1123 by Stephen, later King of England.

OPENING TIMES
Any reasonable time

HOW TO FIND US
Direction: Located ½ mile N of Barrow-in-Furness, on minor road off A590; near to Furness Abbey

BOW BRIDGE
Train: Barrow-in-Furness 1½ miles

Bus: Stagecoach in Cumbria 6/A Barrow-in Furness – Ulverston to within ¾ mile

MAP	Page 266 (7D)
	OS Map 96 (ref SD 224715)

BROUGH CASTLE
CUMBRIA

Commanding a magnificent view of the Pennines, medieval Brough Castle stands within the earthworks of a Roman fort built to guard the strategic Stainmore routeway. The impressive tower-keep dates from c.1200, replacing an earlier stronghold destroyed by William the Lion of Scotland in 1174. Like so many other castles hereabouts, Brough was restored in the 17th century by Lady Anne Clifford: the traces of her kitchen gardens can still be seen.

OPENING TIMES
Any reasonable time

HOW TO FIND US
Direction: 8 miles SE of Appleby S of A66

Train: Kirkby Stephen 6 miles

Bus: Grand Prix 564 Kendal-Brough (passing Kirkby Stephen); Stagecoach in Cumbria/Grand Prix 563 Penrith-Brough (passing Penrith)

MAP	Page 267 (6F)
	OS Map 91 (ref NY 791141)

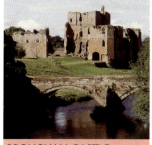

BROUGHAM CASTLE

CUMBRIA – CA10 2AA

Picturesque Brougham Castle was begun in the early 13th century by Robert de Vieuxpont, near the site of a Roman fort guarding the crossing of the River Eamont. His great keep largely survives, reinforced by an impressive double gatehouse and other 14th-century additions made by the powerful Clifford family, Wardens of the Marches. The castle thus became a formidable barrier to Scots invaders.

Though both James I and Charles I stayed here, Brougham was in poor condition by the time of the Civil War. It was thereafter restored as a residence by the indomitable Lady Anne Clifford (see also Brough Castle and the Countess Pillar): she often visited with her travelling 'court', and died here in 1676.

Today, the site features an introductory exhibition, including carved stones from the nearby Roman fort.

The site has good wheelchair access to entry point, toilet, shop and small introductory exhibition. There is a wheelchair route to the castle ruins, which enables visitors to make a circuit of the site and read the interpretation panels. The keep is not accessible to wheelchairs.

BROUGHAM CASTLE

NON-MEMBERS

Adult	£2.60
Concession	£2.00
Child	£1.30

OPENING TIMES

24 Mar-30 Sep, daily	10am-6pm
1-31 Oct, Thu-Mon	10am-4pm

HOW TO FIND US

Direction: 1½ miles SE of Penrith, off A66.

Train: Penrith 2 miles

Local Tourist information
01228 625600

Tel: 01768 862488

MAP	Page 266 (5E)
	OS Map 90 (ref NY 537290)

CARLISLE CASTLE

CUMBRIA   GO TO PAGE 214

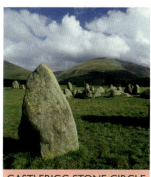

CASTLERIGG STONE CIRCLE

CUMBRIA

The best approach to this atmospheric, enigmatic prehistoric stone circle is along the route used by those who would have dragged the stones to the spot on log rollers. The circle is magnificent and offers a breath-taking panoramic view of the surrounding fells.

Managed by The National Trust.

CASTLERIGG STONE CIRCLE

OPENING TIMES

Any reasonable time

HOW TO FIND US

Direction: 1½ miles E of Keswick

Train: Penrith 16 miles

Bus: Stagecoach in Cumbria X4/5 from 🚆 Penrith to within 1 mile

MAP	Page 266 (5D)
	OS Map 90 (ref NY291236)

CHESTER CASTLE: AGRICOLA TOWER AND CASTLE WALLS

CHESHIRE

Set into the angle of the city walls, this 12th-century tower contains a fine vaulted chapel.

Managed by Chester City Council.

OPENING TIMES

Walls open any reasonable time
Cell block open:

1 Apr-30 Sep, daily	10am-5pm
1 Oct-31 Mar, daily	10am-4pm
Closed	24-26 Dec and 1 Jan

HOW TO FIND US

Direction: Access via Assizes Court car park on Grosvenor St

Train: Chester 1 mile

Bus: From surrounding areas

Disabled access (parts only).

MAP	Page 264 (7C)
	OS Map 117 (ref SJ 405657)

ℹ️

Sign-up on-line for our email Members' Newsletter at
www.english-heritage.org.uk

CARLISLE CASTLE CUMBRIA – CA3 8UR

Impressive and forbidding, Carlisle Castle is a formidable fortress that amply repays anyone wishing to explore its absorbing 900-year history.

Detail of prisoner's carving

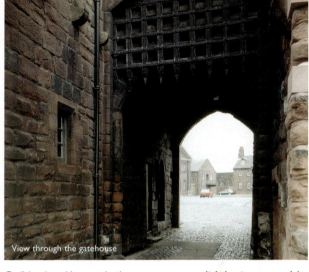
View through the gatehouse

Long commanding the especially turbulent western end of the Anglo-Scottish border, Carlisle has witnessed many conflicts and sieges. The earliest castle was of earth and timber, raised by King William Rufus in c.1092. During the following century it was refortified in stone, possibly by Henry I. The 12th-century stone keep is the oldest surviving structure in the castle, which was frequently updated as befitted a stronghold always in the front line of Anglo-Scottish warfare. In 1315 it triumphantly saw off a determined Scots attack. The rounded 'shot-deflecting' battlements of the keep were added by Henry VIII in c.1540.

Elaborate carvings in a small cell, by captives held here by the future Richard III in 1480, vividly demonstrate that Carlisle Castle was also a prison. Mary Queen of Scots was confined here after her flight from Scotland in 1568: but in 1596 the Border bandit Kinmont Willie Armstrong managed a daring night escape, to the fury of his captors.

Carlisle played its part in the English Civil War. Besieged for eight months by Parliament's Scots allies, its Royalist garrison surrendered in 1645 only after eating rats and even their dogs. A century later in 1746, the castle became the last English fortress ever to suffer a siege, when Bonnie Prince Charlie's High- lander garrison vainly attempted to hold off Butcher Cumberland's Hanoverian army. The castle became their prison: many died here, and others left only for hanging or transportation.

The keep also houses a model of the city in 1745 and an exhibition on Bonnie Prince Charlie and the Jacobite uprising of that year. Visitors can also see the legendary 'licking stones', which parched Jacobite prisoners des- perately licked for moisture in order to stay alive. Admission also includes entry to the King's Own Royal Border Regiment Museum. Another feature of the site is the Carlisle Roman Dig, a fully accessible exhibition displaying the finds from new excavations.

www.english-heritage.org.uk/ carlislecastle

NON-MEMBERS

Adult	£4.00
Concession	£3.00
Child	£2.00

OPENING TIMES

24 Mar-30 Sep, daily	9.30am-6pm
1 Oct-31 Mar, daily	10am-4pm
Closed	24-26 Dec and 1 Jan

HOW TO FIND US

Direction: In Carlisle city centre

Train: Carlisle ½ mile

Bus: From surrounding areas

Tel: 01228 591922

Local tourist information
01228 625600

Disabled access (except interiors).

Dogs on leads (restricted areas only).

Family learning resources available.

Guided tours (available at a small extra charge Apr-Sep; groups please pre-book).

Parking (disabled only, but sign-posted city centre car parks nearby).

MAP	Page 266 (4D)
	OS Map 85 (ref NY 396562)

CHESTER ROMAN AMPHITHEATRE

CHESHIRE

This, the largest Roman amphitheatre in Britain, has been partially excavated. It was used for entertainment and military training by the 20th Legion, based at the fortress of Deva.

Further excavations will be carried out from Jun-Sept 2005.

Managed by Chester City Council.

OPENING TIMES

Any reasonable time

HOW TO FIND US

Direction: On Vicars Lane, beyond Newgate, Chester

Train: Chester ¾ mile

Bus: From surrounding areas

Disabled access (no access to amphitheatre floor).

MAP	Page 264 (7C)
	OS Map 117 (ref SJ 408662)

CLIFTON HALL

CUMBRIA

The surviving tower block of a 15th-century manor house, which was home to the Clifton family for almost 600 years.

CLIFTON HALL

OPENING TIMES

Any reasonable time
(please call at Hall Farm for keys)
Closed   24-26 Dec and 1 Jan

HOW TO FIND US

Direction: Next to Clifton Hall Farm; 2 miles S of Penrith, on A6

Train: Penrith 2½ miles

MAP	Page 266 (5E)
	OS Map 90 (ref NY 530271)

COUNTESS PILLAR

CUMBRIA

A monument erected in 1656 by Lady Anne Clifford (see Brougham Castle), to mark her final parting from her mother.

OPENING TIMES

Any reasonable time

HOW TO FIND US

Direction: ¼ mile E of Brougham

Train: Penrith 2½ miles

Warning (site on a very busy main road).

MAP	Page 266 (5E)
	OS Map 90 (ref NY 546289)

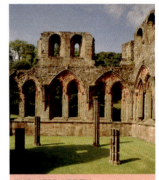

FURNESS ABBEY

CUMBRIA – LA13 0PS

St Mary of Furness was founded in 1123 by Stephen, Count of Blois, who later became King of England. It originally belonged to the Order of Savigny, but passed, in 1147, to the Cistercians. They gradually rebuilt and enlarged the ornate church that the Savigniac order had built. This second church was itself remodelled in the 15th century. The church, set in the 'vale of deadly nightshade', has long been perceived as a very romantic building – Wordsworth visited the abbey on several occasions and referred to it in his *Prelude* of 1805.

An exhibition on the history of the abbey, with a display of elaborately carved stones, can be seen in the visitor centre. (See also Bow Bridge, page 212).

NON-MEMBERS

Adult	£3.30
Concession	£2.50
Child	£1.70

OPENING TIMES

24 Mar-30 Sep, daily	10am-6pm
1 Oct-31 Mar, Thu-Mon	10am-4pm
Closed	24-26 Dec and 1 Jan

www.english-heritage.org.uk/northwest

FURNESS ABBEY

HOW TO FIND US

Direction: Located 1½ miles N of Barrow-in-Furness, off A590

Train: Barrow-in-Furness 2 miles

Bus: Stagecoach in Cumbria 6/A Barrow-in-Furness – Ulverston, to within ¾ mile

Tel: 01229 823420

Audio tours (also available for the visually impaired and those with learning difficulties).

Dogs on leads (restricted areas only).

MAP	Page 266 (7D)
	OS Map 96 (ref SD 218717)

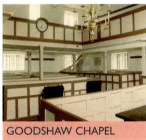

GOODSHAW CHAPEL

LANCASHIRE

This 18th-century Baptist chapel, retaining all its original furnishings, was fully restored in 1985.

OPENING TIMES

Please call the keykeeper for details. Tel 01229 823420

HOW TO FIND US

Direction: In Crawshawbooth, 2 miles N of Rawtenstall; in Goodshaw Ave, off A682

Train: Burnley Manchester Road 4½ miles

Bus: Burnley & Pendle 243 Burnley-Bolton; X43/4 Colne-Manchester. All pass ⟁ Burnley Manchester Road

MAP	Page 264 (4E)
	OS Map 103 (ref SD 814261)

HADRIAN'S WALL

GO TO PAGE 222

HARDKNOTT ROMAN FORT

CUMBRIA

This impressively-sited fort was built AD120-138. Remains include the headquarters building and commandant's house.

Managed by the National Trust.

OPENING TIMES

Any reasonable time

HOW TO FIND US

Direction: 9 miles NE of Ravenglass; at W end of Hardknott Pass

Train: Eskdale (Dalegarth) (Ravenglass & Eskdale Rly) 3 miles

Warning (access may be hazardous during the winter months).

MAP	Page 266 (6C)
	OS Map 90 (ref NY 218015)

KING ARTHUR'S ROUND TABLE

CUMBRIA

Prehistoric circular earthwork, bounded by a ditch and an outer bank.

OPENING TIMES

Any reasonable time

HOW TO FIND US

Direction: Located at Eamont Bridge, 1 mile S of Penrith. Mayburgh Henge is nearby.

Train: Penrith 1½ miles

MAP	Page 266 (5E)
	OS Map 90 (ref NY 523284)

LANERCOST PRIORY

CUMBRIA – CA8 2HQ

Standing close to Hadrian's Wall, the Augustinian priory of Lanercost suffered terribly from Scottish raids, being sacked at least four times. Yet until its final dissolution by Henry VIII in 1537 it was always re-occupied, and today its beautiful 13th-century church remains remarkably well-preserved, standing to its full height: part is now in use as the parish church.

Parish church not managed by English Heritage.

NON-MEMBERS

Adult	£2.60
Concession	£2.00
Child	£1.30

OPENING TIMES

24 Mar-30 Sep, daily	10am-6pm
1-31 Oct, Thu-Mon	10am-4pm

HOW TO FIND US

Direction: Off a minor road S of Lanercost; 2 miles NE of Brampton

Train: Brampton 3 miles

Bus: Stagecoach in Cumbria 685 Carlisle-Newcastle-upon-Tyne to within 1½ miles

Tel: 01697 73030

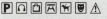

MAP	Page 266 (4E)
	OS Map 86 (ref NY 556637)

MAYBURGH HENGE
CUMBRIA

An impressive prehistoric circular henge, probably a gathering place, with banks up to 4.5 metres (14.8 feet) high, enclosing a central area larger than 6,000 square metres (19,685sq feet), inside which stands a single large stone.

OPENING TIMES
Any reasonable time

HOW TO FIND US
Direction: I mile S of Penrith off A6

Train: Penrith 1½ miles

MAP   Page 266 (5E)
       OS Map 90 (ref NY 519284)

PENRITH CASTLE
CUMBRIA

The mainly 15th-century remains of a castle begun by Bishop Strickland of Carlisle and developed by the Nevilles and Richard III. Set in a park opposite the railway station.

OPENING TIMES
Summer   7.30am-9pm
Winter   7.30am-4.30pm

HOW TO FIND US
Direction: Opposite Penrith railway station

Train: Penrith (adjacent)

MAP   Page 266 (5E)
       OS Map 90 (ref NY 513299)

PIEL CASTLE
CUMBRIA

The ruins of a 14th-century castle with a massive keep, inner and outer baileys, and curtain walls and towers still standing. Piel Castle lies on the south-eastern point of Piel Island at the mouth of the deep-water harbour of Barrow-in-Furness. William Wordsworth wrote about Piel in 1805.

OPENING TIMES
Any reasonable time

HOW TO FIND US
Direction: By small boat: from 11am, from Roa Island, summer only; subject to tides and weather. There is a small charge for this service; for details, call Alan Cleasby on 01229 835809 or 07798 794550, or John Cleasby on 07799 761306

Direction: Piel Island, 3¼ miles SE of Barrow-in-Furness

Train: Barrow-in-Furness 4 miles

Bus: Stagecoach in Cumbria 11 Barrow-in Furness – Ulverston

MAP   Page 266 (7D)
       OS Map 96 (ref SD 233636)

RAVENGLASS ROMAN BATH HOUSE
CUMBRIA

The remains of the bath house of the Roman fort of Ravenglass, established in AD130, are among the most complete in Britain: the walls stand almost 4 metres (13 feet) high. Ravenglass was a key naval base and port for the Roman army.

Managed by the Lake District National Park.

OPENING TIMES
Any reasonable time

HOW TO FIND US
Direction: ¼ mile E of Ravenglass, off minor road leading to A595

Train: Ravenglass (adjacent)

MAP   Page 266 (6C)
       OS Map 96 (ref SD 088959)

NEW FOR 2005

ST GEORGE'S HALL, LIVERPOOL
MERSEYSIDE

A superb neo-Classical building, designed by Harvey Lonsdale Elmes as law courts and a venue for music festivals. Completed in 1855.

ST GEORGE'S HALL, LIVERPOOL

The small Concert Hall is an excellent example of early Victorian design, and the highly decorative Great Hall boasts one of the finest concert organs in the UK.

Entry by guided tour only.

Owned and managed by Liverpool City Council.

NON-MEMBERS

Guided Tours:

Adult	£3.50
Concession	£3.00
Child	£3.00

Discount does not extend to EH corporate partners

OPENING TIMES

For dates and times of guided tours tel: 0151 2335000

HOW TO FIND US

Direction: City Centre, adjacent to Lime Street railway station and Queen Street bus station

Tel: 0151 2333000

Disabled access (for tours; limited). Parking (street).

MAP	Page 264 (6C)
	OS Map 108 (ref SJ 349907)

SANDBACH CROSSES

CHESHIRE

SANDBACH CROSSES

The two massive and elaborately decorated Saxon stone crosses, carved with animals and biblical scenes, including the Nativity of Christ and the Crucifixion, dominate the cobbled market square of Sandbach. They are considered among the finest surviving examples of Anglo-Saxon high crosses, and are believed to date from the 9th century.

OPENING TIMES

Any reasonable time

HOW TO FIND US

Direction: Market Sq, Sandbach

Train: Sandbach 1½ miles

Bus: From surrounding areas

MAP	Page 264 (7D)
	OS Map 118 (ref SJ 759608)

SAWLEY ABBEY

LANCASHIRE

The remains of a Cistercian abbey founded in 1148. After its dissolution in 1536, the monks were returned to the abbey during the Pilgrimage of Grace. They remained in possession until the insurrection's collapse and the execution of their abbot.

SAWLEY ABBEY

The abbey is set on the banks of the Ribble, against a backdrop of dramatic hills.

Managed by the Heritage Trust for the North West.

OPENING TIMES

1 Apr-30 Sep, daily	10am-6pm
1 Oct-31 Mar, daily	10am-4pm
Closed	24-26 Dec and 1 Jan

HOW TO FIND US

Direction: Located at Sawley; 3½ miles N of Clitheroe, off A59

Train: Clitheroe 4 miles

MAP	Page 264 (4D)
	OS Map 103 (ref SD 777464)

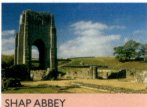

SHAP ABBEY

CUMBRIA

The impressive tower and other remains of a remote abbey inhabited by Premonstratensian 'white canons'.

Managed by the Lake District National Park.

OPENING TIMES

Any reasonable time

HOW TO FIND US

Direction: 1½ miles W of Shap, on the bank of the River Lowther

Train: Penrith 10 miles

Bus: Stagecoach in Cumbria/K&B 106/7, NBM 111 Penrith-Kendal to within 1½ miles

Disabled access (limited views from outside the site).

MAP	Page 266 (6E)
	OS Map 90 (ref NY 548152)

STOTT PARK BOBBIN MILL

CUMBRIA – LA12 8AX

This working mill was built by John Harrison in 1835. The wooden bobbins vital to the spinning and weaving industries of Lancashire were manufactured at Stott Park. It was small compared to some mills – employing up to 250 workers – but still produced a quarter of a million bobbins a week and, in addition, made handles for various tools. Guided tours lasting 45 minutes are included in the admission charge, the last tour begins one hour before closing.

NON-MEMBERS

Adult	£4.00
Concession	£3.00
Child	£2.00
Family ticket	£10.00

OPENING TIMES

24 Mar-30 Sep, daily	10am-6pm
1-31 Oct, daily	10am-5pm
Steam days: Mon-Thu	

HOW TO FIND US

Direction: Located 1½ miles N of Newby Bridge, off A590

Train: Grange-over-Sands 8 miles

STOTT PARK BOBBIN MILL

Ferry: Windermere ferry from Ambleside or Bowness to Lakeside, then 1 mile

Tel: 01539 531087

Local Tourist Information Hawkshead: 01539 436525

Disabled access (ground floor only). Parking (lower car park).

MAP	Page 266 (6D)
	OS Map 97 (ref SD 372881)

WARTON OLD RECTORY

LANCASHIRE

Built in the 14th century and former home to the Washington family, this is a rare medieval stone house with remains of the hall, chambers and domestic rooms.

Managed by Heritage Trust for the North West.

OPENING TIMES

1 Apr-30 Sep, daily	10am-6pm
1-31 Oct, daily	10am-5pm
1 Nov-31 Mar, daily	10am-4pm
Closed	24-26 Dec and 1 Jan

HOW TO FIND US

Direction: At Warton; 1 mile N of Carnforth, on minor road off A6

Train: Carnforth 1 mile

Bus: Carnforth Connect Line 1 from ⇌ Carnforth

MAP	Page 264 (3D)
	OS Map 97 (ref SD 499723)

WETHERAL PRIORY GATEHOUSE

CUMBRIA

The 15th-century gatehouse of a Benedictine priory, preserved after the dissolution ordered by Henry VIII because it then served as the vicarage for the parish church.

WETHERAL PRIORY GATEHOUSE

OPENING TIMES

24 Mar-30 Sep, daily	10am-6pm
1 Oct-31 Mar, daily	10am-5pm
Closed	24-26 Dec and 1 Jan

HOW TO FIND US

Direction: In Wetheral village; 6 miles E of Carlisle, on B6263

Train: Wetheral ½ mile

Bus: Stagecoach in Cumbria 74/5 Carlisle-Wetheral

MAP	Page 266 (4E)
	OS Map 86 (ref NY 468541)

WHALLEY ABBEY GATEHOUSE

LANCASHIRE

The outer gatehouse of the nearby Cistercian abbey, beside the River Calder. There was originally a chapel situated on the first floor.

Managed by Whalley Abbey Council.

OPENING TIMES

Any reasonable time

HOW TO FIND US

Direction: In Whalley; 6 miles NE of Blackburn, on minor road off A59

Train: Whalley ¼ mile

Bus: Lancashire United 225 Bolton-Clitheroe (passes ⇌ Blackburn)

MAP	Page 264 (4D)
	OS Map 103 (ref SD 729362)

DISCOUNTED ENTRY TO OUR MEMBERS (DISCOUNTS MAY NOT APPLY ON EVENT DAYS)

MUNCASTER CASTLE

RAVENGLASS, CUMBRIA

An amazing castle that has been home to the same family, the Penningtons, since 1208.

Managed by Peter and Iona Frost-Pennington.

OPENING TIMES

Please call 01229 717614

www.muncaster.co.uk

Discount for EH members. Discount does not extend to EH Corporate Partners.

MAP   Page 266 (6C)
       OS Map 96 (ref SD 103963)

NORTON PRIORY MUSEUM AND GARDENS

RUNCORN, CHESHIRE

Experience 800 years of history among 38 acres of tranquil, beautiful gardens. The new Medieval Herb Garden – a recreation of the oldest Garden in Britain – featured on BBC 2's 'Hidden Gardens'.

NORTON PRIORY MUSEUM AND GARDENS

ENTRY

Adult	£4.25
Concession	£2.95
Family tickets	£10.00

EH members: 2 adults for the price of 1 full paying adult (not Bank Holidays or with any other offer)

OPENING TIMES

Apr-Oct, Mon-Fri	12pm-5pm
Sat-Sun & Bank Hols	12pm-6pm
Nov-Mar, daily	12pm-4pm
Closed	24-26 Dec and 1 Jan
Tel: 01928 569895	

www.nortonpriory.org

MAP   Page 264 (6D)
       OS Map 108 (ref SJ 548830)

PENDLE HERITAGE CENTRE

BARROWFORD, LANCASHIRE

The centre features an 18th-century walled garden and exhibitions about the area.

Managed by Heritage Trust for the North West.

ENTRY

50% discount for EH members. Discount does not extend to EH Corporate Partners.

OPENING TIMES

Open all year, daily	10am-5pm
Closed	25 Dec
Tel: 01282 661704	

MAP   Page 264 (4E)
       OS Map 103 (ref SD 862398)

SALT MUSUEM

NORTHWICH, CHESHIRE

The museum, housed in a Victorian Workhouse, tells the fascinating history of mid-Cheshire and the industry which shaped the landscape and life of the area.

ENTRY

Adult	£2.40
Concession	£2.00
Child	£1.20

EH members: 1 free entry for every full paying adult (not applicable for group visits)

OPENING TIMES

Tue-Fri	10am-5pm
Sat-Sun	2pm-5pm
Bank holidays	10am-5pm
Tel: 01606 41331	

www.saltmuseum.org.uk

MAP   Page 264 (6D)
       OS Map 118 (ref SJ 658731)

SMITHILLS HALL

BOLTON, LANCASHIRE

Grade I-listed manor house, one of the oldest in the north west region.

ENTRY

Adult	£1.50

Reduction for EH members

OPENING TIMES

Please call 01204 332377

www.smithills.org

MAP   Page 264 (5D)
       OS Map 109 (ref SD 699119)

HADRIAN'S WALL

The Hadrian's Wall World Heritage Site
spans northern England, from the Solway
coast in Cumbria to the Tyne near Newcastle.
Over seventy-five miles long, the Wall was perhaps
the most strongly defended frontier in the whole
Roman Empire. Parts of it remain, often amid
dramatic scenery, where it is easy to imagine
what life was like for the soldiers of Rome.

NORTHUMBERLAND

CUMBRIA

TYNE & WEAR

1 Hare Hill	14 Sewingshields Wall
2 Banks East Turret	15 Temple of Mithras
3 Pike Hill Signal Tower	16 Black Carts Turret
4 Leahill Turret and Piper Sike Turret	17 Chesters Roman Fort
5 Birdoswald Roman Fort	18 Chesters Bridge
6 Harrow's Scar Milecastle and Wall	19 Brunton Turret
7 Willowford Wall, Turrets & Bridge	20 Planetrees Roman Wall
8 Poltross Burn Milecastle	21 Corbridge Roman Site
9 Walltown Crags	22 Heddon-on-the-Wall
10 Cawfields Roman Wall	23 Denton Hall Turret
11 Winshields Wall	24 Benwell Roman Temple and
12 Vindolanda Fort	Vallum Crossing
13 Housesteads Roman Fort	

www.english-heritage.org.uk/hadrianswall

BIRDOSWALD ROMAN FORT
HADRIAN'S WALL

Birdoswald Roman Fort is set high above the River Irthing, in one of the most inspiring and picturesque settings on Hadrian's Wall. A Roman fort, turret and milecastle can all be seen on this excellent stretch of the Wall.

PHOTO: ROGER CLEGG

The remains of the Wall at Birdoswald

Its role as a base for some 1,000 soldiers during the Roman occupation was significant, but the earliest Roman activity at Birdoswald relates to the construction of the earlier turf wall, later replaced in stone.

Archaeological discoveries over the past 150 years have revealed a great deal about Roman military life at Birdoswald. Three of the four main gateways into the fort have been unearthed, as have the outside walls of the fort, two granary buildings and a basilica. The basilica was the exercise and drill hall for soldiers stationed at the fort. The excavations have given archaeologists a great sense of the layout and plan of a Roman fort, but they believe the site still has much to reveal.

At the end of the Roman occupation of Britain, people continued to live at Birdoswald. It is thought that a Dark Age chieftain, possibly ruler of the local lands surrounding

Birdoswald, lived in a large timber hall built over the collapsed Roman granaries. Birdoswald has also been home to a clan of warring Border Reivers, Victorian gentlemen and numerous archaeologists.

The Birdoswald Visitor Centre provides a good introduction to Hadrian's Wall, and tells the intriguing story of Birdoswald and the people who have lived there over the past 2,000 years. There is a cosy tearoom at the site if you need refreshments, and a well-stocked shop for souvenirs.

Accommodation

If you would like to stay within the walls of the fort, there is a 39 bed residential centre, which can be booked for groups. It provides a great base for exploring this and other sites on the Wall, and is an excellent educational resource.

If you would like to find out more about staying at Birdoswald please contact us for a residential pack by calling 01697 747602.

Visitor centre

NON-MEMBERS

Adult	£3.60
Concession	£2.70
Child	£1.80
Family Ticket	£9.00

Education charge applies – ring site for details

OPENING TIMES

1 Mar-9 Nov, daily	10am-5.30pm
Last admission	5.00pm
Winter season (exterior only)	

HOW TO FIND US

Direction: 2¾ miles west of Greenhead off B6318

Tel: 01697 747602

Disabled access (limited).

MAP	Page 266 (4E)
	OS Map 86 (ref NY 615663)

www.english-heritage.org.uk/hadrianswall

View of the strongroom

CHESTERS ROMAN FORT

NORTHUMBERLAND

Chesters Fort was originally built to guard a Roman bridge, which crossed the North Tyne river at this point. It was one of a series of forts added to Hadrian's Wall as the result of a change of plan during construction.

It seems to have been occupied for nearly three centuries, and its six-acre plot would have held a cavalry regiment of around 500 men.

There is much to see on the ground: the four principal gateways are well preserved, as are the short lengths of Hadrian's Wall adjoining them. The entire foundation of the headquarters building is visible, with a court-yard, hall, regimental temple and strongroom clearly laid out.

Down by the river, the changing rooms, steam range and bathing rooms of the garrison's bath house are extremely well preserved, as is the Roman bridge abutment on the opposite bank of the river.

The on-site museum is housed in a smart Edwardian building, and displays a large collection of Roman stonework retrieved by Victorian antiquarian, John Clayton. It includes important early archaeological discoveries relating to the central section of the Wall.

Chesters Bridge abutment

NON-MEMBERS

Adult	£3.60
Concession	£2.70
Child	£1.80

OPENING TIMES

24 Mar-30 Sep, daily 9.30am-6pm
1 Oct-31 Mar, daily 10am-4pm
Closed 24-26 Dec and 1 Jan

HOW TO FIND US

Direction: 1¼ miles W of Chollerford, on B6318

Train: Hexham 5½ miles

Bus: Stagecoach in Cumbria AD122; also Tyne Valley 880/2 from Hexham, to within ½ mile

Tel: 01434 681379

Local Tourist Information Hexham: 01434 652220

Disabled access (limited).
Dogs on leads (restricted areas only).
Family learning resources available.
Tearoom (not managed by EH).

MAP Page 267 (4F)
OS Map 87 (ref NY 912702)

HADRIAN'S WALL

226

www.english-heritage.org.uk/hadrianswall

HOUSESTEADS ROMAN FORT

NORTHUMBERLAND

An important stronghold and now the most popular site on the Wall.

Housesteads is the best preserved and most famous Roman fort on Hadrian's Wall. It lies high on the great volcanic escarpment of Whin Sill, and commands a breathtaking view of the surrounding area.

Like Chesters, it was added to the wall during construction, and

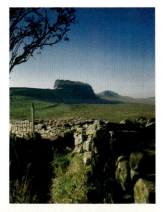

the earlier demolished turret can be seen. Originally it would have contained a garrison of some 1,000 soldiers.

Entry is through a small museum, which holds a complete model of how the site would once have looked. Excavations at the fort have revealed four double-portal gateways, the curtain wall with turrets and latrines, and three barrack blocks. At the centre are the most important buildings: the commanding officer's house, headquarters building and hospital.

The fort lies uphill from the car park (a ten minute walk).

Owned by the National Trust, in the care of EH.

NON-MEMBERS

Adult	£3.60
Concession	£2.70
Child	£1.80
Family	£9.00

OPENING TIMES

24 Mar-30 Sep, daily	10am-6pm
1 Oct-31 Mar, daily	10am-4pm
Closed	24-26 Dec and 1 Jan

HOW TO FIND US

Direction: 2¾ miles NE of Bardon Mill, on B6318

Bus/Train: Tel 0870 608 2608

Bus: Stagecoach in Cumbria AD122; also Tyne Valley 880/2 from 🚆 Hexham, to within ½ mile

Tel: 01434 344363

Local Tourist Information Hexham: 01434 652220

🅿 Ⓜ 🚹 🚽 📷 🏛 🖼 ♿ 🐕 ⚠ 🖲

Disabled access (car park at site; enquire at information centre on main road).

Family learning resources available.

Parking (charge payable to National Park).

MAP	Page 267 (4F)
	OS Map 87 (ref NY 790688)

www.english-heritage.org.uk/hadrianswall

BANKS EAST TURRET

CUMBRIA

Well-preserved turret with adjoining stretches of Hadrian's Wall.

HOW TO FIND US

Direction: On minor road E of Banks village; 3½ miles NE of Brampton

⚠ P

MAP   OS Map 86 (ref NY 575647)

BENWELL ROMAN TEMPLE AND VALLUM CROSSING

TYNE AND WEAR

Remains of a small temple and a stone-built causeway across the Vallum earthwork.

HOW TO FIND US

Direction: Temple located immediately S of A69, at Benwell in Broomridge Ave; Vallum Crossing in Denhill Park

Train: Newcastle 2 miles

Bus: Frequent from centre of Newcastle

MAP   OS Map 88 (ref NZ 217647)

BIRDOSWALD ROMAN FORT

GO TO PAGE 224

BLACK CARTS TURRET

NORTHUMBERLAND

A 460-metre (1,509ft) length of Hadrian's Wall including one turret.

Please note
It is not possible for visitors to park here.

HOW TO FIND US

Direction: 2 miles W of Chollerford on B6318

MAP   OS Map 87 (ref NY 884713)

BRUNTON TURRET

NORTHUMBERLAND

Wall section and a 2.5-metre high turret.

HOW TO FIND US

Direction: ¼ mile S of Low Brunton, off A6079

Train: Hexham 4 miles

Bus: Stagecoach in Cumbria AD122; also Tyne Valley 880/2 from 🚆 Hexham

🐕

MAP   OS Map 87 (ref NY 922698)

CAWFIELDS ROMAN WALL

NORTHUMBERLAND

CAWFIELDS ROMAN WALL

Turrets and an impressive milecastle – along with a fine, consolidated stretch of the Wall itself.

HOW TO FIND US

Direction: 1¼ miles N of Haltwhistle, off B6318

P 🚶 🚹

MAP   OS Map 87 (ref NY 716667)

CHESTERS BRIDGE ABUTMENT

NORTHUMBERLAND

The remains of the bridge which carried Hadrian's Wall across the North Tyne are visible on both banks, but most impressively on the eastern side.

HOW TO FIND US

Direction: ½ mile S of Low Brunton, on A6079

Train: Hexham 4½ miles

Bus: Stagecoach in Cumbria AD122; also Tyne Valley 880/2 from 🚆 Hexham, to within ½ mile

MAP   OS Map 87 (ref NY 914701)

CHESTERS ROMAN FORT

GO TO PAGE 226

CORBRIDGE ROMAN SITE
NORTHUMBERLAND

On the pivotal crossing of Dere Street over the Tyne, Corbridge played a vital role in every Roman campaign in northern Britain. It was founded c. AD85 during the first campaigns into Scotland under Agricola, and was used for the campaigns of Antoninus Pius in the mid 2nd century, and those of Septimius Severus in the early 3rd. It became a busy garrison town.

The remains include a fountain house with an aqueduct, a pair of granaries, and walled compounds for the military, containing barracks, temples, houses and a headquarters building with a below-ground strongroom.

The extensive museum displays a rich selection of Roman finds. An audio tour is provided to guide you around the site.

NON-MEMBERS

Adult	£3.60
Concession	£2.70
Child	£1.80

OPENING TIMES

24 Mar-30 Sep, daily	10am-6pm
1-31 Oct, daily	10am-4pm
1 Nov-31 Mar, Sat-Sun	10am-4pm
Closed	24–26 Dec and 1 Jan

HOW TO FIND US

Direction: ½ mile NW of Corbridge, on minor road, then signposted

Train: Corbridge 1¼ miles

Bus: Arriva Northumbria/ Stagecoach in Cumbria 85, 602, 685 Newcastleupon Tyne – Hexham, to within ½ mile

Tel: 01434 632349

Local Tourist Information
01434 652220

🅿 🏃 🚻 🏪 🏛 📷 ♿ 🏧
🎧 🐕 ⚠ 🚽

Dogs on leads (restricted areas only). Family learning resources available.

MAP   Page 267 (4F)
       OS Map 87 (ref NY 982648)

DENTON HALL TURRET
TYNE AND WEAR

The foundations of a turret and a 65-metre (213ft) length of Wall.

HOW TO FIND US

Direction: 4 miles W of Newcastle upon Tyne city centre, on A69

Train: Blaydon 2 miles

Bus: Frequent from centre of Newcastle

MAP   OS Map 88 (ref NZ 198655)

HARE HILL
CUMBRIA

A short length of Wall that still stands 2.7 metres (8.8ft) high.

HOW TO FIND US

Direction: ¾ mile NE of Lanercost

MAP   OS Map 86 (ref NY 564646)

HARROW'S SCAR MILECASTLE AND WALL

CUMBRIA

The most instructive mile section on the whole Wall. It is linked to Birdoswald Fort.

HOW TO FIND US

Direction: ¼ mile E of Birdoswald, on minor road off B6318

MAP   OS Map 86 (ref NY 620664)

HEDDON-ON-THE-WALL

NORTHUMBERLAND

A stretch of Wall up to 2 metres thick in places.

HOW TO FIND US

Direction: Immediately E of Heddon village; S of A69

Train: Wylam 3 miles

Bus: Go-Northern 684, Arriva Northumbria 685 from Newcastle upon Tyne

MAP   OS Map 88 (ref NZ 137669)

HOUSESTEADS ROMAN FORT

GO TO PAGE 227

LEAHILL TURRET AND PIPER SIKE TURRET

CUMBRIA

Turrets west of Birdoswald.

HOW TO FIND US

Direction: On minor road 2 miles W of Birdoswald Fort

MAP   OS Map 86 (ref NY 586652)

PIKE HILL SIGNAL TOWER

CUMBRIA

Remains of a signal tower, joined to Hadrian's Wall at an angle of 45 degrees.

HOW TO FIND US

Direction: On minor road E of Banks village

MAP   OS Map 86 (ref NY 577648)

PLANETREES ROMAN WALL

NORTHUMBERLAND

A 15-metre (49ft) length of narrow Wall on broad foundations.

HOW TO FIND US

Direction: 1 mile SE of Chollerford on B6318

Train: Hexham 5½ miles

Bus: Stagecoach in Cumbria AD122; also Tyne Valley 880/2 from 🚇 Hexham, to within ¾ mile

MAP   OS Map 87 (ref NY 929696)

POLTROSS BURN MILECASTLE

CUMBRIA

One of the best preserved of the milecastles of Hadrian's Wall. Poltross features an original flight of steps and the remains of its north gateway.

HOW TO FIND US

Direction: Immediately SW of Gilsland village, by old railway station

P
Parking (near the Station Hotel).

MAP   OS Map 86 (ref NY 634662)

SEWINGSHIELDS WALL
NORTHUMBERLAND

A length of Wall with milecastle remains.

HOW TO FIND US

Direction: N of B6318; 1½ miles E of Housesteads Fort

MAP   OS Map 87 (ref NY 805702)

TEMPLE OF MITHRAS, CARRAWBURGH
NORTHUMBERLAND

A 3rd-century temple, with facsimiles of altars found during excavation next to the fort remains at Carrawburgh.

HOW TO FIND US

Direction: 3¾ miles W of Chollerford, on B6318

P

MAP   OS Map 87 (ref NY 859711)

VINDOLANDA FORT
NORTHUMBERLAND

VINDOLANDA FORT

A fort and well-excavated civil settlement.

Owned and managed by Vindolanda Charitable Trust.

ENTRY

Adult	£4.50
Concession	£3.80
Child	£2.90

10% discount for EH members.

OPENING TIMES

12 Feb-31Mar, daily	10am-5pm
1 Apr-30 Sep, daily	10am-6pm
1 Oct-13 Nov, daily	10am-5pm
For winter opening, see website	

HOW TO FIND US

Direction: 1¼ miles SE of Twice Brewed; on minor road off B6318

Tel: 01434 344277

www.vindolanda.com

MAP   OS Map 87 (ref NY 771664)

WALLTOWN CRAGS
NORTHUMBERLAND

One of the best preserved lengths of Wall, snaking over the crags of the Whin Sill.

HOW TO FIND US

Direction: 1 mile NE of Greenhead, off B6318

MAP   OS Map 132 (ref NY 674663)

WILLOWFORD WALL, TURRETS AND BRIDGE
CUMBRIA

914 metres (2,999ft) of Wall, including two turrets and impressive bridge remains.

HOW TO FIND US

Direction: W of minor road, ¾ mile W of Gilsland

MAP   OS Map 132 (ref NY 627664)

WINSHIELDS WALL
NORTHUMBERLAND

Rugged section, including the highest point on the Wall.

HOW TO FIND US

Direction: W of Steel Rigg car park; on minor road off B6318

MAP   OS Map 87 (ref NY 742676)

Sign-up on-line for our email Members' Newsletter at **www.english-heritage.org.uk**

Looking for a unique present?

Why not browse our online shop at **www.english-heritage.org.uk/shopping**

Tynemouth Priory – The Percy Chantry

NORTH EAST

With a savage and fearful past, the breathtaking landscape of
the North East is peppered with once magnificent monuments.
Steeped in thousands of years of history, romance and tradition,
the old kingdom of Northumbria is secluded and mysterious.

233

PROPERTIES

SEE INDIVIDUAL LISTINGS FOR DETAILS

COUNTY DURHAM
Auckland Castle Deer House, Barnard Castle, Bowes Castle, Derwentcote Steel Furnace, Egglestone Abbey, Finchale Priory

NORTHUMBERLAND
Aydon Castle, Belsay Hall, Castle and Gardens, Berwick-upon-Tweed Barracks, Berwick-upon-Tweed Castle, Berwick-upon-Tweed Main Guard, Berwick-upon-Tweed Ramparts, Black Middens Bastle House, Brinkburn Priory, Dunstanburgh Castle, Edlingham Castle, Etal Castle, Lindisfarne Priory, Norham Castle, Prudhoe Castle, Warkworth Castle and Hermitage

REDCAR AND CLEVELAND
Gisborough Priory

TYNE AND WEAR
Bessie Surtees House, Hexham, Hylton Castle, St Paul's Monastery, Tynemouth Priory and Castle

HADRIAN'S WALL
See page 222

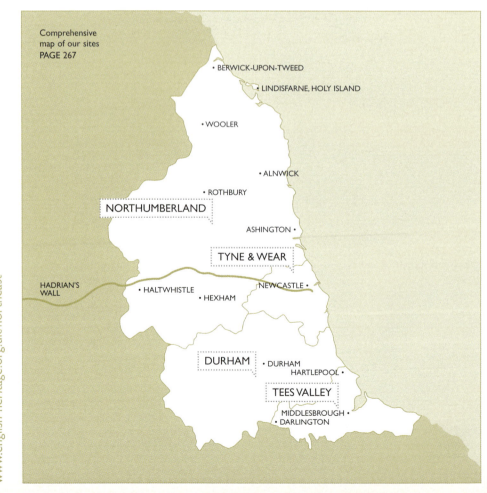

Comprehensive map of our sites
PAGE 267

- BERWICK-UPON-TWEED
- LINDISFARNE, HOLY ISLAND
- WOOLER
- ALNWICK
- ROTHBURY
NORTHUMBERLAND
ASHINGTON -
TYNE & WEAR
HADRIAN'S WALL
- HALTWHISTLE
NEWCASTLE -
- HEXHAM
DURHAM
- DURHAM
HARTLEPOOL -
TEES VALLEY
MIDDLESBROUGH -
- DARLINGTON

www.english-heritage.org.uk/northeast

Holy Island and Lindisfarne Priory

STEP BACK IN TIME

The most famous monument in the North East, and the most important Roman ruin on mainland Britain, is Hadrian's Wall. Some 75 miles long, it runs through spectacular sections of Northumbrian countryside, and is reinforced by many important forts, where Roman soldiers lived while defending their Empire's most northerly frontier.

In contrast to the rugged surroundings of Hadrian's Wall, Belsay Hall is set in 30 acres of unique and atmospheric gardens. The Hall, which was inspired by Classical architecture, the gardens, and the nearby 14th-century castle make a lovely day out for all the family.

To cross the causeway to Holy Island is to step back in time. Impressive Lindisfarne Priory is highly atmospheric, with a strong feeling of its crucial role in the history of Christian Britain. Founded in AD 635 by St.Aidan, it was long the home of St.Cuthbert, greatest of all Northumbrian holy men.

As well as preserving and managing many of the North East's most significant monuments, English Heritage works hard to bring the past to life and engage more people in the heritage of the country.

Over the past year English Heritage has undertaken the restoration of a memorial to Grace Darling, who famously helped her lighthouse-keeper father save nine people wrecked off the Farne Islands in 1838. She died of tuberculosis aged just 26, but her bravery in saving lives at sea won her the nation's adulation and renown in poems, paintings and songs.

The memorial was designed by Anthony Salvin in 1844, and shows an effigy of Grace asleep, with an oar from the boat she used during her daring feat. The neo-Gothic canopied tomb rests in the churchyard of St Aidan's, Bamburgh, where salty winds had taken their toll. Now, thanks to the Grace Darling Conservation Trust and a grant from English Heritage, the monument has been fully repaired, with a new set of storyboards, which tell the amazing Grace Darling story.

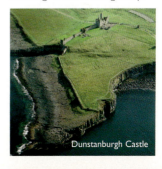

Dunstanburgh Castle

AUCKLAND CASTLE DEER HOUSE

CO. DURHAM

A charming deer house built in 1760 in the park of the Bishops of Durham, to provide deer with shelter and food.

Managed by the Church Commissioners for England. There is a separate charge for members.

OPENING TIMES

Park:
1 Apr-30 Sep, daily   10am-6pm
1 Oct-28 Mar, daily   10am-4pm
Closed   24-26 Dec and 1 Jan

HOW TO FIND US

Direction: Located in Auckland Park, Bishop Auckland; N of town centre on A68

Train: Bishop Auckland 1 mile

MAP   Page 267 (5G)
        OS Map 93 (ref NZ 216304)

AYDON CASTLE

NORTHUMBERLAND – NE45 5PJ

One of the finest examples in England of a 13th-century manor house, Aydon Castle was originally built as an undefended house during a time of unusual peace in the Borders.

AYDON CASTLE

When this ended it was fortified, but was pillaged and burnt by the Scots in 1315, seized by the English rebels two years later and subjected to much modification. In the 17th century Aydon was converted into a farmhouse, remaining so until 1966.

NON-MEMBERS

Adult	£3.30
Concession	£2.50
Child	£1.70

OPENING TIMES

24 Mar-30 Sep, daily   10am-6pm

HOW TO FIND US

Direction: 1 mile NE of Corbridge, on minor road off B6321 or A68

Train: Corbridge 4 miles – approach via bridle path from W side of Aydon Rd, immediately N of Corbridge bypass

Tel: 01434 632450

Disabled access (ground floor only). Dogs on leads (restricted areas only). Family learning resources available.

MAP   Page 267 (4F)
        OS Map 87 (ref NZ 001663)

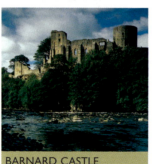

BARNARD CASTLE

CO. DURHAM

Perched high atop a steep bank overlooking the River Tees, Barnard Castle remains an imposing sight.

BARNARD CASTLE

It was damaged in 1630 when Sir Henry Vane bought it to use its stone to rebuild his preferred residence, Raby Castle. The foundations date back to the 12th century. Once one of the largest castles in northern England, it was also the principal residence of the Baliol family and a major power base in the many conflicts between the English and Scottish crowns, the rebellious nobles and the church.

NON-MEMBERS

Adult	£3.30
Concession	£2.50
Child	£1.70

OPENING TIMES

24 Mar-30 Sep, daily   10am-6pm
1-31 Oct, daily   10am-4pm
1 Nov-31 Mar, Thu-Mon 10am-4pm
Closed   24-26 Dec and 1 Jan

HOW TO FIND US

Direction: In Barnard Castle town

Bus: Arriva 75/6 Darlington – Barnard Castle (passes close to ⇌ Darlington)

Tel: 01833 638212

Family learning resources available. Toilets (in town).

MAP   Page 267 (6G)
        OS Map 92 (ref NZ 049165)

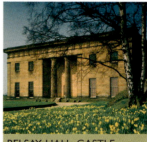

BELSAY HALL, CASTLE AND GARDENS

NORTHUMBERLAND GO TO PAGE 238

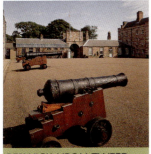

BERWICK-UPON-TWEED BARRACKS & MAIN GUARD

NORTHUMBERLAND

The Berwick Barracks, among the first to be purpose-built, were begun in 1717 based on a sketch by the distinguished court architect Nicholas Hawksmoor. Today, the Barracks hosts a number of attractions, including 'By Beat of Drum' – an exhibition on the life of the British infantryman. While there, visit the Regimental Museum of the King's Own Scottish Borderers, the Contemporary Art Gallery and the Clock Block exhibition.

The Main Guard is a Georgian Guard House near the quay: it displays 'The Story of a Border Garrison Town' exhibition.

The Guard House is managed by Berwick Civic Society.

NON-MEMBERS (BARRACKS)

Adult	£3.30
Concession	£2.50
Child	£1.70

OPENING TIMES

Barracks:
24 Mar-30 Sep, daily 10am-6pm

1-31 Oct, daily 10am-4pm

1 Nov-31 Mar: call site for details

Closed 24-26 Dec, 1 Jan and during Tattoo event – ring for details

BERWICK-UPON-TWEED BARRACKS & MAIN GUARD

HOW TO FIND US

Direction: On the Parade, off Church St in town centre

Train: Berwick-upon-Tweed ¼ mile

Bus: From surrounding areas

Tel: 01289 304493

Disabled access (Main Guard).
Dogs on leads (restricted areas only).
Parking (in town).

MAP Page 267 (1F)
OS Map 75 (Barracks ref NU 001531, Main Guard ref NU 000525)

BERWICK-UPON-TWEED CASTLE & RAMPARTS

NORTHUMBERLAND – TD15 1DF

The intriguing ruin of a 13th to 16th-century castle; the lower part of a keep and a Tudor gun emplacement remain. The Ramparts consist of remarkably complete 16th-century town fortifications, the entire circuit of which can be walked.

OPENING TIMES

Any reasonable time

HOW TO FIND US

Direction: The castle is adjacent to Berwick-upon-Tweed railway station, W of town centre; also accessible from river bank; the ramparts surround the town and can be accessed at various points

Train: Berwick-upon-Tweed

Bus: From surrounding areas

Disabled access (Ramparts).
Parking (Ramparts).

MAP Page 267 (1F)
OS Map 75 (ref NT 993534)

BESSIE SURTEES HOUSE

TYNE AND WEAR – NE1 3JF

These two 16th and 17th-century merchants' houses are examples of Jacobean domestic architecture. The house is best known as the scene of the elopement of Bessie Surtees and John Scott, who later became Lord Chancellor of England. An exhibition illustrating the history of the two buildings is on the first floor.

OPENING TIMES

Year round, Mon-Fri 10am-4pm

Closed Bank Hols and 24 Dec-3 Jan

HOW TO FIND US

Direction: 41-44 Sandhill, Newcastle upon Tyne

Train: Newcastle ½ mile

Metro: Central ½ mile

Bus: From surrounding areas

Tel: 01912 691200

MAP Page 267 (4G)
OS Map 88 (ref NZ 252638))

BISHOP AUCKLANDS DEER HOUSE

SEE AUCKLAND CASTLE DEER HOUSE

Sign-up on-line for our email Members' Newsletter at
www.english-heritage.org.uk

BELSAY HALL, CASTLE AND GARDENS
NORTHUMBERLAND – NE20 0DX

The vast, magnificent gardens provide a stunning setting for Belsay Hall and Castle. They are largely the work of two related men; Sir Charles Monck, who designed the dramatic Quarry Garden with its series of ravines and pinnacles, and his grandson, Sir Arthur Middleton, who enriched it with all manner of rare and exotic plants. The garden is now Grade 1 listed in the Register of Parks and Gardens.

Belsay Castle

Belsay Hall (1807) was designed by Sir Charles Monck in Greek Revival style, inspired by the Temple of Theseus he had visited in Athens, and is of great architectural interest. Sir Charles strove to create a modern country house that still resembled an ancient, Classical temple.

Belsay is definitely a plantsman's garden and much of the original planting survives, including magnificent magnolias, Pieris floribunda and Exochorda giraldii. A wide variety of species of rhododendrons flower for most of the year, and there is also a large Hybrid Rhododendron Garden, which comes into full bloom from late May to June. There are also formal terraces and the amazingly exotic Quarry Garden, as well as the Winter Garden.

Visually impaired visitors may enjoy the heady scent of the hybrid musk roses and pinks, as well as the birdsong which can be heard in the garden throughout the seasons. The level impacted gravel paths and short grass make the gardens suitable for wheelchairs, and there are plenty of seats for everyone to stop and enjoy the stunning setting.

The castle, which can be found beyond the gardens, is a dramatic, well-preserved medieval tower house, to which a Jacobean manor house was added in 1614.

Belsay has something for everyone: a magical mansion with a fascinating history, wonderful additional buildings and a unique garden for all seasons. There is a tearoom in the summer and food and drink can be brought out to the picnic area.

www.english-heritage.org.uk/belsay

The Pillar Hall

NON-MEMBERS

Adult	£5.30
Concession	£4.00
Child	£2.70
Family ticket	£13.30

OPENING TIMES

24 Mar-30 Sep, daily	10am-6pm
1-31 Oct, daily	10am-4pm
1 Nov-31 Mar, Thu-Mon	10am-4pm
Closed	24-26 Dec and 1 Jan

HOW TO FIND US

Direction: In Belsay; 14 miles NW of Newcastle, on A696

Train: Morpeth 10 miles

Bus: Snaith's 808 from Newcastle; Arriva 508 from ⇄ Newcastle (Sun only, Jun-Oct); National Express Newcastle – Edinburgh, to within 1 mile

Tel: 01661 881636

Local Tourist Information Morpeth: 01670 500700

Disabled access (grounds, tea room and ground floor only; toilets).

Dogs on leads (restricted areas only).

Tearooms/restaurant (Belsay Hall Tea room open daily Apr-Oct, Sat-Sun in Mar).

MAP	Page 267 (3G) OS Map 88 (ref NZ 086785)

Great Arch in Quarry Garden

BLACK MIDDENS BASTLE HOUSE

NORTHUMBERLAND

A stone, two-storey fortified farmhouse, built during the 16th century and set in splendid walking country on the Reivers Route.

OPENING TIMES

Any reasonable time

HOW TO FIND US

Direction: 180 metres N of minor road, 7 miles NW of Bellingham; or along a minor road from A68

MAP   Page 267 (3F)
       OS Map 80 (ref NY 773900)

BOWES CASTLE

CO. DURHAM

The massive ruins of Henry II's tower keep, three storeys high and set within the earthworks of a Roman fort, overlooking the valley of the River Greta.

OPENING TIMES

Any reasonable time

HOW TO FIND US

Direction: In Bowes Village off A66; 4 miles W of Barnard Castle town

Bus: Hodgson's 72, 574 from Barnard Castle

MAP   Page 267 (6F)
       OS Map 92 (ref NY 992135)

BRINKBURN PRIORY

NORTHUMBERLAND – NE65 8AR

Brinkburn Priory was founded c.1135 as a monastery of Augustinian canons. The scenic 10 minute walk down from the car park passes some gnarled and ancient trees, which frame the visitor's first view of the church. This, the only complete surviving building of the monastery, was probably begun in the late 12th century. The adjacent post-dissolution manor house also incorporates part of the medieval monastery.

NON-MEMBERS

Adult	£2.30
Concession	£1.70
Child	£1.20

OPENING TIMES

24 Mar-30 Sep, daily   10am-6pm

HOW TO FIND US

Direction: 4½ miles SE of Rothbury, off B6344

Train: Acklington 10 miles

Bus: Arriva/Northumbria Coaches 516 Morpeth – Thropton (passes Morpeth), with connections from Newcastle (passes Tyne & Wear Metro Haymarket) to within ½ mile.

Tel: 01665 570628

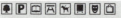

Family learning resources available. Picnic area (¹/₃ mile).

MAP   Page 267 (3G)
       OS Map 81 (ref NZ 116983)

DERWENTCOTE STEEL FURNACE

CO. DURHAM

Built in the 18th century, Derwentcote is the earliest and most complete steel-making furnace to have survived to the present day.

OPENING TIMES

4 Apr-26 Sep, 1st & 3rd Sun of each month   1pm-5pm

HOW TO FIND US

Direction: 10 miles SW of Newcastle, on A694; between Rowland's Gill and Hamsterley

Train: Metro Centre, Gateshead, 7 miles

Bus: Go North East 45/6 Newcastle – Consett

Tel: 0191 269 1200 (Mon-Fri)

Dogs on leads (restricted areas only).

MAP   Page 267 (4G)
       OS Map 88 (ref NZ 130566)

DUNSTANBURGH CASTLE

NORTHUMBERLAND – NE66 3TT

DUNSTANBURGH CASTLE

Dramatic Dunstanburgh Castle was built at a time of political crisis and Anglo-Scottish conflict, when relations soured between King Edward II and his cousin, Thomas Earl of Lancaster, who built the castle. Lancaster began the fortress in 1313 as a remote and secure refuge, but failed to reach it when his rebellion was defeated, being taken and executed in 1322. Thereafter the castle passed eventually to John of Gaunt, who strengthened it against the Scots by converting the great twin-towered gatehouse into a keep. The focus of fierce fighting during the Wars of the Roses, it was twice besieged and captured by Yorkist forces, but subsequently fell into decay: its dramatic ruins still watch over a headland famous for seabirds.

New for 2005
New interpretation panels displaying the results of the recent English Heritage survey of the castle.

Owned by the National Trust, maintained and managed by EH. Free to NT members.

NON-MEMBERS

Adult	£2.60
Concession	£2.00
Child	£1.30

OPENING TIMES

24 Mar-30 Sep, daily	10am-6pm
1-31 Oct, daily	10am-4pm
1 Nov-31 Mar, Thu-Mon	10am-4pm

HOW TO FIND US
Direction: 8 miles NE of Alnwick; on footpaths from Craster or Embleton – 1½ miles flat coastal walk

DUNSTANBURGH CASTLE

Train: Chathill (U), not Sun, 5 miles from Embleton, 7 miles from Castle; Alnmouth, 7 miles from Craster, 8¼ miles from Castle

Bus: Arriva 401, 501 Alnwick – Belford with connections from ⮾ Berwick-upon-Tweed and Newcastle (passing Metro Haymarket); alight Craster, 1½ miles

Tel: 01665 576231

Parking (in Craster village; a charge is payable).

MAP   Page 267 (2G)
       OS Map 75 (ref NU 257219)

EDLINGHAM CASTLE

NORTHUMBERLAND

Set in a beautiful valley, this complex ruin boasts defensive features dating from the 13th to 15th centuries.

Managed by the Parochial Church Council of St John the Baptist, Edlingham, with Bolton Chapel.

OPENING TIMES
Any reasonable time

HOW TO FIND US
Direction: At E end of Edlingham village, on minor road off B6341; 6 miles SW of Alnwick

Train: Alnmouth 9 miles

Note: waterproof footwear is recommended.

MAP   Page 267 (2G)
       OS Map 81 (ref NU 116092)

EGGLESTONE ABBEY

CO. DURHAM

The charming ruins of a small monastery of Premonstratensian 'white canons', founded c.1200 and picturesquely set above a bend in the River Tees near Barnard Castle. Remains include much of the church and a range of living quarters, with traces of their ingenious toilet drainage system.

OPENING TIMES

Daily	10am-6pm

HOW TO FIND US
Direction: 1 mile S of Barnard Castle, on a minor road off B6277

Bus: Arriva 79 Richmond – Barnard Castle; 75/6 Darlington – Barnard Castle (passes close to ⮾ Darlington), then 1½ miles

MAP   Page 267 (6G)
       OS Map 92 (ref NZ 062151)

i

If you would like more information on properties, events and membership please call 0870 333 1181 or email **customers@ english-heritage.org.uk**

241

ETAL CASTLE

NORTHUMBERLAND – TD12 4TN

In 1341, Robert Manners was granted a licence to fortify his home to protect it against the threat of attack from Scottish raiders. In 1513, when an army of 30,000 Scots led by James IV invaded England, Etal Castle fell, but these invaders were then defeated in the bloody battle that ensued on Flodden Field. An award-winning exhibition tells the story of the Battle of Flodden and of the border warfare that existed here before the union of the English and Scottish crowns in 1603.

NON-MEMBERS

Adult	£3.30
Concession	£2.50
Child	£1.70
Family ticket	£8.30

OPENING TIMES

24 Mar-30 Sep, daily   10am-6pm

HOW TO FIND US

Direction: In Etal village, 10 miles SW of Berwick

Train: Berwick-upon-Tweed 10½ miles

Bus: Border Villager 267 Berwick-upon-Tweed – Wooler

ETAL CASTLE

Tel: 01890 820332

Audio (the audio tour guides visitors around the castle and the exhibition).

Dogs on leads (restricted areas only).

Family learning resources available.

Toilets (in village).

MAP	Page 267 (1F)
	OS Map 74 (ref NT 925393)

FINCHALE PRIORY

CO. DURHAM – DH9 5SH

The very extensive remains of a 13th-century priory, founded on the site of a retired pirate's hermitage. Later, part of it served as a holiday retreat for the monks of Durham Cathedral. Beautifully sited by the River Wear, it can be reached from Durham via a delightful riverside and woodland walk.

NON-MEMBERS

Adult	£2.30
Concession	£1.70
Child	£1.20

OPENING TIMES

24 Mar-30 Sep, Sat & Sun
and Bank Hols   10am-6pm

HOW TO FIND US

Direction: 3 miles NE of Durham; on minor road off A167

Train: Durham 5 miles

Tel: 01913 863828

Parking (on south side of river; charge applicable).

Tearoom (not managed by EH).

MAP	Page 267 (4G)
	OS Map 88 (ref NZ 296471)

GISBOROUGH PRIORY

REDCAR AND CLEVELAND

The ruins of an Augustinian priory founded by the Bruce family, afterwards Kings of Scotland. They are dominated by the dramatic skeleton of the 14th-century church's east end.

Managed by Redcar and Cleveland Borough Council.

NON-MEMBERS

Adult	£1.10
Concession	£0.75
Child	£0.55

OPENING TIMES

1 Apr-30 Sep, Tues-Sun	9am-5pm
1 Oct-28 Mar, Wed-Sun	9am-5pm
Closed	24 Dec-1 Jan

HOW TO FIND US

Direction: In Guisborough town, next to the parish church

Train: Marske 4½ miles

Bus: Arriva X56, 65, 93, 765 from Middlesbrough (passes close to ⟶ Middlesbrough)

Tel: 01287 633801

Toilets (in town).

MAP	Page 267 (6H)
	OS Map 94 (ref NZ 617160)

HADRIAN'S WALL

GO TO PAGE 222

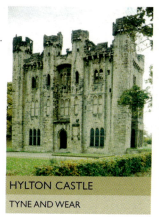

HYLTON CASTLE
TYNE AND WEAR

NORHAM CASTLE
NORTHUMBERLAND – TD15 2JY

NORHAM CASTLE

Train: Berwick-upon-Tweed 7½ miles

Bus: Swan/Buskers 23 ⊠ Berwick-upon-Tweed – Kelso

Tel: 01289 382329

♿ ⬚ ⬚ ⛺ ✕ 🎧 ⚠ 🅿

Disabled access (excluding keep).

MAP	Page 267 (1F)
	OS Map 74 (ref NT 906476)

The remains of a castle built by Sir William Hilton between 1374 and 1420. The keep gatehouse still stands and can be enjoyed today by visitors to the grounds. Adorning the façades is a fine display of medieval heraldic shields.

Managed by Sunderland City Council.

OPENING TIMES

Any reasonable time (grounds only)

HOW TO FIND US

Direction: 3¾ miles W of Sunderland

Train: Seaburn 2½ miles

Bus: From surrounding areas

🅿 ♿ ✕

Disabled access (grounds only). Parking (in town centre).

MAP	Page 267 (4H)
	OS Map 88 (ref NZ 358588)

LINDISFARNE PRIORY

NORTHUMBERLAND GO TO PAGE 244

Norham was one of the strongest of the border castles. Built in the latter half of the 12th century, it came under siege several times during its 400-year history as a military stronghold. Norham's massive walls proved impenetrable during many of these attacks, but when James IV of Scotland stormed it in 1513, it fell and was largely destroyed. The Great Tower shows signs of four building phases spanning the 12th to 16th centuries. Much of what can be seen today dates from the extensive repairs to the castle and the re-roofing of the Great Tower which followed the siege of 1513.

NON-MEMBERS

Adult	£2.60
Concession	£2.00
Child	£1.30

OPENING TIMES

24 Mar-30 Sep, Sun-Mon and Bank Hols   10am-6pm

HOW TO FIND US

Direction: In Norham village; 6 miles SW of Berwick-upon-Tweed, on minor road off B6470 (from A698)

Visit www.english-heritage.org.uk for up-to-date events information and the latest news.

English Heritage membership makes a lovely gift.

Call 0870 333 1181 or visit www.english-heritage.org.uk/gift for more details.

LINDISFARNE PRIORY

NORTHUMBERLAND – TD15 2RX

Lindisfarne Priory on Holy Island was the site of one of the most important centres of early Christianity in Anglo-Saxon England. It is still a place of pilgrimage today, and the dramatic approach across the causeway only adds to the fascination of the site.

St Aidan founded the monastery in AD635, but it is St Cuthbert, Prior of Lindisfarne, who is the most celebrated of the priory's holy men. After many missionary journeys, and 10 years as a hermit on lonely Farne Island, he reluctantly became Bishop before retiring to die on Farne in 687. Buried in the priory, his remains were transferred to a pilgrim shrine there after 11 years, and found still undecayed – a sure sign of sanctity.

From the end of the 8th century, the isolated island with its rich monastery was easy prey for Viking raiders. In 875 the monks left, carrying Cuthbert's remains, which after long wanderings were enshrined in Durham Cathedral in 1104, where they still rest. Only around that time did Durham monks re-establish a priory on Lindisfarne: the small community lived quietly on Holy Island until the suppression of the monastery in 1537.

The causeway floods at high tide, so it is very important to check the tide times before crossing.

www.english-heritage.org.uk/lindisfarne

New for 2005

The museum has been refurbished to offer a clear and lively interpretation of the story of St Cuthbert and the development of Lindisfarne Priory.

NON-MEMBERS

Adult	£3.60
Concession	£2.70
Child	£1.80

OPENING TIMES

24 Mar-30 Sep, daily	9.30am-5pm
1-31 Oct, daily	9.30am-4pm
1 Nov-31 Mar, Sat-Mon	10am-2pm
Closed	24-26 Dec and 1 Jan

HOW TO FIND US

Direction: On Holy Island, only reached at low tide across causeway; tide tables at each end, or details from tourist info

Train: Berwick-upon-Tweed 14 miles, via causeway

Bus: Travelsure 477 from Berwick-upon-Tweed (passes close to ⇄ Berwick-upon-Tweed); times vary with tides

Tel: 01289 389200

Tourist Information Centre 01289 330733

Dogs on leads (restricted areas only). Family learning resources available.

MAP	Page 267 (1G)
	OS Map 75 (ref NU 126417)

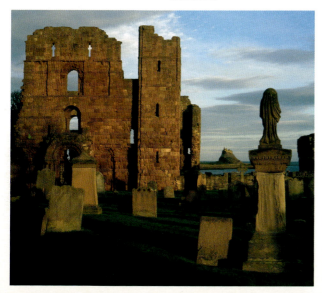

PRUDHOE CASTLE
NORTHUMBERLAND – NE42 6NA

On a wooded hillside overlooking the River Tyne stand the remains of this formidable castle. Archaeological evidence reveals that a defended enclosure existed on the site as early as the mid-11th century. Today, inside the defensive ditches and walls, the Georgian manor house is a dominating feature. The castle was successfully defended against many Scottish attacks, resisting sieges in 1173 and 1174. This was famously recorded by the contemporary chronicler, Jordan Fantosme. There is a brass-rubbing centre and a beautiful picnic spot.

New for 2005
New exhibition and collections explain the development of this medieval castle, and its important role in the history of this border county.

NON-MEMBERS

Adult	£3.30
Concession	£2.50
Child	£1.70

OPENING TIMES
24 Mar-30 Sep, daily   10am-6pm

PRUDHOE CASTLE

HOW TO FIND US
Direction: In Prudhoe, on minor road off A695

Train: Prudhoe ¼ mile

Bus: From surrounding areas

Tel: 01661 833459

Dogs on leads (restricted areas only). Family learning resources available.

MAP	Page 267 (4G) OS Map 88 (ref NZ 091634)

ST PAUL'S MONASTERY, JARROW
TYNE AND WEAR

The home of the Venerable Bede, the Anglo-Saxon church partly survives as the chancel of the parish church. The monastery has become one of the best-understood Anglo-Saxon monastic sites. English Heritage members also receive a discount on the entry fee to the nearby Bede's World Museum.

Managed by Bede's World.

OPENING TIMES
Monastery ruins any reasonable time

ST PAUL'S MONASTERY, JARROW

HOW TO FIND US
Direction: In Jarrow, on minor road N of A185; follow signs for Bede's World

Metro: Bede ¾ miles

Bus: Go North East 527 Newcastle – South Shields

Tel: 01914 897052

MAP	Page 267 (4H) OS Map 88 (ref NZ 339652)

Check *Heritage Today* for news and information on forthcoming events and exclusive members' offers.

English Heritage members can take up to 6 children, as part of a family group, into our properties at no extra cost (see page 6).

TYNEMOUTH PRIORY AND CASTLE

TYNE AND WEAR – NE30 4BZ

The coastal location of Tynemouth, which lies on a promontory between the sea and the river, has long been considered a strategically important site. Perched on the cliff-top near the village are the striking ruins of a Benedictine priory and medieval castle. A burial place of saints and kings, the history of the area combines military and religious significance.

Founded in 1090 on the site of an ancient Anglian monastery, the priory church boasts ornate eastern sections that stand only just short of their original height of 22 metres (72ft).

The castle commands the northern approaches of the River Tyne and has been a valued defence against threats from the Vikings, medieval Scotland, Napoleon and 20th-century Germany. It played a

part in both World Wars, and today you can see the restored magazine of a coastal defence gun battery at weekends.

Tynemouth's vast headland will make a perfect spot to watch the Tall Ships race 2005, part of a world-class maritime event that is taking place at the waterfront at Newcastle/Gateshead from the 25th to 28th July 2005 (Parade of Sail event on 28th July).

The Tall Ships race is one of a series of events which form part of the SeaBritain 2005 Festival. This maritime festival aims to celebrate ways in which the sea touches our lives. Events will take place throughout the country all year. Visit www.seabritain2005.co.uk for more details.

www.english-heritage.org.uk/ tynemouthcastle

NON-MEMBERS

Adult	£3.30
Concession	£2.50
Child	£1.70
Family ticket	£8.30

OPENING TIMES

24 Mar-30 Sep, daily	10am-6pm
1-31 Oct, daily	10am-4pm
1 Nov-31 Mar, Thu-Mon	10am-4pm
Gun Battery: Jun-Aug: Sat & Sun & Bank Hols	10am-6pm
Closed	24-26 Dec and 1 Jan

HOW TO FIND US

Direction: In Tynemouth, near North Pier

Metro: Tynemouth ½ mile

Bus: From surrounding areas

Tel: 0191 257 1090

Disabled access (priory only).
Family learning resources available.

MAP	Page 267 (4H)
	OS Map 88 (ref NZ 373694)

www.english-heritage.org.uk/northeast

WARKWORTH CASTLE AND HERMITAGE

NORTHUMBERLAND – NE65 0UJ

The magnificent cross-shaped keep of Warkworth, crowning a hilltop rising steeply above the River Coquet, dominates one of the largest, strongest and most impressive fortresses in northern England. The castle's most famous owners were the Percy family, whose lion badge can be seen carved on many parts of their stronghold. Wielding almost kingly power in the north, their influence reached its apogee under the first Earl of Northumberland and his son 'Harry Hotspur', hero of many Border ballads as the bane of Scots raiders and a dominant character in Shakespeare's *'Henry IV'*. Having helped to depose Richard II, these turbulent 'kingmakers' both fell victim to Henry IV: the next three Percy earls likewise died violent deaths.

Still roofed and almost complete, the uniquely-planned keep dates mainly from the end of the 14th century. It presides over the extensive remains of a great hall, chapel, fine gatehouse and a virtually intact circuit of towered walls.

Half a mile from the castle, tucked away by the Coquet and accessible only by boat, stands a much more peaceful building: the late medieval cave Hermitage and chapel of a solitary holy man.

There are free tours of the Duke's Rooms in the castle keep on Sun, Wed and Bank Hols, 1 April-30 Sept

www.english-heritage.org.uk/warkworth

NON-MEMBERS (CASTLE)

Adult	£3.30
Concession	£2.50
Child	£1.70
Family ticket	£8.30

NON-MEMBERS (HERMITAGE)

Adult	£2.30
Concession	£1.70
Child	£1.20

OPENING TIMES

Castle:

24 Mar-30 Sep	10am-6pm
1-31 Oct, daily	10am-4pm
1 Nov-31 Mar, Sat-Mon	10am-4pm

Hermitage:

24 Mar-30 Sep, Wed, Sun & Bank Hols	11am-5pm
Closed	24-26 Dec and 1 Jan

HOW TO FIND US

Direction: In Warkworth; 7½ miles S of Alnwick, on A1068

Train: Alnmouth 3½ miles

Bus: Arriva 518 Newcastle – Alnwick

Tel: 01665 711423

Audio tours (also available for the visually impaired and those with learning difficulties).

Disabled access (limited access only).

Dogs on leads (restricted areas only).

Family learning resources available.

MAP	Page 267 (2G)
	OS Map 81 (ref NU 247058)

OTHER HISTORIC ATTRACTIONS

DISCOUNTED ENTRY TO OUR MEMBERS (DISCOUNTS MAY NOT APPLY ON EVENT DAYS)

BEDE'S WORLD MUSEUM
TYNE AND WEAR

Significant site that celebrates the extraordinary life of the Venerable Bede. Interactive museum and recreated Anglo-Saxon farm buildings with rare breed animals.

Managed by Bede's World.

ENTRY

Half-price for English Heritage members. Discount does not extend to EH Corporate Partners

OPENING TIMES

1 Apr-31 Oct
Mon-Sat   10am-5.30pm
Sun   12pm-5.30pm

1 Nov-31 Mar
Mon-Sat   10am-4.30pm
Sun   12pm-4.30pm

Tel: 0191 489 2106

MAP   Page 267 (4H)
       OS Map 88 (ref NZ 388654)

CHESTERS WALLED GARDEN
NORTHUMBERLAND

Historic two acre walled garden famous for herbs and flower filled border, organically grown. A haven of peace, scent and colour.

ENTRY

Concessionary rate for English Heritage members. Please call for details.

OPENING TIMES

Good Fri-31 Oct   10am-5pm

Tel: 01434 681483

MAP   Page 267 (4F)
       OS Map 87 (ref NY 906703)

Don't forget your membership card when you visit any of the properties listed in this handbook.

SEGEDUNUM ROMAN FORT, BATHS AND MUSEUM
TYNE AND WEAR

The reconstruction of a Roman bathhouse and section of Hadrian's Wall, including an Interactive Museum

Managed by Tyne and Wear Museums.

ENTRY

10% reduction for English Heritage members, please call site for details

Discount does not extend to EH Corporate Partners.

OPENING TIMES

1 Apr-31 Aug, daily   9.30am-5pm
1 Sep-31 Oct, daily   10am-5pm
1 Nov-31 Mar, daily 10am-3.30pm

Tel: 0191 236 9347

MAP   Page 267 (4H)
       OS Map 88 (ref NZ 300660)

Looking for a unique present?

Why not browse our online shop at www.english-heritage.org.uk/shopping

OTHER HISTORIC ATTRACTIONS

SCOTLAND, WALES AND THE ISLE OF MAN

In addition to free admission to English Heritage properties featured in this handbook, members of English Heritage are also entitled to free or reduced-price entry to a host of other historic attractions in Scotland, Wales and on the Isle of Man. Entry is discounted in the first year of membership and free in subsequent years.

MANX NATIONAL HERITAGE

English Heritage members can gain half-price admission to Manx National Heritage attractions during the first year of membership and free entry in subsequent years.

For more details please write to:
Manx National Heritage, Douglas, Isle of Man IM1 3LY

Please call **01624 648000** or you can visit the Manx National Heritage website at **www.gov.im/mnh**

Castle Rushen
Castletown

Cregneash Folk Village
Cregneash

The Grove Rural Life Museum
Ramsey

House of Manannan
Peel

Laxey Wheel and Mines Trail
Laxey

Manx Museum
Douglas

Nautical Museum
Castletown

Old Grammar School
Castletown

Old House of Keys
Castletown

Peel Castle
Peel

Rushen Abbey
Ballasalla

Sound Visitor Centre
Port St Mary

Laxey Wheel

English Heritage members can gain half-price admission to Cadw attractions during the first year of membership and free entry in subsequent years.

For more details on Cadw, write to:
Plas Carew, Unit 5/7 Cefn Coed, Parc Nantgarw, Cardiff, CF15 7QQ

Please call **01443 336000** or you can visit the Cadw website at **www.cadw.wales.gov.uk**

PHOTO: CADW WELSH HISTORIC MONUMENTS

Tintern Abbey

Beaumaris Castle,
Anglesey
Tel: 01248 810361

Blaenavon Ironworks,
Nr Pontypool,
Torfaen
Tel: 01495 792615

Caerleon Roman
Fortress, Caerleon,
Newport
Tel: 01633 422518

Caernarfon Castle,
Caernarfon,
Gwynedd
Tel: 01286 677617

Caerphilly Castle,
Caerphilly
Tel: 02920 883143

Carreg Cennen Castle,
Nr Trapp,
Carmarthenshire
Tel: 01558 822291

Castell Coch, Cardiff
Tel: 02920 810101

Chepstow Castle,
Chepstow,
Monmouthshire
Tel: 01291 624065

Cilgerran Castle,
Nr Cardigan,
Ceredigion
Tel: 01239 615007

Conwy Castle, Conwy
Tel: 01492 592358

Criccieth Castle,
Nr Criccieth, Gwynedd
Tel: 01766 522227

Dolwyddelan Castle,
Dolwyddelan,
Gwynedd
Tel: 01690 750366

Harlech Castle,
Harlech, Gwynedd
Tel: 01766 780552

Kidwelly Castle,
Kidwelly,
Carmarthenshire
Tel: 01554 890104

Laugharne Castle,
Laugharne,
Carmarthenshire
Tel: 01994 427906

Oxwich Castle,
Oxwich, Swansea
Tel: 01792 390359

Plas Mawr, Conwy,
Tel: 01492 580167

Raglan Castle,
Nr Raglan,
Monmouthshire
Tel: 01291 690228

Rhuddlan Castle,
Rhuddlan, Denbighshire
Tel: 01745 590777

Rug Chapel and
Llangar Church,
Corwen, Denbighshire
Tel: 01490 412025

St Davids Bishop's
Palace, St Davids,
Pembrokeshire
Tel: 01437 720517

Strata Florida Abbey,
Pontrhydfendigaid,
Ceredigion
Tel: 01974 831261

Tintern Abbey,
Tintern,
Monmouthshire
Tel: 01291 689251

Tretower Court
and Castle,
Tretower,
Powys
Tel: 01874 730279

Valle Crucis Abbey,
Nr Llangollen,
Denbighshire
Tel: 01978 860326

Weobley Castle,
Nr Llanrhidian, Swansea
Tel: 01792 390012

White Castle,
Nr Abergavenny,
Monmouthshire
Tel: 01600 780380

HISTORIC SCOTLAND

English Heritage members can gain half-price admission to Historic Scotland attractions during the first year of membership and free entry in subsequent years.

For more details on Historic Scotland, write to:

Longmore House, Salisbury Place, Edinburgh EH9 1SH

Please call **0131 668 8999** or you can visit the Historic Scotland website at www.historic-scotland.gov.uk

Edinburgh Castle

Aberdour Castle and Garden, Aberdour, Fife
Tel: 01383 860519

Arbroath Abbey, Angus
Tel: 01241 878756

Argyll's Lodging, Stirling, Central
Tel: 01786 431319

Balvenie Castle, Dufftown, Grampian
Tel: 01340 820121

Bishop's and Earl's Palaces, Kirkwall, Orkney
Tel: 01856 871918

The Black House, Arnol, Lewis, Western Isles
Tel: 01851 710395

Blackness Castle, Firth of Forth, Edinburgh and Lothians
Tel: 01506 834807

Bonawe Historic Iron Furnace, Taynuilt, Argyll
Tel: 01866 822432

Bothwell Castle, Bothwell, Greater Glasgow
Tel: 01698 816894

Broch of Gurness, Aikerness, Orkney
Tel: 01856 751414

Caerlaverock Castle, Nr Dumfries, Dumfries and Galloway
Tel: 01387 770244

Cairnpapple Hill, Torphichen, Edinburgh and Lothians
Tel: 01506 634622

Calanais Standing Stones, Isle of Lewis, Western Isles
Tel: 01851 621422

Cardoness Castle, Nr Fleet, Dumfries and Galloway
Tel: 01557 814427

Castle Campbell, Dollar Glen, Central
Tel: 01259 742408

Corgarff Castle, Nr Strathdon, Grampian
Tel: 01975 651460

Craigmillar Castle, Edinburgh and Lothians
Tel: 0131 6614445

Craignethan Castle, Lanark, Greater Glasgow
Tel: 01555 860364

Crichton Castle, Nr Pathhead, Edinburgh and Lothians
Tel: 01875 320017

Crossraguel Abbey, Nr Maybole, Greater Glasgow
Tel: 01655 883113

Dallas Dhu Historic Distillery, Nr Forres, Grampian
Tel: 01309 676548

Dirleton Castle and Gardens, Dirleton, Edinburgh and Lothians
Tel: 01620 850330

Doune Castle, Doune, Central
Tel: 01786 841742

Dryburgh Abbey, Nr Melrose, Borders
Tel: 01835 822381

Dumbarton Castle, Dumbarton, Greater Glasgow
Tel: 01389 732167

Dundonald Castle, Dundonald, Greater Glasgow
Tel: 01563 851489

Dundrennan Abbey, Nr Kirkcudbright, Dumfries and Galloway
Tel: 01557 500262

Dunfermline Palace and Abbey, Dunfermline, Fife
Tel: 01383 739026

Dunstaffnage Castle, Nr Oban, Argyll
Tel: 01631 562465

Edinburgh Castle, Edinburgh and Lothians
Tel: 0131 225 9846

Edzell Castle and Garden, Edzell, Angus
Tel: 01356 648631

Elcho Castle, Nr Bridge of Earn, Perthshire
Tel: 01738 639998

Elgin Cathedral, Elgin, Grampian
Tel: 01343 547171

Fort George, Nr Ardersier village, Highlands
Tel: 01667 460232

Glasgow Cathedral, Glasgow
Tel: 0141 552 6891

Glenluce Abbey, Nr Glenluce, Dumfries and Galloway
Tel: 01581 300541

Hackness Martello Tower and Battery, Hoy, Orkney
Tel: 01856 811397

Hermitage Castle, Nr Newcastleton, Borders
Tel: 01387 376222

Huntingtower Castle, Nr Perth, Perthshire
Tel: 01738 627231

Huntly Castle, Huntly, Grampian
Tel: 01466 793191

Inchcolm Abbey,
Firth of Forth,
Fife
Tel: 01383 823332

Inchmahome Priory,
Lake of Menteith,
Central
Tel: 01877 385294

Iona Abbey and
Nunnery,
Island of Iona, Central
Tel: 01681 700512

Jarlshof Prehistoric
and Norse Settlement,
Sumburgh Head,
Shetland
Tel: 01950 460112

Jedburgh Abbey
and Visitor Centre,
Jedburgh, Borders
Tel: 01835 863925

Kildrummy Castle
Nr Alford,
Grampian
Tel: 01975 571331

Kinnaird Head Castle,
Lighthouse and Museum,
Fraserburgh,
Grampian
Tel: 01346 511022

Kisimul Castle,
Isle of Barra,
Western Isles
Tel: 01871 810313

Linlithgow Palace,
Linlithgow, Edinburgh
and Lothians
Tel: 01506 842896

Lochleven Castle,
Lochleven, Perthshire
Tel: 07778 040483

MacLellan's Castle,
Kirkcudbright, Dumfries
and Galloway
Tel: 01557 331856

Maeshowe Chambered
Cairn, Nr Kirkwall,
Orkney
Tel: 01856 761606

Meigle Sculptured
Stone Museum,
Meigle, Angus
Tel: 01828 640612

Melrose Abbey,
Melrose, Borders
Tel: 01896 822562

New Abbey Corn Mill,
New Abbey, Dumfries
and Galloway
Tel: 01387 850260

Newark Castle,
Port Glasgow,
Greater Glasgow
Tel: 01475 741858

Rothesay Castle,
Rothesay, Isle of Bute
Tel: 01700 502691

St Andrews Castle,
St Andrews, Fife
Tel: 01334 477196

St Andrews Cathedral,
St Andrews, Fife
Tel: 01334 472563

St Serf's Church and
Dupplin Cross,
Dunning, Perthshire
Tel: 01764 684497

Seton Collegiate
Church, Nr Cockenzie,
Edinburgh and Lothians
Tel: 01875 813334

Skara Brae and
Skaill House,
Nr Kirkwall,
Orkney
Tel: 01856 841815

Smailholm Tower,
Near Smailholm,
Borders
Tel: 01573 460365

Spynie Palace,
Nr Elgin, Grampian
Tel: 01343 546358

Stirling Castle,
Stirling, Central
Tel: 01786 450000

Sweetheart Abbey,
New Abbey,
Dumfries
and Galloway
Tel: 01387 850397

Tantallon Castle,
Nr North Berwick,
Edinburgh and Lothians
Tel: 01620 892727

Threave Castle,
Nr Castle Douglas,
Dumfries and Galloway
Tel: 07711 223101

Tolquhon Castle,
Nr Aberdeen,
Grampian
Tel: 01651 851286

Urquhart Castle,
Drumnadrochit,
Highlands
Tel: 01456 450551

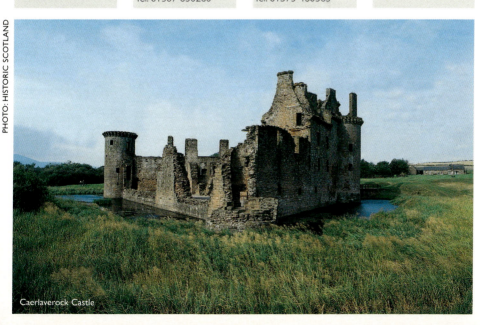

Caerlaverock Castle

Ayshford Chapel, Devon

THE FRIENDS OF FRIENDLESS CHURCHES

The Friends own redundant but beautiful places of worship that would otherwise have been demolished or left to ruin. We now have 34 Grade II* and Grade I buildings in England and Wales. In 2004 we finished work on the tower to our church at Boveney on the banks of the Thames near Eton, with the help of an enormous English Heritage grant of £150,000. Without this grant the tower might well have collapsed.

Matlock Bath, Derbyshire

THE FRIENDS OF FRIENDLESS CHURCHES
St. Ann's Vestry Hall, 2 Church Entry, London EC4V 5HB

Tel: 020 7236 3934
Email: office@friendsoffriend
lesschurches.org.uk

www.friendsoffriendless
churches.org.uk

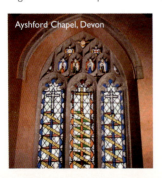
Ayshford Chapel, Devon

We are a small, voluntary organisation which welcomes visitors. Our churches are places for quiet study and contemplation. We do not claim sophistication in terms of parking, toilets, attendants or shops, and access may require approach to a key-keeper. You can support our work by becoming a member.

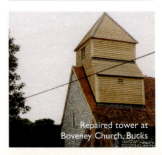
Repaired tower at Boveney Church, Bucks

Little Witchingham, Norfolk

THE CHURCHES CONSERVATION TRUST

The Churches Conservation Trust conserves England's beautiful and historic churches which are no longer needed for regular worship. It promotes public enjoyment of these churches, and encourages their use as an educational and community resource. Many are open all year round, others have a keyholder nearby; all are free.

English Heritage and CCT work closely together on a range of issues concerning historic church buildings such as joint provision of learning activities at Wroxeter, Shropshire.

Many churches host concerts and festivals, drama groups and exhibitions. English Heritage members looking for a venue are welcome to contact us.

Next time you visit an English Heritage property why not take in a nearby Trust church? One example of many is Audley End House, where a fine series of monuments to the Audley family and a superb hammerbeam roof can be found in the nearby Trust chapel at St Michael's, Berechurch. And if you live nearby, why not volunteer to help us keep the church open?

THE CHURCHES CONSERVATION TRUST

1 West Smithfield
London EC1A 9EE

Tel: 020 7213 0660
Fax: 020 7213 0678
Email: central@tcct.org.uk

www.visitchurches.org.uk

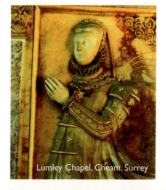

St John the Baptist, Inglesham, Wiltshire

Lumley Chapel, Cheam, Surrey

SOUTH WEST

BRISTOL
CORNWALL
DEVON
DORSET
GLOUCESTER
ISLES OF SCILLY
SOMERSET
WILTSHIRE

⚅ English Heritage Sites
▲ Other Historic Attractions

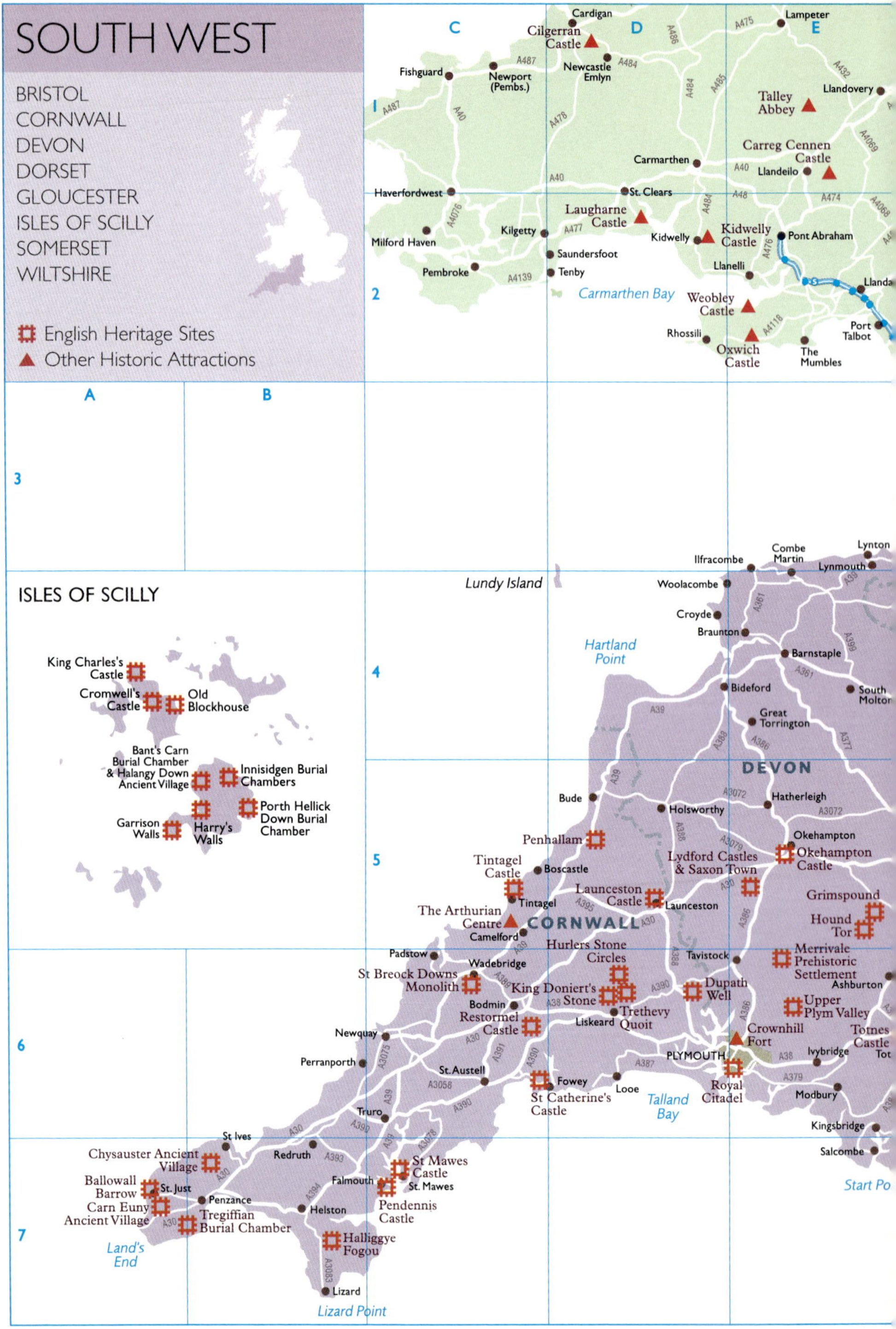

A **B** **C** **D** **E**

1
Cardigan
Cilgerran Castle ▲
Fishguard
Newport (Pembs.)
Newcastle Emlyn
A487
A40
A478
Lampeter
A475
Llandovery
Talley Abbey ▲
Carreg Cennen Castle ▲
Carmarthen
Llandeilo
Haverfordwest
St. Clears
A40
Milford Haven
Kilgetty
Laugharne Castle ▲
Kidwelly
Kidwelly Castle ▲
Pont Abraham
Llanda
2
Pembroke
Saundersfoot
Tenby
A4139
Carmarthen Bay
Llanelli
Weobley Castle ▲
Port Talbot
Rhossili
Oxwich Castle ▲
The Mumbles

3

ISLES OF SCILLY

King Charles's Castle ⚅
Cromwell's Castle ⚅
Old Blockhouse ⚅
Bant's Carn Burial Chamber & Halangy Down Ancient Village ⚅
Innisidgen Burial Chambers ⚅
Garrison Walls ⚅
Harry's Walls ⚅
Porth Hellick Down Burial Chamber ⚅

4
Lundy Island
Ilfracombe
Combe Martin
Lynton
Lynmouth
Woolacombe
Croyde
Braunton
Hartland Point
Barnstaple
Bideford
South Molton
Great Torrington
DEVON
Bude
Holsworthy
Hatherleigh
Okehampton
5
Penhallam ⚅
Lydford Castles & Saxon Town ⚅
Okehampton Castle ⚅
Tintagel Castle ⚅
Boscastle
Launceston Castle ⚅
Launceston
Grimspound
Hound Tor ⚅
The Arthurian Centre ▲
Tintagel
Camelford
CORNWALL
Hurlers Stone Circles ⚅
Tavistock
Merrivale Prehistoric Settlement ⚅
Ashburton
Padstow
Wadebridge
King Doniert's Stone ⚅
Dupath Well ⚅
Upper Plym Valley ⚅
St Breock Downs Monolith ⚅
Bodmin
Trethevy Quoit ⚅
Restormel Castle ⚅
Liskeard
Newquay
Crownhill Fort ▲
Totnes Castle ⚅
Perranporth
PLYMOUTH
Ivybridge
6
St. Austell
Fowey
Looe
Royal Citadel ⚅
Modbury
Truro
St Catherine's Castle ⚅
Talland Bay
Kingsbridge
St Ives
Redruth
Salcombe
Chysauster Ancient Village ⚅
Falmouth
St Mawes Castle ⚅
St Mawes
Start Po
Ballowall Barrow ⚅
St. Just
Penzance
Helston
Pendennis Castle ⚅
Carn Euny Ancient Village ⚅
Tregiffian Burial Chamber ⚅
7
Land's End
Halliggye Fogou ⚅
Lizard
Lizard Point

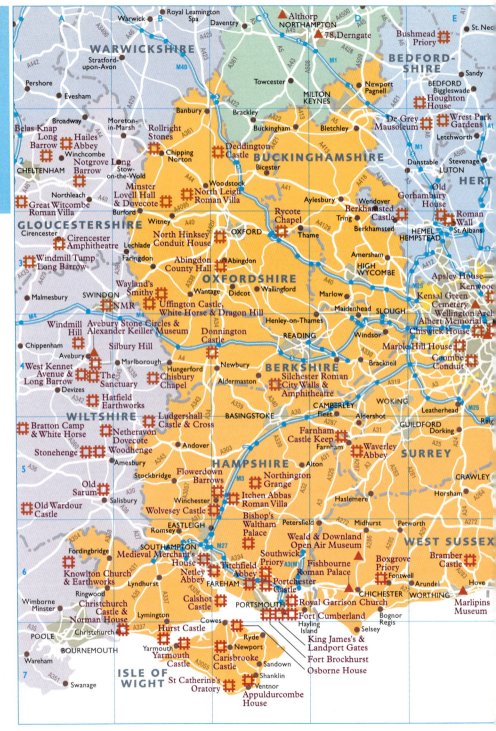

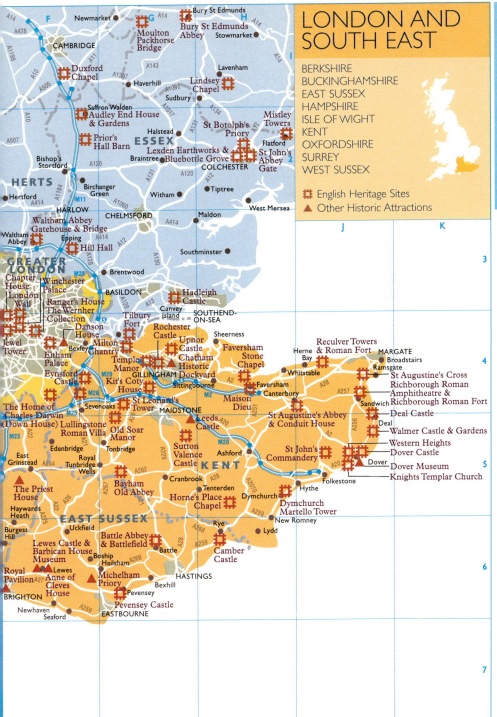

LONDON AND SOUTH EAST

BERKSHIRE
BUCKINGHAMSHIRE
EAST SUSSEX
HAMPSHIRE
ISLE OF WIGHT
KENT
OXFORDSHIRE
SURREY
WEST SUSSEX

⌗ English Heritage Sites
▲ Other Historic Attractions

F · G · H · I
J · K

2

3

4

5

6

7

Newmarket

Bury St Edmunds
Bury St Edmunds Abbey
Stowmarket

CAMBRIDGE

Moulton Packhorse Bridge

A14
A428
A1198
A14

A143
Lavenham

Duxford Chapel

A505
A10
A1307
Haverhill
A1092

Lindsey Chapel

Sudbury

A134

Saffron Walden
Audley End House & Gardens

Prior's Hall Barn

Halstead
Braintree

Mistley Towers

A131

Flatford
St John's Abbey Gate

A120

ESSEX

Lexden Earthworks & Bluebottle Grove
COLCHESTER

St Botolph's Priory

Bishop's Stortford

A120
A12

Tiptree

HERTS

Birchanger Green

Hertford
A414
A1184

Witham

West Mersea

HARLOW
CHELMSFORD

M11

Waltham Abbey
Gatehouse & Bridge

Maldon

A414

Epping
Hill Hall

Waltham Abbey

Southminster

GREATER LONDON

Chapter House
London Wall

Winchester Palace

Ranger's House
The Wernher Collection

Jewel Tower

Danson House

Brentwood

M25

BASILDON

A128
A13

Hadleigh Castle

Canvey Island

SOUTHEND-ON-SEA

Tilbury Fort

Rochester Castle

Upnor Castle

Sheerness

Reculver Towers & Roman Fort

MARGATE

Milton Chantry

Bexley

Chatham Historic Dockyard

Faversham Stone Chapel

Herne Bay

Broadstairs

Ramsgate

Eltham Palace

Temple Manor

GILLINGHAM

Whitstable

St Augustine's Cross

Eynsford Castle

M20

Kit's Coty House

Sittingbourne

A2

Faversham

A28

Richborough Roman Amphitheatre & Richborough Roman Fort

M26

M2

Canterbury

A257

Sandwich

The Home of Charles Darwin (Down House)

Sevenoaks

St Leonard's Tower

MAIDSTONE

Maison Dieu

A251

St Augustine's Abbey & Conduit House

Deal Castle

M25

Lullingstone Roman Villa

Old Soar Manor

Leeds Castle

A20

A2

A256

Deal

Walmer Castle & Gardens

M23
A22

Edenbridge

Royal Tunbridge Wells

Tonbridge

Sutton Valence Castle

Ashford

St John's Commandery

A20

Western Heights
Dover Castle

A2

East Grinstead
A264

A229

KENT

A2070

Dover

Dover Museum

Knights Templar Church

The Priest House

Cranbrook

Tenterden

A28

Hythe

Folkestone

Haywards Heath

A275

Bayham Old Abbey

A262

Dymchurch

Horne's Place Chapel

A259

Dymchurch Martello Tower

Burgess Hill

Uckfield

EAST SUSSEX

Rye

New Romney

Royal Pavilion

Lewes Castle & Barbican House Museum

Boship
Hailsham

A269

Battle

Lydd

Camber Castle

BRIGHTON

A27

Lewes
Anne of Cleves House

Michelham Priory

Battle Abbey & Battlefield

A259

HASTINGS

Bexhill

Newhaven
Seaford

A259

Pevensey

EASTBOURNE

Pevensey Castle

EAST OF ENGLAND

BEDFORDSHIRE
CAMBRIDGESHIRE
ESSEX
HERTFORDSHIRE
NORFOLK
SUFFOLK

⌗ English Heritage Sites
▲ Other Historic Attractions

Mansfield   C   Rufford Abbey   D   Woodhall Spa   E
Newark-on-Trent   Coningsby   Tattershall College
A616   A617   A612   A46   A17   A15   A153
A60   Papplewick Pumping Station   Sleaford   A1121
M1   NOTTINGHAMSHIRE   A1   A153
NOTTINGHAM   West Bridgford   A52   Grantham   A607   Spalding
A453   A52   Belvoir Castle   A52   A151   A16
A6006   A60   A606   Melton Mowbray   A607   A1   A132
Loughborough   A6   A607   A606   Rutland Water   Stamford   A1073
LEICESTERSHIRE   Oakham   RUTLAND
Kirby Muxloe Castle   LEICESTER   Longthorpe Tower
Jewry Wall   Lyddington Bede House   Kirby Hall   PETERBOROUGH   Flag Fen Excavations
TAMWORTH   A47   A47   Corby   A427   Oundle   CAMBS.
WOLVERHAMPTON   Bosworth Battlefield   Market Harborough   Rushton Triangular Lodge   Eleanor Cross
WALSALL   M42   Hinckley   M69   A14   Kettering   A14   Huntingdon
WEST MIDLANDS   NUNEATON   M1   A508   A43   Chichele College
DUDLEY   BIRMINGHAM   A45   Lutterworth   A4304   NORTHAMPTON-SHIRE   Wellingborough   St. Neots
Merry Hill   SOLIHULL   COVENTRY   M6   RUGBY   M1   M428   Althorp   A4500   Bushmead Priory
Kenilworth Castle   Kenilworth   Stoneleigh Abbey   Chichele College   Sandy
Bromsgrove   Warwick   Royal Leamington Spa   78,Derngate   BEDFORD-SHIRE
WORCS.   Droitwich Spa   Daventry   NORTHAMPTON   BIGGLESWADE   Houghton House
WARWICKSHIRE   A361   Towcester   MILTON KEYNES   Newport Pagnell   De Grey Mausoleum   Wrest Park
Pershore   Stratford-upon-Avon   M40   Banbury   Brackley   Buckingham   Bletchley   Letchworth
Evesham   Belas Knap Long Barrow   Moreton-in-Marsh   Rollright Stones   BUCKINGHAMSHIRE   Dunstable   LUTON   Stevenage
Broadway   Hailes Abbey   Winchcombe   Chipping Norton   Deddington Castle   Bicester   HERTS.
CHELTENHAM   Stow-on-the-Wold   Notgrove Long Barrow   Woodstock   Aylesbury   Old Gorhambury House
Great Witcombe Roman Villa   Northleach   Minster Lovell Hall & Dovecote   North Leigh Roman Villa   Berkhamsted Castle   Roman Wall
GLOUS.   Cirencester   Burford   Witney   Rycote Chapel   Wendover   Tring   St. Albans
Cirencester Amphitheatre   Lechlade   North Hinksey Conduit House   OXFORD   Thame   Berkhamsted   HEMEL HEMPSTEAD
Windmill Tump Long Barrow   Faringdon   Abingdon County Hall   Abingdon   Amersham   HIGH WYCOMBE   Apsley House
Malmesbury   Wayland's Smithy   OXFORDSHIRE   Wantage   Didcot   Wallingford   Marlow   SLOUGH   Kensal Green Cemetery   Kenwood
SWINDON   NMR   Uffington Castle, White Horse & Dragon Hill   Maidenhead   Albert Memorial   Wellington Arch
Windmill Hill   Avebury Stone Circles & Alexander Keiller Museum   Donnington Castle   Henley-on-Thames   READING   Windsor   Chiswick House
Chippenham   Silbury Hill   Hungerford   Newbury   BERKSHIRE   Bracknell   Marble Hill House   Coombe Conduit
Avebury   West Kennet Avenue & Long Barrow   Marlborough   Chisbury Chapel   Aldermaston
The Sanctuary

F   G   H   J   K

Sibsey Trader Windmill

Boston

Blakeney Guildhall

Wells-next-the-Sea

Sheringham   Cromer

Holt

Hunstanton

Creake Abbey

Baconsthorpe Castle

The Wash

Binham Priory   Binham Wayside Cross

Mundesley

Holbeach

Long Sutton

Fakenham

Aylsham

North Walsham

Castle Rising Castle

King's Lynn

Castle Acre Bailey Gate   Castle Acre Castle

North Elmham Chapel

Hoveton

Great Yarmouth Row Houses & Greyfriars' Cloisters

Hemsby

Caister Roman Site

Great Yarmouth

Wisbech

Castle Acre Priory

East Dereham

Cow Tower

NORWICH

Berney Arms Windmill

Time & Tide Museum

Downham Market

Swaffham

NORFOLK

Wymondham

Loddon

Burgh Castle

March

Grimes Graves

Attleborough

St Olave's Priory

LOWESTOFT

CAMBRIDGESHIRE

Weeting Castle

Thetford Warren Lodge

Bungay

Beccles

Chatteris

Isleham Priory Church

Brandon

Thetford Priory   Thetford

Diss

Kessingland

Ely

Church of the Holy Sepulchre

SUFFOLK

Halesworth

Southwold

Denny Abbey & the Farmland Museum

Bury St Edmunds Abbey

Saxtead Green Post Mill

Framlingham Castle

Newmarket

Bury St Edmunds

Stowmarket

Leiston Abbey

CAMBRIDGE

Moulton Packhorse Bridge

Aldeburgh

Duxford Chapel

Lavenham

Woodbridge

Orford Castle

Haverhill

Lindsey/St James's Chapel

IPSWICH

Orford

Sudbury

Saffron Walden

Audley End House & Gardens

Halstead

St Botolph's Priory

Mistley Towers   Felixstowe

Felixstowe Museum

Landguard Fort

Prior's Hall Barn

ESSEX

Lexden Earthworks & Bluebottle Grove

St John's Abbey Gate

Flatford

Harwich

Bishop's Stortford

COLCHESTER

Walton-on-the-Naze

HERTS.

Braintree

Frinton-on-Sea

Hertford

Birchanger Green

Witham

Tiptree

Clacton-on-Sea

HARLOW

CHELMSFORD

West Mersea

Waltham Abbey Gatehouse & Bridge

Epping

Maldon

Waltham Abbey

Hill Hall

Southminster

Brentwood

GREATER LONDON

Chapter House

BASILDON

Hadleigh Castle

Islington

London Wall

Tilbury Fort

Canvey Island

SOUTHEND-ON-SEA

Winchester Palace

Bexley

Rochester Castle

Sheerness

Greenwich

Milton Chantry

Reculver Towers & Roman Fort

Eltham Palace

Upnor Castle

Faversham

Herne Bay

MARGATE

Jewel Tower

The Wernher Collection

Temple Manor

Chatham Historic Dockyard

Stone Chapel

Broadstairs

Ramsgate

Eynsford Castle

GILLINGHAM

Whitstable

St Augustine's Cross

MAPS: CREATED BY ARKA LTD. FOR ENGLISH HERITAGE. ©12/04

WEST MIDLANDS

HEREFORDSHIRE
SHROPSHIRE
STAFFORDSHIRE
WARWICKSHIRE
WEST MIDLANDS
WORCESTERSHIRE

⌗ English Heritage Sites
▲ Other Historic Attractions

262

GREATER MANCHESTER
DERBYSHIRE
STAFFORDSHIRE
SHROPSHIRE
WEST MIDLANDS
WARWICKSHIRE
WORCESTERSHIRE
HEREFORDSHIRE

Smithills Hall
BOLTON
BURY
Manchester North
OLDHAM
Holmfirth
Monk Bretton Priory
BARNSLEY
SALFORD
MANCHESTER
Ashton-under-Lyne
Glossop
SHEFFIELD
Warrington
WARRINGTON
STOCKPORT
Altrincham
Peveril Castle
CHESTERFIELD
Knutsford
Macclesfield
Buxton
Hob Hurst's House
Northwich
Winsford
Sandbach
Congleton
Bakewell
Nine Ladies Stone Circle
Arbor Low Stone Circle & Gib Hill Barrow
Matlock
Wingfield Manor
Sandbach Crosses
Crewe
Leek
Gib Hill Barrow
DERBYSHIRE
Gresford
Nantwich
NEWCASTLE-UNDER-LYME
STOKE-ON-TRENT
Ashbourne
Ripley
Rug Chapel & Llangar Church
Wrexham
Croxden Abbey
Valle Crucis Abbey
Whitchurch
Corwen
Llangollen
Old Oswestry Hill Fort
Market Drayton
Stone
DERBY
Oswestry
Ellesmere
STAFFORDSHIRE
Uttoxeter
Moreton Corbet Castle
Ashby de la Zouch Museum
Llanfyllin
Haughmond Abbey
Lilleshall Abbey
STAFFORD
Burton-upon-Trent
Ashby de la Zouch Castle
SHREWSBURY
TELFORD
Boscobel House & the Royal Oak
CANNOCK
Ashby de la Zouch
Welshpool
Wroxeter Roman City
Buildwas Abbey
White Ladies Priory
Lichfield
Moira Furnace
Cantlop Bridge
Ironbridge Iron Bridge
Wall Roman Site
TAMWORTH
Mitchell's Fold Stone Circle
Acton Burnell Castle
WOLVERHAMPTON
WALSALL
Bosworth Battlefield
Church Stretton
Langley Chapel
Wenlock Priory
Bridgnorth
WEST MIDLANDS
NUNEATON
Newtown
SHROPSHIRE
DUDLEY
BIRMINGHAM
COVENTRY
Clun Castle
Stokesay Castle
Merry Hill
SOLIHULL
Stoneleigh Abbey
Knighton
Ludlow
KIDDERMINSTER
Kenilworth Castle
Wigmore Castle
Bromsgrove
Kenilworth
Mortimer's Cross Water Mill
WORCESTERSHIRE
Royal Leamington Spa
Presteigne
Witley Court
Droitwich Spa
Warwick
Llandrindod Wells
Edvin Loach Old Church
WORCESTER
Builth Wells
Leominster
Bromyard
Leigh Court Barn
Stratford-upon-Avon
Queenswood
Great Malvern
Pershore
WARWICKSHIRE
Hay-on-Wye
HEREFORDSHIRE
Evesham
Arthur's Stone
Hereford
Upton-upon-Severn
Broadway
Moreton-in-Marsh
Longtown Castle
Rotherwas Chapel
Ledbury
Belas Knap Long Barrow
Hailes Abbey
Rollright Stones
Brecon
St Mary's Church Kempley
Tewkesbury
Winchcombe
Chipping Norton
Tretower
Odda's Chapel
Newent
CHELTENHAM
Stow-on-the-Wold
North Leigh Roman Villa
Tretower Castle
Crickhowell
Ross-on-Wye
Over Bridge
Notgrove Long Barrow
Tretower Court
White Castle
Goodrich Castle
Blackfriars & Greyfriars
GLOUCESTER
Northleach
Monmouth

EAST MIDLANDS

DERBYSHIRE
LEICESTERSHIRE
LINCOLNSHIRE
NORTHAMPTONSHIRE
NOTTINGHAMSHIRE
RUTLAND

⊞ English Heritage Sites
▲ Other Historic Attractions

Created by Arka Cartographics Ltd. for English Heritage. © 12/04.

NORTH WEST (BOTTOM)

CHESHIRE
GREATER MANCHESTER
LANCASHIRE
MERSEYSIDE

⌗ English Heritage Sites
▲ Other Historic Attractions

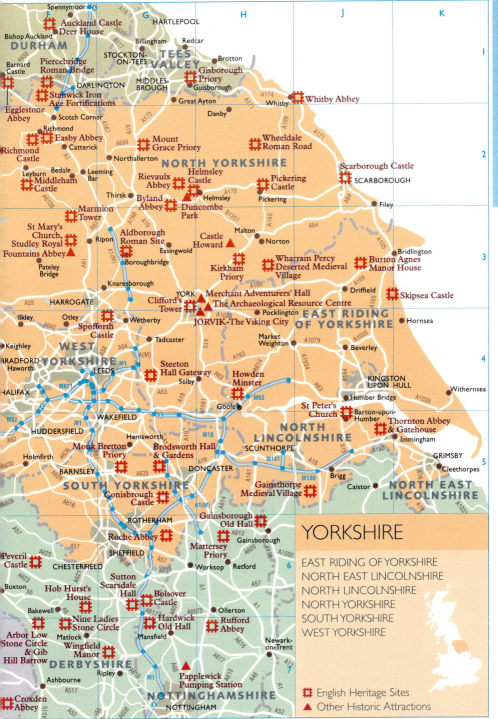

F · G · HARTLEPOOL · H · J · K

1

Spennymoor
Auckland Castle
Deer House
Bishop Auckland
DURHAM
Barnard Castle
Piercebridge
Roman Bridge
DARLINGTON
Stanwick Iron
Age Fortifications
Egglestone
Abbey
Scotch Corner
Richmond
Easby Abbey
Richmond
Castle
Catterick
Leyburn Bedale Leeming Bar
Middleham
Castle
Marmion Tower
St Mary's Church, Studley Royal
Fountains Abbey
Ripon
Pateley Bridge

Billingham Redcar
STOCKTON-ON-TEES
MIDDLES-BROUGH
Brotton
Gisborough Priory
Guisborough
TEES VALLEY
Great Ayton
A174
Whitby
Whitby Abbey
Danby

Mount Grace Priory
Northallerton
NORTH YORKSHIRE
Wheeldale
Roman Road
Helmsley
Castle
Rievaulx
Abbey
Pickering
Castle
Scarborough Castle
SCARBOROUGH
Thirsk
Byland
Abbey
Duncombe
Park
Helmsley
Pickering
Filey

2

Aldborough
Roman Site
Boroughbridge
Easingwold
Castle
Howard
Malton
Norton
Kirkham
Priory
Wharram Percy
Deserted Medieval
Village
Bridlington
Burton Agnes
Manor House
Driffield
Skipsea Castle

3

Knaresborough
HARROGATE
A59
Ilkley Otley
Spofforth
Castle
Wetherby
YORK
Clifford's
Tower
Merchant Adventurers' Hall
The Archaeological Resource Centre
Pocklington
JORVIK-The Viking City
EAST RIDING
OF YORKSHIRE
Hornsea

4

BRADFORD
Haworth
WEST
YORKSHIRE
LEEDS
Tadcaster
Steeton
Hall Gateway
Selby
Howden
Minster
Goole
Market
Weighton
Beverley
KINGSTON
UPON HULL
Humber Bridge
Withernsea
HALIFAX
HUDDERSFIELD
WAKEFIELD
St Peter's
Church
Barton-upon-Humber
Thornton Abbey
& Gatehouse
Immingham

5

Holmfirth
Monk Bretton
Priory
Hemsworth
Brodsworth Hall
& Gardens
DONCASTER
NORTH
LINCOLNSHIRE
SCUNTHORPE
GRIMSBY
Cleethorpes
BARNSLEY
SOUTH YORKSHIRE
Conisbrough
Castle
ROTHERHAM
Gainsthorpe
Medieval Village
Brigg
Caistor
NORTH EAST
LINCOLNSHIRE
Roche Abbey
SHEFFIELD

6

Peveril
Castle
CHESTERFIELD
Mattersey
Priory
Worksop Retford
Gainsborough
Old Hall
Gainsborough
Buxton
Hob Hurst's
House
Sutton
Scarsdale
Hall
Bolsover
Castle
Hardwick
Old Hall
Ollerton
Rufford
Abbey
Bakewell
Nine Ladies
Stone Circle
Matlock
Mansfield
Newark-on-Trent

7

Arbor Low
Stone Circle
& Gib
Hill Barrow
Wingfield
Manor
Ripley
Papplewick
Pumping Station
Croxden
Abbey
Ashbourne
NOTTINGHAMSHIRE
NOTTINGHAM
DERBYSHIRE

YORKSHIRE

EAST RIDING OF YORKSHIRE
NORTH EAST LINCOLNSHIRE
NORTH LINCOLNSHIRE
NORTH YORKSHIRE
SOUTH YORKSHIRE
WEST YORKSHIRE

English Heritage Sites
▲ Other Historic Attractions

MAPS: CREATED BY ARKA LTD. FOR ENGLISH HERITAGE. ©12/04

NORTH WEST (TOP)

CUMBRIA

⬡ English Heritage Sites

▲ Other Historic Attractions

A737 A77 A726 A723 A72 A8 A71 A702 A702 A71 A72 A697 E

A Bothwell Castle Hamilton **B** **C** **D** **E**

M77

Dundonald Castle

Craignethan Castle M74 Lanark

Prestwick

Muirkirk Biggar

Cumnock

Sanquhar Abington

Moffat

Peebles

A72

Galashiels Melrose

Selkirk

Hawick

Crichton Castle

Melrose Abbey Smailholm Tower

Dryburgh Abbey Kelso

Jedburgh Abbey & Visitor Centre Jedburgh

Hermitage Castle

Kielder

A74(M)

Dumfries

Sweetheart Abbey

New Abbey Corn Mill

Caerlaverock Castle

Gretna Green

Longtown Birdoswald Roman Fort Once Brewed

Brampton Lanercost Priory Haltwhistle

Hadrian's Wall

Carlisle Castle **CARLISLE**

Wetheral Priory Gatehouse

Wetheral

Silloth-on-Solway

Wigton Southwaite Alston

Allonby

Maryport

CUMBRIA

Cockermouth

Workington

Keswick Penrith Castle **PENRITH**

Mayburgh Henge

Brougham Castle

Clifton Hall Countess Pillar

Castlerigg Stone Circle King Arthur's Round Table Appleby-in-Westmorland

Whitehaven

Ullswater

Egremont

Seatoller Barn

Shap Abbey

Grasmere Ambleside

Waterhead Ambleside Roman Fort

Hardknott Roman Fort

Sellafield Hawkshead Windermere

Ravenglass

Ravenglass Roman Bath House Muncaster Castle

Coniston Kendal

Broughton-in-Furness

Bootle

Stott Park Bobbin Mill

Tebay

Sedbergh

Kirkby Lonsdale

Millom

Bride

Ramsey Gibbs of the Grove

The Great Laxey Wheel & Mines Trail

Laxey

The Island's Treasure House

Douglas

Ulverston Grange-over-Sands Ingleton

High Bentham

Furness Abbey

Bow Bridge **BARROW-IN-FURNESS**

Piel Castle

Piel Island

Warton Old Rectory

Carnforth

Morecambe

Morecambe Lancaster

Bay

NORTH EAST

COUNTY DURHAM
NORTHUMBERLAND
TYNE AND WEAR
TEES VALLEY

✥ English Heritage Sites
▲ Other Historic Attractions

Berwick-upon-Tweed Barracks & Main Guard
Berwick-upon-Tweed
Berwick-upon-Tweed Castle & Ramparts
Norham Castle
Coldstream
Lindisfarne Priory
Etal Castle
Belford
Seahouses
Adderstone
Wooler
Dunstanburgh Castle
Craster
Alnwick
Edlingham Castle
Warkworth Castle & Hermitage
Rothbury
Amble
NORTHUMBERLAND
Black Middens Bastle House
Brinkburn Priory
Otterburn
ASHINGTON
Morpeth
Newbiggin-by-the-Sea
Bellingham
Chesters Roman Fort
Blyth
Chesters Walled Garden
Belsay Hall
Whitley Bay
Bessie Surtees House
Tynemouth Priory & Castle
▲ **Segedunum Roman Fort**
Chesters Bridge Abutment
NEWCASTLE UPON TYNE
▲ **St Paul's Monastery**
Housesteads Roman Fort
Aydon Castle
Prudhoe Castle
GATESHEAD
▲ **Bede's World Museum**
Haydon Bridge
Hexham
Prudhoe
A6127(M)
TYNE & WEAR
Corbridge Roman Site
Derwentcote Steel Furnace
SUNDERLAND
Hylton Castle
Beamish
Consett
Finchale Priory
A1(M)
Stanhope
DURHAM
Peterlee
Auckland Castle Deer House
Spennymoor
HARTLEPOOL
Bishop Auckland
Billingham
Redcar
A689
STOCKTON-ON-TEES
Brotton
Piercebridge Roman Bridge
TEES VALLEY
Gisborough Priory
Barnard Castle
Barnard Castle
DARLINGTON
MIDDLES-BROUGH
Guisborough
Brough
Bowes Castle
Bowes
Stanwick Iron Age Fortifications
Great Ayton
A174
Whitby Abbey
Whitby
Brough Castle
Kirkby Stephen
Egglestone Abbey
Scotch Corner
Danby
Richmond
Reeth
Easby Abbey
Catterick
Mount Grace Priory
A169
Richmond Castle
Northallerton
Wheeldale Roman Road
Hawes
Aysgarth Falls
Leyburn
Bedale
Leeming Bar
NORTH YORKSHIRE
Scarborough Castle
Middleham Castle
Rievaulx Abbey
Helmsley Castle
Pickering Castle
SCARBOROUGH
Thirsk
Helmsley
A170
Pickering
A64
Filey
Horton-in-Ribblesdale
Marmion Tower
Byland Abbey
Duncombe Park
Malton
B1257
A169
Burton Agnes Manor House
Clapham
St Mary's Church, Studley Royal ▲ Fountains Abbey
Ripon
Aldborough Roman Site
▲ **Castle Howard**
Norton
Settle
Grassington
Pateley Bridge
Easingwold
Kirkham Priory
Wharram Percy Deserted Medieval Village
Malham
Boroughbridge

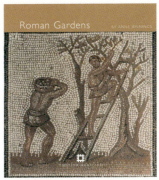

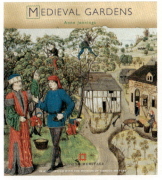

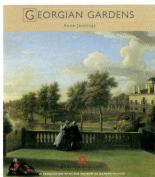

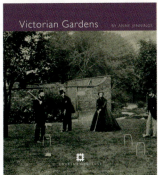

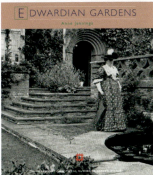

New books from
English Heritage

273

This publication is produced on UPM Star Matt 70 gsm paper from a mill which has ISO14001 and EMAS certification.

The mill also has a PEFC Certified Chain of Custody Certificate. 67% of the fibre used at the mill during 2003 originated from PEFC certified sources.